The Buddha

The Buddha

Biography of a Myth

DONALD S. LOPEZ JR.

Yale UNIVERSITY PRESS
New Haven and London

Published with assistance from the Louis Stern Memorial Fund.

Yale University Press books may be purchased in quantity for educational, business, or promotional use. For information, please e-mail sales.press@yale.edu (U.S. office) or sales@yaleup.co.uk (U.K. office).

Set in Minion Pro type by IDS Infotech Ltd.
Printed in the United States of America.

ISBN 978-0-300-23427-5
Library of Congress Control Number: 2024952451
A catalogue record for this book is available from the British Library.

Authorized Representative in the EU: Easy Access System Europe, Mustamäe tee 50, 10621 Tallinn, Estonia, gpsr.requests@easproject.com

10 9 8 7 6 5 4 3 2 1

MIX
Paper | Supporting responsible forestry
FSC® C008955
FSC www.fsc.org

Contents

Preface *ix*

Introduction 1

Part 1: The Buddha Tells His Tale

ONE. The Appearance of the Buddha 17

TWO. A Child Is Born 26

THREE. The Prince in the Palace 43

FOUR. The Great Departure 51

FIVE. Six Years of Austerities 69

SIX. The Attack of Māra 79

SEVEN. The Night of Enlightenment 88

EIGHT. Seven Weeks in the Forest 105

NINE. To the Deer Park 114

TEN. Passage to Nirvāṇa 124

Part 2: Did the Buddha Exist?

The Buddha

Preface

In 2023, the Metropolitan Museum of Art in New York hosted an exhibition of early Indian Buddhist sculpture. Called "Tree and Serpent: Early Buddhist Art, 200 BCE to 400 CE," it presented an extraordinary array of pieces, many never displayed in the West before. It ran from July 21 to November 13. Before the opening, John Guy, the Met's senior curator for South Asian art, who conceived and curated the show, invited me to serve as the "second voice" on the audio guide and the video tour that the Met produces for its major exhibitions. That gave me the rare opportunity to spend time in the galleries before the show opened. Once it did open, I must have given twenty tours to various friends, students, and fellow scholars.

During those five months, I was deep into the days of writing this book, walking across Central Park on beautiful summer and fall days to see the trees and the serpents, walking back across the park a couple of hours later, often pulling out my phone along the way to record thoughts inspired by the exhibition, turning those thoughts into sentences when I returned to my apartment on Riverside Drive.

The exhibition traced the movement of Indian Buddhist sculpture from its "aniconic" phase, when the Buddha was not depicted in the form that we know today, to the iconic phase, some centuries later, when he was. In that first phase, trees were depicted, tree spirits (*yakṣa*) were depicted, serpents (*nāga*) were depicted, but the Buddha was not. Yet if you know the story that the scene depicts, you know that he is somehow there. Two small footprints on a cushion held by a beautiful woman represent his birth from the right side of his mother, Queen Māyā. A riderless horse with an open parasol perched upright on the saddle is his loyal steed Kaṇṭhaka carrying Prince Siddhārtha out of the palace under the cover of darkness as he sets out in search of enlightenment. A tree festooned with garlands and worshipped by gods is the Bodhi Tree, the site of his enlightenment. A seat enwrapped by a giant hooded snake is the *nāga* Mucilinda protecting the newly enlightened Buddha from a rainstorm in the first weeks after he achieved buddhahood. In each case, I knew the story and I knew the history; I could not see the hero. This book is my attempt to find him.

Introduction

In 1972, the Buddhist Publication Society posthumously published *The Life of the Buddha According to the Pāli Canon* by the Buddhist monk Ñāṇamoli (1905–1960). He had been born in England as Osbert Moore, serving in the British Army in the Second World War. While stationed in Italy, he read a book about Buddhism and decided to become a monk, ordaining in Sri Lanka in 1949, spending the rest of his life in a hermitage on an island in a lagoon. Ñāṇamoli wrote at a time when most scholars believed that the Pāli canon included the earliest Buddhist texts and hence the most authentic record of the Buddha's life and teachings. Like other scholars of the nineteenth and early twentieth centuries, he preferred the simplicity of the Pāli accounts of the life of the Buddha to what he called "the ornate and florid later versions" composed in Sanskrit. Indeed, he praises the Pāli account of the life of the Buddha up to his enlightenment as being "as lean and polished as a rapier, a candle flame or an uncarved ivory tusk."[1] Yet before the Pāli canon had been written on palm leaves—said to have taken place in a cave in Sri Lanka in the last years before the Common Era—events from the life of the Buddha that do not appear in that canon had been carved in stone. In the centuries that followed, fuller biographies of the Buddha, some of them indeed ornate, would be composed and gain great fame. Thus, sadly for the biographer of the Buddha, there are many more voices—indeed, at times it seems a cacophony—to be heard.

In my books *From Stone to Flesh: A Short History of the Buddha* and *Strange Tales of an Oriental Idol,* I have catalogued European descriptions of the Buddha, beginning with Clement of Alexandria circa 200 CE and ending with Eugène Burnouf in 1844. In these books, I took it as my task not to depict the Buddha but to document how Europeans over the course of several centuries sought to depict him. In this book I take on what might seem to be a simpler task but in fact is far more complicated: to depict the Buddha myself.

A Buddhist sūtra with the inspiring title *Introduction to the Domain of the Inconceivable Qualities and Wisdom of the Tathāgatas* explains that the Buddha appears to the members of his audience in the way that they want, or perhaps more accurately, in the way that they need. The text says that they see him in different moments of his biography, at different heights (ranging from six feet to thousands of miles), with a body of different colors, the colors of different jewels, like rubies, beryl, sapphire, and crystal.[2] Knowing the capacities and predispositions of each member of his audience, the Buddha causes them to see him in these different ways. And the text makes clear that the Buddha does this spontaneously, without the need for thought. I cite this passage simply to note how ancient Buddhist texts anticipated various visions of the Buddha that would appear again and again, often in less poetic terms, over the millennia.

Since the Buddha was first mentioned by Clement of Alexandria around 200 CE, Europeans have had their own views, wildly varying views, of the Buddha, seeing him for centuries as an idol and as a purveyor of idolatry. Only in the nineteenth century did he come to be admired as a prophet of a latter-day

Enlightenment, preaching liberty from suffering, fraternity of the brotherhood of monks, and equality of members of all castes. For others he became a romantic hero rhapsodizing in iambic pentameter. And for still others, the Buddha was merely a myth. He never existed at all.

These various views and their long history obviously present challenges to the biographer. Beginning in the second century of the Common Era, and therefore centuries after his death, biographies of the Buddha began to appear in India. These were translated in China and Tibet, where additional biographies would be composed, a process that continues in Buddhist countries until the present day. Between 1972 and 1983 the Japanese artist Osamu Tezuka produced an eight-volume graphic novel of the life of the Buddha. An entire volume could be written about the history of Buddhist lives of the Buddha. This is not that book.

In Europe, versions of the life of the Buddha begin with some of the first travelers to Asia. One of the earliest, most detailed, and most positive appears in Marco Polo's account of his travels. Describing "Sagamoni Borcan" (the Mongolian name of the Buddha that he learned at the court of Kublai Khan), who is worshipped by "the idolators," he writes in part, "So what did he one night but take his departure from the palace privily, and betake himself to certain lofty and pathless mountains. And there he did abide, leading a life of great hardship and sanctity, and keeping great abstinence, just as if he had been a Christian. Indeed, and he had but been so, he would have been a great saint of Our Lord Jesus Christ, so good and pure was the life he led. And when he died they found his body and brought it to his father. And when the father saw dead before him that son whom he loved better than himself, he was near going distraught with sorrow. And he caused an image in the similitude of his son to be wrought in gold and precious stones, and caused all his people to adore it. And they all declared him to be a god; and so they still say."[3]

Numerous accounts of his life have appeared in the reports of missionaries, soldiers, and colonial officials over the centuries.[4] In the nineteenth century, as Sanskrit and Chinese began to be taught in the universities of Europe and then America, biographies drawing directly from Sanskrit, Pāli, Chinese, and Tibetan texts appeared, inspiring in turn biographies of the Buddha in European languages by authors who did not read the canonical Buddhist languages. Indeed, an entire book could be written about those biographies. This also is not that book. That is not to say, however, that those European biographies of the Buddha were unimportant and unworthy of our study. Indeed, one could argue that the portrait of the Buddha that is best known today, both in Europe and in Asia, was painted in Europe in the nineteenth century.

If the cliché is that every English professor wants to write a novel, perhaps every scholar of Buddhism wants to write a biography of the Buddha. Certainly, many have. But where to begin? Many of the most famous Buddhist biographies begin in the distant past—including the Pāli *Account of Origins* (*Nidānakathā*) and *Chronicle of the Buddha* (*Buddhavaṃsa*) as well as the Sanskrit *Great Matter* (*Mahāvastu*). In the *Buddhavaṃsa,* twenty-four previous buddhas are described before we get to Gotama; in the *Mahāvastu,* the Buddha is not born until the second of the three volumes. I have argued that the Buddha as we think of him today—the atheist philosopher who offered the path to nirvāṇa to all who sought it, regardless of their social class; the opponent of ritual and priestcraft—is a product of nineteenth-century Paris and the work of Eugène Burnouf (1801–1852), who saw the Buddha as a figure of history in a land of myth.[5] This demythologized Buddha was then portrayed by Hermann Oldenberg—with generations of scholars returning to the myths, in some cases to date them, in many cases to explain them away—inspired by the field of New Testament studies and especially *The Life of Jesus, Critically Examined,* published in 1835 by David Strauss, who wrote of the Gospels, "It is not however to be imagined that any one individual seated himself at his table to invent them out of his own head, and write them down, as he would a poem: on the contrary, these narratives like all other legends were fashioned by degrees, by steps which can no longer be traced; gradually acquired consistency, and at length received a fixed form in our written Gospels."[6]

Yet there is no fixed form for the life of the Buddha. Only one of the famous Sanskrit and Pāli biographies considered here takes him from his descent into his mother's womb to his passage into nirvāṇa, and it says very little about the forty-five years between his enlightenment and death. The traditional biographies cannot, therefore, provide an ancient model for a modern life. The Buddha appears in hundreds of scenes in the monastic code, as a monk or nun commits a misdeed, and the Buddha makes a rule. But which of these to choose, and which is biographical? The modern biographer is compelled to have a vision of the Buddha before beginning, and then to include those elements that conform to that vision and exclude those that do not: the rationalist philosopher, the meditating mystic, the eternal cosmic reality, the compassionate savior, the tantric master. The Buddha has been portrayed as all of these. Yet how could he be them all? The Buddhist answer, as our sūtra suggests, is that the Buddha appears in the way that is most meaningful to each of us, taking on a different form, speaking in a different language, providing different advice, depending on our capacities and our needs. This is inspiring to the aspirant, vexing to the biographer. The biographer must first select a frame before painting the portrait.

There is no model for that frame in ancient Buddhist texts; although there are occasional biographical passages, there is no biography in the canon, and the post-canonical biographies are all deficient in one way or another, either ending long before his death or skipping over decades of his life between his enlightenment at age thirty-five and his death at age eighty. I have decided to seek my frame in an unusual time and place: in nineteenth-century Paris and in the work of Gustave Flaubert (1821–1880), arguably the greatest French novelist of that century, best known for two masterpieces: *Madame Bovary* and *A Sentimental Education.* However, the work that Flaubert considered his greatest achievement, the work that he devoted his adult life to researching and writing, was *La Tentation de Saint Antoine* (*The Temptation of Saint Anthony*), about the famous Desert Father Saint Anthony of Egypt (251–356 CE), whose visions in the wilderness have inspired painters for centuries. Indeed, Flaubert was himself inspired to begin the project when he saw a painting attributed to Pieter Bruegel the Elder (d. 1569) in 1845. Captivated by Saint Anthony for decades, Flaubert published his book in 1874. Painters from Bosch to Salvador Dalí have depicted the temptations that Saint Anthony suffered during his days and nights in the desert, as demons appeared, some to seduce him, others to assail him. Flaubert expands Saint Anthony's visions to include not just demons but a pantheon of gods and pagan philosophers from across the centuries. The pagan philosopher that Flaubert depicts in the greatest detail is the Buddha.

We know that Flaubert was a serious student of Buddhism, but with the sensibility that characterizes so much of his work. In his *Dictionary of Received Ideas,* a collection of silly definitions (Omega is defined as "second letter of the Greek alphabet"), he took the definition of Buddhism from the *Dictionnaire universel d'histoire et de géographie* (better known as the *Dictionnaire Bouillet,* first published in 1842): "False religion of India." Flaubert had clearly read Burnouf's 897-page translation and study of the *Lotus Sūtra,* published in 1852, with its twenty-one appendices providing the most detailed description of the qualities of the Buddha available in a European language. He had also read the French translation of the *Lalitavistara,* a famous biography of the Buddha, translated from the Tibetan by Burnouf's student Édouard Foucaux (1811–1894) and published in 1848. On June 24, 1871—in the final stages of his work on *The Temptation of Saint Anthony*—Flaubert wrote to his childhood friend Frédéric Baudry, a philologist, student of Sanskrit, translator of the Brothers Grimm, and a student of Burnouf:

> O Bodhisattva! O son of good family! O perfect Buddha!
> Like an old stork, my spirit is sad and gloomy; like an old elephant fallen into the quagmire, I have no strength.
> My meditation is so vehement that sweat pours out and drips from my armpits.
> I need, O son of good family, the fourth of the medicinal plants that provide well-being in any situation, whatever it might be.
> I have read the *Lalitavistara,* O Bodhisattva—I have read *The Lotus of the Good Law,* O son of good family!
> But I would pass countless hundreds of myriads of *koṭis* of *kalpas*
> Without understanding, O holy name of God, what the Buddha is.
> I look at myself to see if I have the thirty-two qualities of an imbecile.[7]

The translation used here is not *The Temptation of Saint Antony,* the scholarly translation by Kitty Mrosovsky from 1980, but the first English translation by Lafcadio Hearn (1850–1904), published in 1904.[8] Hearn was a remarkable figure, born to a Greek mother and an Irish father on the Greek island of

Lefkada (the inspiration for his name). Spending his youth in Ireland and England, in 1869 he sailed to the United States, where he worked as a journalist and translator, first in Cincinnati and then in New Orleans; he was fired from his post at the *Cincinnati Daily Enquirer* for marrying Alethea Foley, a Black woman. They were divorced in 1877. Hearn later moved to New Orleans, where he encountered Japanese culture at the World's Industrial and Cotton Centennial Exposition of 1884. After several years in Martinique, in 1890 he sailed to Japan, where he spent the rest of his life and produced the work for which he is best remembered. There, he married a Japanese woman named Koizumi Setsu, took a Japanese name himself (Koizumi Yakumo), became a Buddhist, and wrote extensively about Japanese culture, including in a book called *Gleanings from the Buddha Fields* (1897). He is best remembered today for *Kwaidan* (1904), a collection of Japanese ghost stories, made into a classic Japanese horror film in 1964. Hearn was sufficiently captivated by Flaubert's *Saint Anthony* to begin his translation in the year following its publication while he was living in Cincinnati. It was not published until the year of his death, in 1904.

In the pages that follow, Flaubert's depiction of the Buddha in *Saint Anthony* will provide this portrait of the Buddha with its frame, with Hearn's translation cited at the beginning of each chapter. The contents of that frame, the colors and the shading, are drawn from many Buddhist sources, relying particularly on five of the most famous. Each of these texts is renowned, each is important, each is different from the others. When these texts are cited, it is not in an effort to provide some kind of concordance but to draw from each at various points to provide a compelling narrative, using that narrative to ponder the mysterious figure that we call the Buddha.

The first of those texts is the *Mahāvastu,* a title that might be translated as the *Great Matter* or, more colloquially, the *Big*

Deal. The text is found in the vinaya (the section of the canon concerned with the monastic code) of one of the early schools of Buddhism, the Lokottaravāda ("transcendentalist") branch of the Mahāsaṅghika ("majority"), the school that broke away from what would come to be known as the Sthavira ("elders") at the Second Council. It shows many signs of being compiled over several centuries, with numerous interpolations, beginning as early as the second century BCE. Those elements of the text that might be considered a biography of the Buddha begin in the second of its three volumes, with other scenes interspersed in the first and third. As part of the *tripiṭaka* ("three baskets") of a Buddhist school, the *Mahāvastu* is regarded as canonical, although it does not bear the title "sūtra." The next two texts are sūtras, and thus traditionally regarded as having been spoken by the Buddha.

The first of these is called the *Abhiniṣkramaṇa,* or *Great Renunciation,* the term used to describe Prince Siddhārtha's departure from the palace and quest for enlightenment. Only part of the text might be called a biography of the Buddha, a lengthy section that describes the events from his birth to his first teaching, the exposition of the four truths to the "group of five" in the Deer Park at Sarnath. Much of the rest of the text is devoted to stories of some of the Buddha's most famous disciples, with the Buddha appearing in those accounts. It was one of the first biographies of the Buddha to be translated into a European language, by Samuel Beal in 1875 as *The Romantic Legend of Sâkya Buddha.*

The other sūtra is the *Lalitavistara,* a title rendered here as the *Play in Full.* Here, the life of the Buddha is essentially a play, a dramatic performance by a being who was already enlightened long ago. The sūtra likely dates from the third or fourth century CE. Like the other texts mentioned, it is also associated with one of the early schools of Buddhism, the Sarvāstivāda ("those who say that everything exists"), although there are Mahāyāna elements that seem to have been interpolated into the text. Like the previous text, it ends with the Buddha's first teaching at the age of thirty-five.

The final two sources are biographies by famous Buddhist authors. The first is the *Nidānakathā*, the *Account of Origins,* attributed to the great fifth-century monk and scholar Buddhaghosa. Best known for his massive compendium on meditation practice, the *Path of Purification* (*Visuddhimagga*), he wrote many important commentaries. The *Account of Origins* is in a way a commentary, meant to serve as an introduction to the *jātaka* collection, the stories of the Buddha's past lives. It is in three parts. It begins eons ago when the future buddha makes a vow in the presence of a previous buddha to achieve enlightenment in the distant future. All of the *jātaka* stories are thus said to have taken place between that lifetime and his birth as Prince Siddhārtha. The second part of Buddhaghosa's text jumps to the story of the bodhisattva's descent into his mother's womb and continues to his achievement of enlightenment. This is followed by the third and final section, which begins with the seven eventful weeks after the Buddha's enlightenment, continuing to his first teaching and his return to his home city for the first time since the great departure, and ends when he is given the monastery of Jetavana in the city of Śrāvastī, said to have occurred in the third year after his enlightenment.

It is noteworthy that none of these four texts deal directly with the last forty-two years of the Buddha's life; none take him to his passage into final nirvāṇa. It is unclear why this is the case. It is true that not a great deal of narrative consequence happens between the Buddha's first teachings and establishment of the order of monks and nuns in the first years after his enlightenment (said to have occurred when he was thirty-five) and his final days at age eighty. It is also true that those days are recounted in detail in two texts, one in Pāli, one in Sanskrit (very different from each other), called the *Great*

Discourse on the Final Nirvāṇa (*Mahāparinibbāna Sutta* in Pāli and *Mahāparinirvāṇa Sūtra* in Sanskrit).

The final source here is the only one that describes his life from birth to death. It is the *Deeds of the Buddha* (*Buddha-carita*), by the great second-century Indian poet Aśvaghoṣa. This masterpiece of Sanskrit literature is considered the first full biography of the Buddha, beginning with his birth and ending with his passage into nirvāṇa and the distribution of his relics. It is these five texts that provide much of the source material for the biography of the Buddha given here.

Most of the sources for this book were first translated into a European language (in whole or part) during the nineteenth century by such figures as the American Pāli scholar Henry Clarke Warren; the French scholar Philippe Édouard Foucaux, a student of Burnouf; as well as a number of British scholars, including J. J. Jones, deputy keeper in the department of printed books at the National Library of Wales; E. B. Cowell, the first professor of Sanskrit at Cambridge; and Samuel Beal, "Chaplain in Her Majesty's Fleet." His translation *The Romantic Legend of Sâkya Buddha* in 1875 would serve as the foundation for Edwin Arnold's Victorian bestseller *The Light of Asia*. The sources for this book also include the work of a range of European and Asian authors of the twentieth and twenty-first centuries who have sought to refine our understanding of the life of the Buddha.

The names of these more recent authors will be found for the most part in the source notes. Many of the names of authors that appear in the body of the text do not typically occur in biographies of the Buddha, names like David Strauss, Gustave Flaubert, Patrick Lafcadio Hearn, Joris-Karl Huysmans, and Oscar Wilde. Ostensibly, they share little in common apart from the fact that they are all European and they all lived in the nineteenth century, the time, as I argued in *From Stone to Flesh*, when the Buddha as we know him was born.

The story of the Buddha has been told many times, and each of those retellings can be read in so many ways. While he was composing *The Temptation of Saint Anthony,* Flaubert wrote to a friend, "How lovingly I chiselled the beads of my necklace! I left out one thing and that's the string."[9] I therefore decided to let Flaubert provide the string. This, however, is the string woven by the artist, not the string discovered by the historian. When we seek to find the historical string on which to place the beads of the Buddha's life, we find only broken threads. If the Buddha is a literary creation, one whose current incarnation owes much to European scholars of the nineteenth century, it seemed appropriate to base this biography on one of that century's most striking creations, Flaubert's portrayal of the Buddha in Chapter 5 of *The Temptation of Saint Anthony.* Like Flaubert's strange masterpiece, this book seeks to remythologize the Buddha.

The year 1835 marks an important moment in Western efforts to compose a biography of the Buddha. This was the year that the German theologian David Strauss published his *Life of Jesus.* It sent shockwaves through the world of biblical studies in Europe. Its tremors were felt in the infant world of Buddhist studies, where Strauss's "quest for the historical Jesus" inspired a "quest for the historical Buddha," a search that began, at least in book-length form, in 1881, with the publication in German of Hermann Oldenberg's *The Buddha: His Life, His Doctrine, His Order.* The search continues to the present day.

Any linear biography of the Buddha creates a creature made from parts, requiring that many other pieces of the puzzle be left in the box. In the final chapter, I try to imagine what the completed puzzle might look like. Over the almost two centuries since Strauss, many biographers of the Buddha have attempted to turn story into history to create the Buddha they long to see, not the mystic or the miracle maker, but the rationalist philosopher, a figure who somehow went unrecognized by Buddhists across

Asia over the past two and a half millennia. The portrait of this philosopher is painted by selecting some elements of the canon and ignoring many others. Indeed, such biographies arrive at the historical Buddha by a process of subtraction, eliminating one by one the qualities that strain credulity. In order to do so, they silence the Buddha by cutting off his long tongue, one of the thirty-two marks of a superman that adorn all buddhas, a tongue so long that he can lick behind his ears, said to be the karmic effect of lifetimes of refraining from harsh speech. The portrait of the rationalist also eliminates the Buddha's most famous defeat of six rival philosophers, the "twin miracle" at Śrāvastī. Here, the Buddha did not debate about the self. Instead, he rose into the sky shooting flames and jets of water from his body. The Buddhist devil Māra can cite, or not cite, sūtras for his purpose.

Those who seek to demythologize the Buddha, stripping away the superhuman in an effort to reveal the human, should know that they do so at their peril. In the *Great Discourse on the Lion's Roar* (*Mahāsīhanāda Sutta*), a famous text from the Pāli canon, the collection that, according to many, best represents his teachings, the Buddha declares, "Should anyone say of me: 'The recluse Gotama does not have any superhuman states, any distinction in knowledge and vision worthy of the noble ones. The recluse Gotama teaches a Dhamma [merely] hammered out by reasoning, following his own line of inquiry as it occurs to him'—unless he abandons that assertion and that state of mind and relinquishes that view, then as [surely as if he has been] carried off and put there, he will wind up in hell."[10]

The goal of so many biographies of the Buddha is to find the man behind the myth. I argue in this book that that man cannot be found. And I argue that the man that some claim to find, the philosopher who died from an attack of dysentery, is not the man from whom Buddhists have sought refuge from suffering for more than two millennia. After listening to presentations of current scholarship on the origins of the Mahāyāna sūtras (which scholars place centuries after the death of the Buddha), the Dalai Lama once told me, "If I believed what they said, the Buddha would only be a nice person, and I know he is much more than that."

It is that "much more" that this book seeks to restore. It seeks to give some sense of the often hallucinogenic wonders that surround the Buddha like a shimmering aura. It seeks to celebrate the human imagination and its power to conjure a figure of such marvel; to see the various lives of the Buddha not as a cacophony of contractions but as a chorus that together inspires us to remythologize the Buddha and allow ourselves to delight in myth, to be moved, to be inspired, to be liberated. As Frederic Prokosch wrote in *The Seven Who Fled*, "It is not history that survives, but legend. What does our past matter, except as it has fashioned our spirit? It is legend which is the history of the spirit. What signifies is not a great battle or the death of an emperor or the fall of a city a thousand years ago, but the poetry and wisdom which men have created from these, and which blossom in our minds forever, and move us to serene reflections."[11]

But can we say that to decide that the Buddha was not a historical figure is ultimately liberating? We would no longer need to endlessly obsess over his dates. We would no longer need to endlessly search for relics, dreaming about a technology that would allow us to date them down to the decade. We would no longer need to stratify the stories, seeking to identify those that are history and those that are myth. In a real sense, to argue that the Buddha in all his glory, like all the buddhas that preceded him in all their glory, was not a historical figure is an argument that is authentically Buddhist. We need not abandon the search in despair. Instead, we renounce the search for a self that was never there.

I

The Buddha Tells His Tale

1

The Appearance of the Buddha

In Chapter 5 of *The Temptation of Saint Anthony*, all manner of ancient gods and idols appear to Anthony and Hilarion. First are various unnamed idols from the Antediluvian Age, damaged and covered with seaweed, then demonic figures receiving human sacrifice. This is followed by a large number of Hindu gods, described but unnamed by Flaubert. Thus, Ganeśa is "The god who rubs his abdomen with his elephant-trunk, is the solar Deity, the inspiring spirit of wisdom." Not only are they unnamed, they do not speak. Then:

> All upon a sudden appears a Naked Man seated in the midst of the sand, with legs crossed. A large halo vibrates, suspended in air behind him. The little ringlets of his black hair in which blueish tints shift symmetrically surround a protuberance upon the summit of his skull. His arms, which are very long, hang down against his sides. His two hands rest flat upon his thighs, with the palms open. The

> soles of his feet are like the faces of two blazing suns; and he remains completely motionless—before Anthony and Hilarion—with all the gods around him, rising in tiers above the rocks, as if upon the benches of some vast circus. His lips, half-open; and he speaks in a deep voice.[1]

Flaubert begins not with the teachings of the Buddha but with his body. For so many around the world and across the centuries, the Buddha is first known by his image rather than his words, by his body rather than by his voice. In Flaubert's rendition, the Buddha appears at the end of a long sequence of idols, who then surround him as he begins to speak. And we recall that for centuries, Europeans referred to Buddhists simply as "idolaters." According to the *Oxford English Dictionary,* the first occurrence of the word "Buddhism" (spelled "Boudhism") in English was in 1801.

Although Mahāvīra, the founder of Jainism, said to be a contemporary of the Buddha, is depicted naked, the Buddha is not. He is almost always depicted in the robes of a monk. Flaubert surely knew this, perhaps making him naked to mark the Buddha's lack of artifice and concealment; the Buddha is famously said to have never taught with a closed fist.

The remainder of the description of the body of the Buddha is quite accurate. The Buddha's body is said to be adorned with the thirty-two signs or marks (*lakṣana*) of a *mahāpuruṣa,* literally a "great person" or perhaps "superman." His body also has eighty "secondary marks" (*anuvyañjana*). In Buddhism, these physical marks are said to be unique to a buddha and to a universal monarch (or *cakravartin,* discussed below). And as we will see, it was these marks on the body of the infant Prince Siddhārtha that caused the royal astrologers to predict that he was destined to be one or the other.

The list of these physical attributes is strange, at least to the modern reader. We find, for example, that the Buddha has webbed fingers and toes, forty teeth, a circle of hair between the eyebrows, a tongue so broad and long that it can cover his entire face, and a retractable penis. A Pāli sutta, appropriately entitled *Sūtra on the Marks* (*Lakkhaṇa Sutta*), describes the deeds that the future buddha had done in the past that resulted in these physical marks. The webbed fingers and toes are the result of generosity, pleasant speech, and purposeful deeds. The forty teeth are the result of reconciling enemies and encouraging friends. The retractable penis is the result of reuniting friends and family members.[2] Like so many elements of the life and person of the Buddha, the "major and minor marks," as they are often called, seem to be yet another case of accretion, perhaps never meant to be compiled. Yet, having been assembled from many pieces, like Frankenstein's monster, they create an odd, in some ways frightening, figure. This will be discussed in the final chapter.

The origins of these physical qualities have been the subject of much speculation, with precedent found for some of them in Hindu works. Some, like the webbed fingers, may be cases of art producing doctrine. Because of the difficulty of carving separate fingers from stone without breaking them, a thin layer of stone was sometimes left between them; the Buddha's skills as a swimmer are not mentioned in the sūtras. However, the most obvious example of art becoming doctrine—and in this case, a famous doctrine—is the familiar bump on top of the Buddha's head; the Sanskrit term *uṣṇīṣa* (which means "turban" or "diadem") is more respectfully rendered in the case of the Buddha as "crown protrusion."

Some of the earliest sculptures of the Buddha come from Gandhāra, a region of what was once northwest India and is today parts of Pakistan and Afghanistan. In the aftermath of

Alexander the Great's invasion in 327 BCE, much of the region remained under Greek or "Indo-Greek" control until the beginning of the Common Era. Many of the statues of the Buddha from this region show him with his hair pulled up into a chignon or topknot, tied with a cord. Statues from around the same period from Mathura in central India show him with his hair coiled at the top of his head, or in the more familiar ringlets; one of the thirty-two marks of the Buddha is that his hair curls to the right. Eventually, however, likely from its depiction in statuary, this topknot became a fleshy protuberance or even a bone. Thus, when the Chinese monk Faxian went to India in 399, he visited a shrine in what is today Afghanistan that housed the relic of the "*uṣṇīṣa* bone." Chinese translations of *uṣṇīṣa* include *ding gu* ("bone on the crown of the head") and *rou ji gu* ("bone of flesh topknot"). The "crown protrusion" would come to be invested with great meaning. It is said to have originated when Prince Siddhārtha drew his sword, cut off his long princely locks, and threw them up into the sky, saying that if they came down, he would not become a buddha. They were caught by a god in the Heaven of the Thirty-three atop Mount Meru, where they were enshrined. The *uṣṇīṣa* was considered so potent that a kind of no-fly zone extended above it, preventing gods from flying over the Buddha. Although it was perfectly proportional to the Buddha's head, it was impossible to measure its circumference. It would eventually take on a life of its own, embodied as an important tantric goddess called Uṣṇīṣavijayā, or "Victorious Crown Protrusion."[3]

That the Buddha, like all buddhas, has an aura, that his hair is curly, and that he has the crown protrusion are all known to Flaubert. He was familiar with Eugène Burnouf's 1852 translation of the *Lotus Sūtra* where, in the eighth of its twenty-one appendices, he would have found a detailed discussion of each of the thirty-two marks of a superman. There he would have learned, as he says, that the Buddha's arms are "very long, hang down against his sides." The Buddhist sources are explicit about this, saying that while standing erect, the Buddha's arms extend to his knees, allowing him to rub his knees without bending over. But Flaubert's Buddha is not standing. He is seated with his legs crossed in the lotus posture, his hands resting on his thighs. Here Flaubert is likely describing the position of the Buddha's hands as he sits in meditation, his right hand resting on his left, each resting on his thighs. In his visit to the Desert Father, Flaubert has the Buddha seated on the desert sands, not on a pile of grass, where he sat on the night of his enlightenment, not on a throne, as he is so often depicted in Buddhist art.

Buddhist texts often describe all manner of deities attending the teachings of the Buddha, but it is the Buddha who holds the place of honor; one of his epithets is *devātideva,* "god above the gods." Flaubert has him sitting below, with the gods arrayed above him, "as if upon the benches of some vast circus." And then he opens his red lips (described in the texts as the color of a bimba fruit) and speaks. Among the eighty secondary marks, we find that the voice of the Buddha resonates like that of an elephant and like thunder, and yet is sweet, pleasing, and gentle. Elsewhere, we find that his voice has the sixty qualities of melodious speech. For Flaubert, it is only "deep."

> I am the Master of great charities, the succor of all creatures; and not less to the profane than to believers, do I expound the law.[4]

The first words that Flaubert has the Buddha speak are that he is, in Hearn's translation, "the master of great charities," perhaps, in a more Buddhist vocabulary, "great alms" (*la grande aumône*). This is not a traditional description of the Buddha and its meaning is not immediately clear, since the Buddha, like all monks and nuns, is a recipient rather than a donor of alms. Flaubert's reference, and Hearn's translation, may mean that the Buddha is the agent rather than the object of charity, as is clear from the six or ten perfections (*pāramitā*) that all bodhisattvas practice over the course of their long path to buddhahood: giving, ethics, patience, effort, concentration, and wisdom, with giving often extolled above the others. That this is Flaubert's meaning is suggested by the Buddha's description of himself as the "succor," *secours* (we note that Flaubert chooses not to use the term "savior," *sauveur*), or rescuer of all creatures, who offers protection to all sentient beings. This is a more familiar Buddhist image, indeed evoking the sentence that has been on the lips of millions of Buddhists over the centuries: "I go for refuge to the Buddha."

A Buddhist is traditionally defined as someone who "goes for refuge" to the "three jewels"—the Buddha, the dharma, and the saṅgha—seeking their protection from the storms of the realms of rebirth in search of the safe haven of nirvāṇa. Among the many descriptions of the three jewels and their relation, the Buddha is depicted as the person who discovers that safe haven and then leads others to it. Flaubert notes that he does so "not less to the profane than to believers." Again, this does not evoke a particular Buddhist trope apart from the fact that the Buddha was said to teach all who came to hear him, regardless of their own religious beliefs or social status. In this case, "profane" refers to those who do not belong to any particular religion, a condition that is rarely mentioned in Buddhist sources but would apply widely to Flaubert's readers, so many of whom had rejected the Roman Catholic church. That the Buddha seemed to welcome all to his teachings and to ordain all into his community has been a reason for his particular appeal in the West since the nineteenth century.

The Buddha leads all creatures to the refuge of nirvāṇa by teaching them the dharma, the second of the three jewels, in

Flaubert's words "expounding the law." The word *dharma* in Sanskrit has many meanings. In the late eighteenth century, officials of the British East India Company undertook a study of Hindu and Muslim texts from which they might derive a legal system to rule the two major religions of the subcontinent. For Hinduism, they turned to a genre of caste regulations called "treatises on dharma" (*dharmaśāstra*), and the most famous of these texts came to be known in English as the *Laws of Manu*. From that point on, "law" became a standard translation of *dharma*, regardless of the context. In Buddhism, it has many meanings, the most important of which is the teachings of the Buddha; when he is dying, he tells the monk Ānanda that when he is gone the monks should turn to the *dharma* and the *vinaya*, the doctrine and the discipline, his teachings and the monastic code, for guidance.

As we shall see in the final chapter, *dharma* can also mean a quality; many qualities of the Buddha have been compiled. Finally, it can mean reality, in the sense of the fundamental principle or truth of the universe. Flaubert is able to evoke two of these in his statement. His phrase is *j'expose la loi*, meaning that he does not merely "expound" it as Hearn translates it, but that he also reveals it. There is a famous statement that whether or not buddhas appear in the world, the nature of the dharma remains the same; that is, the dharma (in the sense of the truth) is not something that is the creation of the Buddha but something that he discovered and then revealed to the world, as previous buddhas had done in the past and as future buddhas will do after his passing.

Indeed, across the geographical range and chronological durée of the Buddhist traditions, there has remained the shared belief that the nature of reality was discovered long ago by the Buddha and, before him, by the buddhas of the distant past, and that that same reality was understood by all buddhas in its entirety and its fullness. This reality, therefore, is not something that the Buddha was the first to discover but that he rediscovered. In a famous parable, the Buddha describes a traveler who arrives at an ancient city at the end of the ancient path through the great forest, a once great city, now deserted and in ruins. The traveler informs the king, who rebuilds the city, restoring it to its former glory. The Buddha is that traveler, traversing the same path to the city of reality that the buddhas of the past had found. Thus, in Buddhism, the truth is something that is found, and then lost, and then found again.

This is why it is said that the next buddha does not appear in the world until the teachings of the previous buddha have been forgotten. As long as the path to the city of reality remains passable and the city itself remains prosperous, there is no reason for repair. But when the city falls into ruins and the path is overgrown with oblivion, then the path must be cleared again and the city restored. This is what the buddhas have done, again and again, over the eons. This is what the next buddhas will do in the future. Whether Flaubert knew this parable or not, all of this is evoked by his phrase *j'expose la loi*.

Prior to the appearance of the Buddha, Anthony declares, "If matter can contain such power, it must surely contain a spirit. The souls of the Gods are attached to their images."[5] Flaubert has Anthony say this, likely not knowing that in the Buddhist world, a new image of the Buddha, whether in the three dimensions of sculpture or two dimensions of painting, is not regarded as complete until it has been consecrated. In Japan, a compartment is carved in the back of a wooden statue and silk viscera inserted, the image animated with the inclusion of a relic. In Tibet, something called a "life stick" is wrapped with scrolls of mantras to fill the hollow image from crown to base. Monks then invite the Buddha to enter the image and implore him to remain there for the benefit of beings. The image is one of descent, with immortal spirit inhabiting mortal matter.

In Thailand, there are consecration manuals, manuals that monks, seated before a newly crafted image, recite all night to animate the image through remembrance, first by listing the various qualities of the Buddha—his three knowledges, the seven factors of enlightenment, the thirty-two major marks, the eighty secondary marks. Next they recount the life of the Buddha, telling the image the story of the Buddha's life. In each case they ask that these elements remain in the image of the Buddha as long as his teaching remains in the world. The model here is not one of embodiment, but of reanimation, of resuscitation, or revival, like reading a diary to a person who has emerged from a coma. The logical and temporal sequence is reversed, as biography becomes autobiography.[6]

Here, having announced himself, the Buddha, so long considered an idol, now tells Saint Anthony, Hilarion, and the assembled idols his life story.

2

A Child Is Born

> That I might deliver the world, I resolved to be born among men. The gods wept when I departed from them. I sought me first a woman worthy to give me birth: a woman of warrior race, the wife of a king, exceedingly good, excessively beautiful, with body firm as adamant;—and at time of the full moon, without the auxiliation of any male, I entered her womb. I issued from it by the right side. Stars stopped in their courses. And seeing the star, they rejoiced with exceeding great joy![1]

Flaubert next turns to the story of the birth of the Buddha. Although he did not describe the Buddha with the term "savior" in the previous passage, here his choice of words explicitly evokes the birth of Jesus and the incarnation of Christ. He begins, "That I might deliver the world, I resolved to be born among men." However, in Buddhism, the birth of the Buddha is not the incarnation of God, of the word becoming flesh, but the final stage along the long road to perfection.

According to the account in the Pāli tradition of Sri Lanka and Southeast Asia, eons ago a wealthy brahmin named Sumedha concluded that there must be a state free from birth, aging, sickness, and death. He thus renounced the world and went into the forest, living under a tree, dressed only in tree bark, subsisting only on fruit. Through the practice of meditation, he gained certain supernormal powers, including the ability to fly. One day, he was flying through the sky when he saw a crowd gathering on the ground below. When he landed and asked a passerby the reason, he was told that the buddha Dīpaṅkara would soon arrive. When he heard the word "buddha," he experienced a moment of frisson. As the Buddha and his entourage approached, Sumedha noticed that he was walking toward a mud puddle. In order that the Buddha not soil his feet, he laid face down on the ground and spread his long and matted dreadlocks over the mud. As the Buddha approached, Sumedha reflected that if he were to become the disciple of Dīpaṅkara, he could achieve liberation from rebirth in that very lifetime. But then the thought occurred to him—as rendered in 1896 by Henry Clarke Warren (1854–1899), one of the first American translators of Buddhist texts—"But why thus in an unknown guise / Should I the Doctrine's fruit secure? / Omniscience first will I achieve / And be a Buddha in the world." Dīpaṅkara paused before the prone ascetic and said, "Behold ye now this monk austere, / His matted locks, his penance fierce! / Lo! he, unnumbered cycles hence, / A Buddha in this world shall be."[2] He then went on to predict the future Buddha's birthplace, his parents' names, the place of his enlightenment, the names of his chief disciples, and his own name: Gotama.

This story is regarded as the origin account, or the creation myth, of our buddha, known as Gotama Buddha in Pāli (Gautama Buddha or Śākyamuni—"sage of the Śākya clan"—in Sanskrit). He is presented as an ordinary Indian yogin who is wandering the world in search of a state beyond. He knows the goal; he does not know how to reach it. That path is known only to a buddha. Through his good fortune, the yogin encounters a buddha and knows that he is sufficiently advanced in the practice of meditation that if he were to follow that buddha's instructions, he would be liberated in that lifetime, becoming what in Buddhism is called an *arhat* ("worthy one"), and that he would escape the beginningless round of rebirth and enter nirvāṇa upon his death. Yet he decides not to do so, vowing instead to find the path to liberation on his own when there is no buddha in the world, when the teachings of Dīpaṅkara and any intervening buddhas have been forgotten. In keeping with the parable, he will rediscover the path to the city of nirvāṇa and reveal it to others.

However, becoming a buddha when a buddha and his teachings are not present in the world is infinitely more difficult than becoming an arhat as a disciple of a buddha, and the path is infinitely longer. In Sumedha's case, he could become an arhat in a matter of days, months, or years. In order to become a buddha, he would need to perfect himself over eons, four incalculable eons and one hundred thousand eons to be precise. An incalculable eon is in fact calculable, said to last 10^{140} years. This is the time required to accumulate the vast stores of merit and wisdom necessary to discover the path to nirvāṇa on one's own, without the benefit of a teacher. The person who makes such a vow is called a *bodhisattva*. Despite its fame, the precise derivation of this term is not known. It refers, however, to someone who seeks *bodhi* (often translated as "enlightenment" or "awakening), with *bodhi* in this context referring not to the enlightenment of an arhat, but to the enlightenment of a buddha.

There is much else that might be noted in the story of Sumedha, elements beyond his making this heroic vow. Commentators have explained that the vow must be taken by someone capable of achieving the state of the arhat in the lifetime when the vow is taken, that the vow must be taken in the presence of a buddha, that that buddha must make a prophecy of the future successful achievement of the goal by the person taking the vow, that the person who makes the vow must be someone who has already renounced the world and attained deep meditative states and gained supernormal powers, and that the person who makes the vow must be a male.[3]

The vast sweeps of time described here serve an important polemical purpose. The dominant religious tradition in India during the time of the Buddha was once referred to by European scholars as "Brahminism" because it was the religion of brahmin priests who performed fire sacrifices to various gods. Today, it is often called "Vedic Hinduism," that is, the tradition based on a body of texts called the Vedas, the earliest of which, the *Ṛg Veda,* is dated to around 1500 BCE, a millennium before the rise of Buddhism. However, according to the Hindu tradition, the Vedas have no date and they have no author. They also have always existed as sound, coming to be known by humans when those sounds were heard by the ancient sages of the past. Among the various proofs given for their eternity is that no one can remember who composed them. They are considered infallible precisely because they were not composed by fallible humans.

Thus, any religion or philosophy that seeks to challenge the authority of the Vedas requires its own antiquity; a thirty-five-year-old Indian prince cannot simply announce that he has become the Enlightened One after meditating under a tree one night. Instead, he has perfected himself over the course of many billions of years. However, even this cannot equal the antiquity of the Vedas. And so it is said that he took a vow from a previous buddha, who had in turn taken a vow from a previous buddha, passing backward in time to a time immemorial. The ancient city in the forest was never built, it is only restored. And so, in Jainism, another challenger to Vedic authority, their founder Mahāvīra, possibly a contemporary of the Buddha, is the twenty-fourth *tīrthaṅkara,* or "maker of the ford," their equivalent of a buddha. And "our buddha," Gotama Buddha, was the fourth, the seventh, or the twenty-fifth, but this only refers to our world system. There have been previous buddhas in previous worlds, worlds that all passed through the four stages of creation, abiding, destruction, and nothingness. And each of those buddhas taught the same truth, the same path to liberation from suffering. And each of those buddhas perfected themselves over billions of lifetimes. In their penultimate lifetime, they are all reborn in one of the Buddhist heavens located in the sky above the central mountain in the Buddhist cosmos, called Mount Meru. It is a heaven called Tuṣita, or "Joyous," where they await their final birth.

It is here that we find Flaubert's Buddha, who declares: "That I might deliver the world, I resolved to be born among men. The gods wept when I departed from them." The gods did indeed weep. According to some versions, one of those weeping gods was the Buddha's successor, the bodhisattva Maitreya ("Kindness"), who will not descend to our world to achieve buddhahood until the teachings of our buddha have completely disappeared from the world. According to the standard Buddhist cosmology, the advent of Maitreya will occur when the human lifespan has decreased to ten years of age and then has slowly increased to eighty thousand years.[4] That means that Maitreya will have a long wait in Tuṣita, calculated, according to one system, at 5.67 billion years after the passing of Śākyamuni. As Maitreya wept at the descent of the future buddha into the world of humans, the soon-to-be Buddha comforted him, telling him not to be overcome by sadness. One of the epithets of Maitreya is therefore Ajita (Undefeated).

It was now time for the future buddha to determine when and where he would be reborn. The first consideration was the time. According to Buddhist cosmology, the human lifespan falls and rises in cycles, falling as low as ten years and rising as high as eighty thousand years. The future buddha therefore had to consider the appropriate period in the fluctuating human lifespan to enter the world. According to the Pāli account, he concluded that anything over one hundred thousand years was too long because it would take too long for the sufferings of aging and death to be apparent to those with such long lives. If the lifespan was under a hundred years, a period described as a time of moral depravity, it would be too short for his disciples to progress on the path. He therefore concluded that a buddha should appear in the world when the lifespan was between one hundred thousand and one hundred years. He selected the latter figure. Next was the place. According to Buddhist cosmology, we live on a flat world consisting of four island continents around a central mountain. Buddhas are only born on the southern continent, called Jambudvīpa; on that continent, he chose the country of Madhyadeśa, the Middle Country, one of the five traditional regions of ancient India.

Next, he chose his caste. The Buddha is often portrayed—inaccurately in modern sources—as an opponent of the caste system, the division of Indian society into four hereditary castes: *brahmins,* that is, priests; *kṣatriya,* warriors and rulers; *vaiśya,* merchants and landowners; and *śudra,* laborers. That the Buddha makes this one of his five considerations indicates its importance. It is said that buddhas are only born into the first two castes, depending on which is more highly respected at the time. We recall that Sumedha was a member of the brahmin caste. In the intervening eons its seems that the kṣatriya had ascended, because the bodhisattva declares that he will be born into the warrior caste. That the descriptions of his decision stress this point is further evidence of his future contentious relations with brahmin priests, the chief competitors of Buddhist monks for daily alms and royal patronage.

The fourth consideration is about the mother; she must be "neither wanton nor addicted to drink." Finally, the future buddha must decide on the lifespan of his future mother, how long she will live after he enters her womb. He says that it will be ten months (the period of gestation following the lunar calendar) and seven days. That is, she will live for seven days after his birth.[5] We will return to the demise of Queen Māyā.

Flaubert mentions none of this, focusing on the beauty of the mother, clearly evoking the Virgin Mary with a mildly erotic piety: "I sought me first a woman worthy to give me birth: a woman of warrior race, the wife of a king, exceedingly good, excessively beautiful, with body firm as adamant;—and at time of the full moon, without the auxiliation of any male, I entered her womb." However, the Buddhist sources do not describe Queen Māyā as a virgin. It is the case that in the account of the bodhisattva's conception, King Śuddhodana is not present, such that the conception took place "without the auxiliation of any male." In order not to spoil the sense of coincidence between the Buddha and Jesus, to which Flaubert will return in the passages ahead, he does not mention that the embryonic buddha did not enter his mother's womb in the form of an infant carrying a tiny cross, as we see in Robert Campin's fifteenth-century *Merode Altarpiece* depicting the Annunciation, but as a white elephant who enters her right side.[6]

From here, Flaubert jumps directly to the Buddha's birth: "I issued from it by the right side. Stars stopped in their courses." Buddhist texts often describe the human body as a site of almost unspeakable disgust and the womb as a fetid prison where the fetus undergoes all manner of suffering over the course of ten lunar months, ending in the horrific experience of birth, described in lurid detail. We note that the four sufferings most often mentioned in Buddhism are birth, aging, sickness, and death. The bodhisattva must be reborn as a human in his last lifetime, yet as an exalted being who has perfected himself over the course of billions of lifetimes, he cannot be depicted as undergoing a typical birth. Indeed, one of the early Buddhist schools argued that when in the womb, the bodhisattva does not go through the fetal stages called the oblong, the oval, and the lumplike. And his mother's womb is not a dank prison but a perfumed palace made of jewels where the future buddha and all manner of visiting gods may walk about at their leisure, without his mother's body changing size or her feeling the slightest discomfort.[7]

One might ask why, if the future buddha is such an exalted being, does he need to spend ten lunar months in a womb, albeit a womb of such splendor? Why did he not appear in the world fully formed? In Buddhism, many beings, including both gods and the denizens of the various hells, appear as what are called "apparitional beings," with no need to go through the tedious stages of gestation, birth, and maturation. This very question was taken up by a Buddhist author of the fifth century, who explained that buddhas enter a womb so that they will have a body that can be cremated when they pass into nirvāṇa, thereby producing relics that can be worshipped by the faithful.[8]

The Buddha continues: "I issued from it by the right side." This refers to the future Buddha's unusual birth. As just noted, he entered his mother's womb not through vaginal intercourse but through the right side of her body, painlessly, despite the fact that he had taken the form of a six-tusked white elephant. After ten lunar months, he emerged from the same side, the auspicious side of the body in ancient India.

In the story that is often told, Queen Māyā had decided to give birth to her child at the home of her parents and so traveled with her retinue from the capital of Kapilavastu toward the city of Devadaha. En route, in a place called Lumbinī Garden, she felt birth pangs and raised her right arm to grasp the branch of a tree. The child emerged from under her right arm. This momentous scene is often depicted in Buddhist art. In many works of art, the infant future Buddha already has a full head of hair and an *uṣṇīṣa*. The two most important gods of the Indian pantheon, Indra and Brahmā, descended to earth for the momentous event, catching the infant in a pearled skein while other deities rained down water from the sky to wash the newborn (despite his having spent ten months in the immaculate palace of his mother's womb). However, the child did not need to be held; he could already walk and talk. He took seven steps to the north, with a lotus blossoming under his foot with each step. Pointing to the sky above and the earth below, he announced, "In heaven and on earth, I alone am worthy of worship." When this scene is depicted in Buddhist art, the newborn is wearing a loincloth. Queen Māyā returned to the city with her infant son, who was presented to King Śuddhodana.

The emergence of a child from under its mother arm is the kind of arresting image that would have intrigued Flaubert, but he describes it only in one sentence ("I issued from it by the right side"), and in such a way that its meaning would not be clear to a reader unfamiliar with the story. The story, however, was known in Europe in the seventeenth century by the renowned German Jesuit Athanasius Kircher (1602–1680), who excoriated the Buddha as a purveyor of idolatry. Knowing that the infant Buddha emerged from his mother's right side and that his mother died seven days after his birth, Kircher explained that the infant had murdered his mother by gnawing his way out of her womb.[9]

Flaubert goes on to say, "Stars stopped in their courses." The Buddhist sources do not say this, but Burnouf's *Introduction to the History of Indian Buddhism* of 1844, which Flaubert would have known, describes an account given by a goddess who witnessed the birth, saying that the sky was "brilliant with a miraculous light, resplendent with gold, pleasant to the eyes."[10] And, as we shall see, the gods did rejoice. Flaubert's insertion of this stellar miracle seems part of his continuing attempt in this section to link the Buddha and the Christ. In his translation, Lafcadio Hearn reminds the reader with a footnote referencing the Gospel of Matthew.

Scholars speculate that the four primary places of pilgrimage in Buddhism—the sites of the Buddha's birth, enlightenment, first teaching, and passage into nirvāṇa—were established long after his death and that some of them may not have been the actual sites of those events. The great French scholar of Indian Buddhism André Bareau (1921–1993) speculated that the Buddha was born in the city of Kapilavastu. However, in order to encourage pilgrimage, a major source of support for the monastic community, his birthplace was moved to nearby Lumbinī, already the site of a tree cult, associating Queen Māyā with the local tree spirit (*yakṣī*). As we will see in Part 2, archaeologists have discovered an ancient tree shrine at Lumbinī, one that may predate the fifth-century BCE date that many scholars give for the birth of the Buddha. Bareau speculated that the Buddhists decided to place the Buddha's birth there, with his mysterious mother, who would die seven days after his birth, holding a branch of a sacred tree (the tree that already had its own cultus) as the bodhisattva emerged from her right side.[11] Regardless of whether this theory is correct, Lumbinī was identified as the birthplace of the Buddha. And it became a site of Buddhist pilgrimage relatively quickly, significant enough that the Emperor Aśoka himself visited some one hundred and fifty years after the death of the Buddha, assuming that we knew when he died.

> From the furthest recesses of the Himalayas, a holy man one hundred years of age, hurried to see me.
> Hilarion: "A man named Simeon . . . who should not see death, before he had seen the Christ of the Lord."[12]

With the stars, Flaubert has intimated the comparison of the Buddha to Jesus, a comparison that had been made negatively by Christian missionaries for centuries. Thus, the Jesuit missionary to Tibet Ippolito Desideri (1684–1773) described the future Buddha's choice of his mother in these terms, laying the blame on Satan himself: "The special gifts and perfections he sought in the woman whom he had to choose as his mother are also like another copy made by the said infernal monkey of what our ascetics and contemplatives are wont to say about the Divine Word's election of the Most Holy Virgin to be elevated to the great dignity of the Mother of God Incarnate."[13]

Flaubert's somewhat more nuanced comparison of the Buddha to Jesus is made explicit here with the story of a holy man from the Himalayas, whom Flaubert does not name. His name is Asita (also Kāḷadevala in some Pāli sources). There are several versions of his story. In the Pāli sources, he is a brahmin priest who served as court chaplain to King Śuddhodana's father and was both Śuddhodana's teacher during his youth and the court chaplain early in his reign. Later in life, Asita receives permission from the king to renounce his official duties to practice meditation, eventually developing supernormal powers that allow him to travel to various heavens. On a visit to the Heaven of the Thirty-three on the summit of Mount Meru he finds the gods celebrating the birth on earth of the future buddha. Returning to the palace, he examines Śuddhodana's infant son, seeing that he possesses the physical signs of a buddha—the thirty-two marks and the eighty secondary marks. He rejoices at being in the presence of the future buddha but knows that he will not live long enough to receive his teachings after the prince achieves enlightenment. Asita has attained a state of meditative concentration such that when he dies, he will be reborn in the Formless Realm, a region of the Buddhist cosmos where, as the name suggests, the beings are only consciousness, without physical form. The karmic result of achieving such a state in this life is so powerful that one cannot avoid rebirth there, a rebirth that lasts for many millennia. The only way to avoid such a fate is to achieve liberation from rebirth before one's death, and at the time, this was impossible because the future buddha had yet to achieve enlightenment and teach the path to liberation. We will discuss these states of meditation in more detail below in the context of Prince Siddhārtha's meditation practice.

Flaubert's source for the story of Asita is found in the *Play in Full* (*Lalitavistara*). Here Asita is not the king's chaplain living on the grounds of the palace, but a sage living in the Himalayas with his nephew. He sees gods rejoicing in the sky and uses his "divine eye" (one of the five supernormal powers) to see that a prince has been born whose body bears the thirty-two major marks and eighty secondary marks indicating that he will become either a universal monarch (*cakravartin*) or a buddha. He and his nephew then fly to Kapilavastu, where they ask to see the prince. The king informs them that the child is sleeping. Asita replies that great beings do not sleep long. The king goes and gets his son and hands him to Asita, who places him on his lap. Holding the child, Asita bursts into tears. The king, fearing that a terrible fate awaits his son, becomes alarmed, but Asita says that he is lamenting his own fate, for he will die before the prince achieves buddhahood. He then gives a long speech in which he enumerates each of the thirty-two marks and eighty secondary marks that he saw on the infant (apparently born with all forty teeth, one of the major marks).

Yet a third version contains more grisly imagery. When Śuddhodana shows his newborn son to Asita, the king performs the traditional form of obeisance of touching the baby's head to the sage's feet. Before he can do so, however, the infant twists in his father's arms so that his feet touch Asita's head. It is explained that this was a compassionate act by the baby; if the future buddha's head had touched Asita's feet, Asita's head would have exploded into seven pieces.[14] This is the kind of detail that Flaubert certainly would have included if he knew this source.

It is at this point that Flaubert makes his first direct reference to Jesus. Saint Hilarion (291–371), a contemporary and sometime disciple of Saint Anthony, speaks of "A man named Simeon . . . who should not see death, before he had seen the Christ of the Lord." He is referring here to the story, found in the Gospel of Luke, of an old man in Jerusalem named Simeon who is informed by the Holy Spirit that he will not die until he has seen the Christ. This leads him to go to the temple, where Mary and Joseph have taken the infant Jesus for what is known in Christian sources as "the presentation at the temple," the performance of the ritual of the purification of the first-born son. There, they meet Simeon, a stranger and not a priest, who takes the child in his arms and says (in the King James Version, Luke 2:29–32), "Lord, now lettest thou thy servant depart in peace, according to thy word: For mine eyes have seen thy salvation, which thou hast prepared before the face of all people; a light to lighten the Gentiles, and the glory of thy people Israel." He goes on to give a rather cryptic prophecy that this will not occur without difficulty. Unlike the story of Asita, it is a brief scene and one in which there is no lamentation or shedding of tears. Instead, Simeon simply rejoices that he can now die in peace for redemption is at hand.

Flaubert leaves the prognostication of the infant's future to Asita. He does not provide a more elaborate and well-known scene, in which the king summons eight brahmin priests to prophesy his son's future and give him a name. Like Asita, they examine the marks on the infant's body and recognize them as signs of both a buddha and a *cakravartin.* At the conclusion of their examination, seven of them hold up two fingers, indicating that he will be one or the other. The eighth, and youngest, an expert in physiognomic prognostication named Kauṇḍinya (Koṇdañña in Pāli), holds up one finger, declaring that it is certain that the child will be a buddha. Thirty-five years later, Kauṇḍinya and the sons of four of the seven other priests will become the first disciples of the Buddha, the famous "group of five" (*pañcavargika*). The infant is given the name Siddhārtha, "he who achieves his goal."

The *cakravartin* figures as a kind of doppelganger of the Buddha, one the perfect king, one the perfect ascetic; world conqueror and world renouncer, as one scholar has described them. The term literally means "wheel turning," and refers to the most important of his seven treasures, a magic wheel. In order to expand their domains and display their power, kings in Vedic India performed the "horse sacrifice" (*aśvamedha*). A stallion would be let loose to wander, accompanied by an army. Whatever territory the horse traversed was claimed by the king; his warriors would do battle with those who disputed the claim. The horse would wander in this way for a year, after which it would be led home, where it would be purified and then sacrificed (along with several hundred other animals), with the king declared the ruler of all the lands where the horse had set foot during his travels.

We see elements of the horse sacrifice in the *cakravartin.* Although one of his seven possessions is a horse, he also has a self-propelled wheel that magically rolls across the regions of the world, bringing them under his rule. When the wheel is not rolling around the world, it floats in the sky, spinning. Buddhist texts describe four kinds of wheel-turning kings, based on the substance of their wheel and the extent of their domain. As noted, Buddhism has a flat-earth cosmology, with four island continents surrounding a central mountain. The king with a wheel of gold rules all four continents without the need for an army; the rulers of the lands crossed by the wheel surrender without a fight. The king with a wheel of silver rules three continents (all except the northern continent), with the local kings yielding at the threat of invasion. The king with a wheel of copper becomes the ruler of two continents (the southern and the eastern) after a brief battle with those who resist. The king with an iron wheel rules only our southern continent and achieves victory only after protracted warfare.[15] Evoking the movement, ideally without opposition, of the *cakravartin*'s precious possession, the Buddha's teaching is referred to as his "turning of the wheel of the dharma."

Although the Buddha is revered today for his teachings, the marks that Asita and the eight astrologers saw on his infant body were extolled over the centuries, with commentaries explaining what he had done in a past life to result, for example, in his having eyelashes like a bull. Those marks, however, do not simply evoke either celebration or anxiety; they can be interpreted in many ways. His feet, marked with the patterns of a wheel on each sole, suggest the movement of Buddhism across Asia, where footprints of the Buddha are often found. His retractable penis suggests Buddhism's complicated relationship to gender and sexuality.[16] His webbed fingers suggest the difficulties that attended the first depictions of the Buddha in sculpture. His jaw like that of a lion evokes his teaching, called the "lion's roar," which silences the lesser teachers of the land. His long tongue suggests his remarkable powers of speech, which allow him to teach in multiple languages at once. His long earlobes, stretched by the earrings he wore as a prince, signify his princely pedigree and his proud membership in the warrior caste of ancient India. The curls on his head, which never needed to be cut, set him apart from dreadlocked Hindu yogins and his own shaven-headed monks and nuns. The circle of hair between his eyes is the source of a beam of light that illuminates distant worlds and their denizens, suggesting the vastness of the Buddhist universe. The bump on his head, the "crown protrusion," originally just a topknot, was considered so numinous that it became a deity itself.

The prophesies of the eight brahmin priests present the first moment of dramatic tension in the biography of the Buddha; his descent into the womb, gestation, and birth have all been occasions of divine and human happiness. Now, seven of the brahmins have said that the prince will become either a buddha or a *cakravartin,* and Kauṇḍinya (and Asita in the other version) has declared that he will definitely become a buddha. One might imagine that any father would be delighted at either destiny, but King Śuddhodana is depicted as alarmed at the thought that his son and heir might abandon his future throne, renounce his royal duties, and ignore his familial responsibilities, leaving instead to meditate in the forest. Assuming, perhaps correctly, that one turns to the religious life as a result of existential despair, he devises a plan to prevent it, famously building a palace where never is heard a discouraging word. He therefore keeps his son under a luxurious form of house arrest for twenty-nine years. Having been told by the eight prognosticators that the prince would renounce the world if he ever saw the four omens—an old person, a sick person, a corpse, or a mendicant—the king takes steps to ensure that none of these will be allowed into the presence of the prince; Śuddhodana has his troops set up a defensive perimeter around the palace.[17] Thus begins the chapter of the future buddha's life in the palace.

Almost immediately, however, a death occurred that the king could not prevent. The prophecy of the priests is said to have taken place five days after the prince's birth. The accounts of these days generally fail to mention that his mother, Queen Māyā, died two days later, as the future buddha had foreseen before he descended into her womb. The child would be nursed and raised by her sister, Mahāprajāpatī, also married to the king. Several reasons, none particularly satisfying to the modern reader, are given for the queen's demise. One is that she suffered a fatal case of joy when she learned of the predictions of her son's future fame. A second describes a kind of postpartum depression, in which she dies because she can no longer experience the joy she felt when the future buddha was in her resplendent womb. A third is that she died after seven days because otherwise she would have done so when he abandoned her, and the world, twenty-nine years later. It is also explained that the mothers of all buddhas die after seven days because the sacred womb that had been occupied by a future buddha could never house another child, nor was it appropriate for the mother of a buddha to subsequently have sexual intercourse. And so, it seems, she had to die.[18]

Mahāmāyā thus remains a strangely minor figure in the drama of the Buddha's life, depicted more in sculpture and painting than in words, with none of the dimension and detail that we find in the cult of the Virgin Mary as *theotokos,* from her ancestry to her birth, her youth, her marriage, her death, and her assumption. Mahāmāyā had her own assumption, being reborn as a (according to some versions, male) deity in Tuṣita, the Joyous Heaven, the same heaven from which her son had descended into her womb ten lunar months and seven days before. And he would meet her again, years later, teaching her the dharma in a different heaven, although, as will be discussed in Part 2, this encounter serves a number of doctrinal purposes beyond the expression of filial piety.

3
The Prince in the Palace

> I was led unto the schools; and it was found that I knew more than the teachers. . . . In the midst of the doctors . . . and all that heard him were astonished at his wisdom![1]

On his first day of school, Prince Siddhārtha knows more than the teacher, listing the sixty-four scripts that he can read, scripts that the teacher has never heard of, with Hilarion offering another parallel to the life of Jesus. After alluding to the story of Simeon when the infant Jesus was taken to the temple of Jerusalem, he now evokes the scene, also from the Gospel of Luke, of the twelve-year-old Jesus debating with the elders in the temple. The future buddha, however, does not need to debate. His teacher defers to the child's great knowledge. When the teacher next begins to teach the children the alphabet, illustrating each letter with a sentence beginning with it, the future buddha magically causes each of those sentences to be a statement of Buddhist doctrine. Hence, for the letter *a*, he says, "Every conditioned thing is impermanent (*anityaḥ sarvasaṃskārah*)." And so on, for each of the forty-six letters of the Sanskrit alphabet.

> Continually did I meditate in the gardens. The shadows of the trees turned with the turning of the sun; but the shadow of that which sheltered me turned not.[2]

This passage refers to an odd scene during Prince Siddhārtha's youth. Each spring, there was a plowing festival in which the king and his ministers would leave the city and go into the countryside, each with a festooned plow. There, they would join the local farmers in plowing the fields to inaugurate the growing season. The king was accompanied with a large retinue, including the prince and his nursemaids. The story implies that he was quite young, because a kind of tent was set up for him under a rose apple (*jambu*) tree, where he and his nursemaids were protected from the sun, and from public view. At some point, the women left the prince and went to watch the festivities, becoming so absorbed in the day's events that they left him alone for several hours. When they looked back at the tree, they saw the shadows of the other nearby trees had all shifted over the course of the day, but the shadow of the tree that shaded the prince had not moved from the time they had left him. Racing to the tree, they pulled back the curtain that surrounded him and saw the child seated in the lotus posture meditating.

The texts relate that he achieved the first concentration that day. In Buddhist meditation theory, there are four levels of concentration (*dhyāna*), simply named first, second, third, and fourth. The architectonics of the Buddhist interior universe will be described in Chapter 5 in the context of the prince's practice of austerities. Here, we can say that the first concentration achieved by the boy prince is the lowest of the levels of concentration that are needed as the foundation for achievement of enlightenment. Nonetheless, it is an important achievement.

Although Flaubert suggests that the prince practiced meditation often, with the shade of the trees protecting him in each case, the biography of the Buddha that he consulted does not say this, mentioning only this scene at the plowing festival. The scene was sufficiently famous that, according to some sources, later in life, when the Buddha is asked to allow his image to be made, he authorizes an image of himself not as the Buddha but as the prince meditating under the rose apple tree.[3]

And so the young prince does not participate in the plowing festival, perhaps because he is too young, and does not observe it, as a young child might like to do. Instead, he is physically separated and shielded from it, seated in meditation under a tree, as he would famously do some years hence. As has been often noted, the scene thus prefigures his enlightenment after meditating all night under a different tree. Indeed, according to one account, it was essential to this later achievement. In a Pāli text called *Great Discourse to Saccaka* (*Mahāsaccaka Sutta*), the Buddha recounts that during his six years of practicing austerities, his various physical privations did not lead to deep states of meditation. He then says, "I recall that when my father the Sakyan was occupied, while I was sitting in the cool shade of a rose-apple tree, quite secluded from sensual pleasures, secluded from unwholesome states, I entered upon and abided in the first jhāna [concentration], which is accompanied by applied and sustained thought, with rapture and pleasure born of seclusion. Could that be the path to enlightenment?"[4] Inspired by this memory, he concludes that it is.

Still, this story raises an interesting question as we attempt, perhaps vainly, to impose a consistent identity onto the prince, not only from one lifetime to the next but even over the course of his final lifetime. There is no mention of anyone teaching

Prince Siddhārtha how to meditate before his departure from the palace. Having achieved advanced meditative states in numerous past lives, was his ability in his final life from a memory of a past practice? Yet he is not said to have remembered his past lives until the night of his enlightenment. And what motivated him to meditate during the plowing festival? Was it simply boredom?

A version of the story that appears in both the *Sūtra on the Great Renunciation* (*Abhiniṣkramaṇa Sūtra*) and the *Buddhacarita* provides a more elaborate account of the event, where the young prince is confronted with suffering prior to his famous four chariot rides. Here, he sees the yoked oxen being beaten by the farmers as they plow, the upturned earth in the furrows exposing insects who are quickly devoured by birds. It is this vision of suffering that causes the prince to turn away and sit down beneath the tree to meditate.[5]

> None could equal me in the knowledge of the Scriptures, the enumeration of atoms, the conduct of elephants, the working of wax, astronomy, poetry, pugilism, all the exercises and all the arts![6]

In a *Twilight Zone* episode called "A Nice Place to Visit," a man dies and finds himself in a luxurious apartment (with a Buddhist statue on the mantlepiece) where he has the best of everything. He wears the finest clothes, eats the finest food, and the drawers of the tables are stuffed with cash. He drives a Cadillac convertible. Beautiful women dance for him (as they do for the Buddha). In the casino, when he plays roulette, he wins every time. When he plays poker, he gets a royal flush in every hand. When he plays pool, he sinks every ball on the break. The future Buddha's life in the palace is very much like this.

He displays his mathematical skills by immediately and correctly multiplying astronomical figures without the use of a calculator, in each case giving the correct name for the resulting number. He even is able to calculate what is perhaps the most common example of the innumerable in Indian literature, the number of grains of sand in the river Ganges. From the immense, he turns to the minute, explaining how many of the smallest particles (*paramāṇu*) constitute a particle (*aṇu*), how many water particles constitute one particle of dust, and so on. This is Flaubert's reference to "the enumeration of atoms." Flaubert's other references come from this paragraph from the *Play in Full:*

> He was superior in leaping, and likewise in writing, finger counting, computation, arithmetic, wrestling, archery, running, rowing, swimming, elephant mounting, horsemanship, carriage driving, bow-and-arrow skills, balance and strength, heroics, gymnastics, elephant driving, lassoing, rising, advancing, retreating, gripping with the hand, gripping using the foot, gripping using the top of the head, cutting, cleaving, breaking, rubbing, target shooting without causing injury, target shooting at vital points, target shooting through only hearing the target, striking hard, playing dice, poetry composition, prose composition, painting, drama, dramatic action, tactical analysis, attending the sacred fire, playing the lute, playing other musical instruments, dancing, singing, chanting, storytelling, comedy, dancing to music, dramatic dancing, mimicry, garland stringing, cooling with a fan, dying precious gems, dying clothes, creating optical illusions, dream analysis, bird sounds, analysis of women,

> analysis of men, analysis of horses, analysis of elephants, analysis of cattle, analysis of goats, analysis of sheep, analysis of dogs, ritual science and its related lexicon, revealed scripture, ancient stories, history, the Vedas, grammar, etymologies, phonetics, metrics and composition, rules for conducting rituals, astrology, the Sāṃkhya philosophical system, the Yoga philosophical system, ceremonies, the art of courtesans, the Vaiśeṣika philosophical system, economics, ethics, hydraulics, knowledge of demigods, knowledge of game animals, knowledge of bird sounds, logic, hydromechanics, beeswax crafts, sewing, wickerwork, leaf cutting, and perfume making.[7]

Prince Siddhārtha is an excellent athlete, defeating his cousins in a wrestling match. In an archery competition, like Odysseus, he raises a bow that no one else can bend and fires an arrow that, according to different accounts, pierces five iron drums, each a greater distance from the one before it, and seven palm trees. The arrow then strikes the earth, causing water to flow.[8] This creates the River of the Arrow described by the seventh-century Chinese pilgrim Xuanzang; Kipling made it the goal of the Teshoo Lama's quest in *Kim*. Prince Siddhārtha's cousin Devadatta is so strong that he kills an elephant with a blow of his fist. But the corpse of the great beast blocks the city gates and Devadatta cannot lift it. Prince Siddhārtha flips it over the city walls with his foot.[9] The stories of the Buddha's youth are thus very much of a piece. He is always the best, always has the most.

In the *Twilight Zone* episode, the man eventually becomes bored with what seems an unending chain of success, where every wish is fulfilled, telling the man who brought him there that he had always imagined heaven to be like this, but he had become bored. He asks if he might go to "the other place," to hell. His guide informs him that this *is* the other place; he is in hell. The episode ends with the guide laughing diabolically. The same success that bores the reader of the stories of Prince Siddhārtha's youth seems to have bored the prince, for he eventually, after twenty-nine long years in the palace, seeks to escape. But first, he gets married.

> In accordance with custom, I took to myself a wife; and I passed the days in my kingly palace;—clad in pearls, under a rain of perfumes, refreshed by the fans of thirty thousand women,—watching my people from the height of my terraces adorned with fringes of resonant bells.[10]

When Prince Siddhārtha is sixteen, his father decides that he should marry. The prince contemplates the dangers of desire and acknowledges his preference for a solitary life in the forest. In some versions of the life of the Buddha, the prince seems to have a foreknowledge of his destiny. That is the case in Flaubert's source, the *Play in Full*. And so, recalling that previous buddhas had wives and families, he agrees to his father's request, describing in verse the qualities that his bride should possess, including that she be "loving like a sister" yet "as adept as a courtesan in knowing the arts of love."[11] The king announces that the prince will select a bride in seven days, inviting all eligible women of the city to assemble at the palace. He has jewelry made for the prince to give to each of the women, instructing his ministers to observe the eye contact that takes place in the exchange. The women assemble and approach the prince one by one, receiving their gift. All but one averts her eyes. She is Yaśodharā. However, by this time, the prince has given away all the jewelry. And so he takes off his own ring and gives it to her. The royal spies report this to the king and the marriage is arranged.

In the story as it appears in the *Play in Full,* when the king goes to Yaśodharā's father to arrange the marriage, her father protests that the prince has lived a life of leisure and thus lacks skills in the manly arts, like swordsmanship, archery, and wrestling. Those tests of skill are then arranged, with the prince, of course, triumphant in all events. Perhaps in the interests of concision, Flaubert reverses the order of events in his account, placing the feats of strength before the marriage. His interest, clearly, is in getting the prince out of the palace.

Yaśodharā is not a finely drawn figure in many of the canonical sources. In some texts, she is called Gopā, in others Bimbā. In Pāli sources she is simply called Rāhulamātā, "Rāhula's Mother," signifying her main role in the biography of the Buddha: to give birth to his son. However, as we shall see, she will have much to say upon her husband's departure from the palace and upon his return as the Buddha. In some versions, the prince has two other wives; in one account he has sixty thousand wives. And this is not to mention the women of the inner chamber, numbered in the Pāli biography at forty thousand, always ready to dance, sing, and perform for him.

4
The Great Departure

> But the sight of the miseries of the world turned me away from pleasure. I fled.[1]

Flaubert reduces some of the most famous scenes in Buddhist literature, and certainly the most moving scenes in the life of the Buddha, to sixteen words. Before the Buddha could save the world, the prince Siddhārtha first had to renounce it.

He is married at age sixteen and nothing of note seems to happen for the next thirteen years. It is only when he is twenty-nine, as the story goes, that he grows curious about life outside the palace walls and asks his father for permission to take a chariot ride outside the palace. His father at first refuses, and then eventually relents, but only after taking a series of precautions. He has his army conduct a sweep of the city, gathering anyone who is old, sick, or ugly and placing them in detention for the day. He then covers the route of the excursion with flowers and incense, placing flags and flowers in all the trees. The chariots of ancient India were similar to those of ancient Rome, with room for a driver and a passenger. Prince Siddhārtha's driver is the royal groom, Chandaka.

Departing the city from the eastern gate, they soon encounter an old man who apparently was missed in the detention of the decrepit. The man has gray hair and decayed teeth. He walks unsteadily, supported by a cane, his body bent and quivering with palsy. Never having seen such a being before, the prince asks his charioteer who it is. Chandaka replies that it is an old man. The prince asks whether he has always been like that. Chandaka replies that the man once drank his mother's milk, crawled on the ground, and became a handsome youth. "Slayer of beauty, ravager of strength, / the womb of sorrow, the end of pleasures, / Destroyer of memory, foe of the sense organs— / this is called old age."[2] The prince then asks whether this is *the* old man, that is, is he the only person so afflicted, or will everyone one day grow old. When the prince learns that old age is the fate of all, he reacts like a bull hearing lightning strike nearby.

He tells Chandaka to drive him back to the palace. He eventually overcomes his despair and rides forth from the palace three more times, departing from the southern, then the western, then the northern gate. Despite the king taking precautions, on the second of his four excursions, he sees a sick person. Learning of the ubiquity of illness, he returns to the palace. On the third excursion, he sees a man covered in cloth being carried on the shoulders of four men, the members of his family walking behind, weeping and throwing dust on their heads. His charioteer explains that this is a dead man: "This is someone his dearest ones discard, / though they nurtured him and guarded him with care."[3] Learning that death is not something that struck only this man but is inevitable for all, he returns to the palace, telling his charioteer, "This is the inevitable end of all men; / yet the world rashly revels, casting fear aside; / the hearts of men, I suspect, must indeed be hard, / that they journey along this road so unperturbed."[4]

It of course seems preposterous that someone, even with such wealth and privilege, could remain oblivious to the existence of old age, sickness, and death for the first twenty-eight years of his life. Still, there may be a psychological truth here. Some of us are blessed with the good fortune to avoid serious illness ourselves during our youth and may not encounter debilitating old age and death among members of our family until around the age of thirty, a time when our grandparents begin to die. The age of twenty-nine is an unusual number in Indian literature, and the stories of the Buddha's life say little about what occurred between his marriage at sixteen and his departure from the palace at twenty-nine; as we shall see, he did not start a family, as one might expect that he would. Perhaps, then, the chariot rides are meant to represent the moment in life when we start to ponder the great questions of birth and death in a serious way.

On his fourth excursion, through the northern gate, he sees a monk meditating under a tree. Asking who he is, the prince is told by his charioteer that he is someone who has renounced the world. The Pāli biography notes that because there was no buddha at the time, there were no monks; the monk that the prince sees is an apparition created by the gods, with the gods empowering the charioteer to describe what the prince saw as a monk.[5] Inspired by this vision, the prince returns to the palace. This, at least, is the way the story is most often told. We find a different version in the *Deeds of the Buddha*.

This text, called the *Buddhacarita* in Sanskrit, ascribed to the famous poet Aśvaghoṣa, is considered the earliest freestanding and complete biography of the Buddha. It is renowned for the beauty of its verse, a masterpiece of Sanskrit court poetry, replete with allusions to Indian myth and adorned with all manner of figures of speech. In Aśvaghoṣa's text, there is much that is erotic and, in the case of the Buddha, there is an association of alluring women with death. This occurs in two scenes. In the first, after his third chariot ride, where the prince has learned for the first time that everyone will one day die, the prince passes through a pleasure grove on his way back to the palace, where he finds a crowd of beautiful women awaiting him. Aśvaghoṣa describes them in erotic detail and their various attempts to seduce the prince, flashing their girdles, exposing their breasts, singing alluring songs, binding him with garlands. As the title of chapter, "Rebuffing the Women," suggests, the prince is unmoved.

His friend Udāyin urges him to reconsider, providing example after example of famous sages of the past who had succumbed to carnal pleasures. The prince responds with a long speech, saying that he would gladly indulge if the bodies of the women remained beautiful. "But when these lovely forms of theirs / will have been consumed by old age, / They'll be repulsive even to themselves; it is delusion to delight in them."[6] He declares that as long as old age, sickness, and death exist, he can take no delight in the pleasures of the senses. He returns to the palace.

Later in the same text, with his father's consent, he leaves the palace for a fourth time, not in a chariot with a charioteer, but alone on his loyal steed Kaṇṭhaka. He comes across some farmers tilling the soil and, as the boy prince does in the *Great Renunciation,* he sees the farmers toiling, the oxen straining, the ground covered with dead insects unearthed by the plow. He feels compassion for them all, grieving for the dead insects as if a kinsman had been killed, crying out, "How wretched, indeed, is this world."

It is then in Aśvaghoṣa's version that he sits down to meditate for the first time, not as the child at the plowing festival but as a married prince. It is then that he achieves the first concentration. And as he emerges from meditation, he encounters a mendicant, not on a fourth chariot ride, as in the more standard version, but alone in the forest. When the prince asks him who he is, he replies that he has been frightened by birth and death, that he has given up both love and hate for the objects of the senses, and that he is in search of a deathless state, living the life of a mendicant, without a home or possessions, eating only alms. Having said that, the man then flies into the sky; he is in fact a deity of long life who has seen previous buddhas and thus is seeking to inspire the next one. The prince then returns to the city. As he enters, a woman who was watching him declares that the wife of such a husband is certainly happy and fulfilled. The word she uses for "fulfilled" is *nirvṛtā* in Sanskrit. The prince hears what she says and immediately feels calm, not because of the compliment but because it sounds like *nirvāṇa*.

This would be the prince's last day in the palace; that night he would make what is celebrated in Buddhist literature and art as the "great departure." In some ways, it is the most momentous day in the history of our age. Billions of years ago, Sumedha had made his vow and the former Buddha had made his prophecy. But the bodhisattva had to perfect himself, according to the Pāli tradition, for four immeasurable eons and one thousand ordinary eons. He has done so. Now the prince needs only to leave the palace and find the truth. And so, this day, in which a man abandons his throne, his wife, and his newborn child, is celebrated, even by the gods.

Much happens on that last day and night. Upon his return to the palace after meeting the mendicant, a courtier comes to the prince with the happy news that Yaśodharā has given birth to a son. However, instead of being delighted, the prince despairs, saying, *rāhu jāto bandhanam jātam*, "A fetter is born; an impediment [*bandha* is a cognate of 'bond'] has arisen." Thinking that the prince is naming the child, the courtier reports this to the princess, who dutifully names the child Rāhula, or "fetter."

Prince Siddhārtha has by now seen the "four omens" prophesied at his birth—the existence of old age, sickness, and death, and those who seek a state beyond them—the four facts that his father had sought to shield him from. And so perhaps the king is not surprised when his son comes to him and asks his father's permission to leave the palace and renounce the world. The king refuses and tries to dissuade him, telling him that the time is not right; indeed, it is more fitting that the king, his duty to his people now done, should give up the throne to the prince and prepare for his own death. But the prince is unmoved. Finally, his father says that he will offer him anything if only he will stay. In some versions, the prince asks that his father promise him four things: that he (the prince) will never die, become ill, grow old, or lose his fortune. In the *Mahāvastu,* he asks for eight: "Grant me, father, these eight boons: that old age does not overtake my youth; that disease does not overtake my health; that death does not take away my life; that I shall not be bereft of your company; that this harem of women like the Apsarases and my numerous kinsfolk do not disappear; that this kingdom and realm experience no reverse or any other evil vicissitude; that those who at my birth were invited to partake of ambrosial joy should all have their lusts quelled, and that for me there be an end of birth, old age and death."[7]

Whether four or eight, this, of course, is beyond the powers of even the king. The prince tells his father that he should not try to stop him, "for it is not right to obstruct a man / Who's trying to escape from a burning house."[8] He argues that it is inevitable that death will separate him from the world; it is far better that he separate from the world at a time of his own choosing so that he might reach his goal. His goal, of course, is to find the place beyond death.

Hoping that his son might be distracted from his quest, the king orders that the women of the inner chamber, the courtesans, attend the prince in his private quarters. Yet knowing that this may not succeed, the king also posts guards at the city gates. Skilled not only in the arts of love, the women perform for him, playing musical instruments, dancing, and singing, dressed in their finery. The prince sits impassively on his throne; in the Pāli biography, he falls asleep briefly. As the night wears on, they become weary, one by one falling asleep on the floor. Some begin drooling, others grind their teeth, still others talk in their sleep. Their mouths are agape, their carefully coiffed hair becomes disheveled, their robes are all askew, their bodies contorted in embarrassing postures. Surveying the scene, the prince sees the women as corpses, the floor of his palace transformed into a charnel ground, the bodies of the women a source not of lust but of disgust. Once again, we see the association of women with death. After the prince saw the corpse being carried to the cremation ground, learning of death for the first time, he encountered beautiful women seeking to seduce him. Now, to distract him from his goal, his father sends in beautiful women to seduce his son. But they become exhausted and fall asleep. The prince sees only cadavers.

There is a second encounter with women, or a woman, on that fateful night, this with his wife Yaśodharā. There are several versions of the scene. In one, as the prince is making his final preparations to escape the palace, he experiences a rare moment of particular love, not the universal love for all sentient beings that would be extolled in Buddhist texts for centuries, but the natural love for his wife and for his newborn child. He goes into Yaśodharā's chamber, where he finds her sleeping with Rāhula by her side (according to some versions one week old, according to others, born that day). He wants to pick up his son and hold him one last time, but he fears that if he does so he will wake his wife, and he will lose his resolve to renounce them. Among the five senses, Buddhism privileges, both in its practice and in its poetry, sight and hearing. There is danger in touch. And so the prince sees, but does not touch, what he is about to leave behind. We shall return to that backward glance.

According to another version of the Buddha's life, there is a further urgency that he leave the palace, beyond the fear that his love for his wife and child might keep him there, an urgency that recalls the famous prognostications at the time of his birth, when the king's astrologers predicted that the infant prince would become either a *cakravartin* or a buddha, a world conqueror or a world renouncer. Now, twenty-nine years later, a god appears to the prince and tells him that if he does not renounce the world in seven days, he will become a *cakravartin*. The seven treasures of this universal monarch will descend from the sky, "And you will have a full thousand sons who will be valiant, brave, comely, overpowering the armies of their enemies, and noble. You will hold and occupy in justice, without opposition, without trouble, without recourse to violence and without oppression, these four great continents."[9]

According to the Pāli account, the god who informs the prince is Māra, the deity of desire and death, making his first appearance in the story, expressing it not as a warning to leave but as an enticement to stay. The Buddha's nemesis, Māra will appear again and again at crucial moments in the story. The version of the story read by Flaubert does not include this detail. Otherwise, he would have certainly had Hilarion note the parallel with the story in the Gospel of Matthew when Jesus, wandering in the wilderness for forty days and forty nights, encounters Satan, who takes him to a mountaintop where they survey the kingdoms of the world. Satan tells him that he will make Jesus the ruler of the world if only he will worship him.

The story of the prince's final moments with his wife and infant son is one that plays on our emotions, providing a moment of doubt, a moment of emotion, a moment of tension, in what is presented as a triumphal scene in the drama, an epochal moment in the history of the world: the departure from the palace of the world in search of the entrance to the city of nirvāṇa, six years hence.

Yet another version of the parting with Yaśodharā sends us to the bookcase, reaching for a volume of Freud. For in this version, Rāhula is not born on the day of his father's departure; he is conceived. The Buddha's attitude toward sexual intercourse is made particularly clear in the story of the requirement of celibacy for the order of monks and nuns. As is well known, the Buddha did not institute the hundreds of vows that they keep in a single proclamation. Instead, the monastic code is presented as evolving organically; as misdeeds are done, the Buddha declares them to henceforth be infractions. The first of those misdeeds is sexual intercourse, resulting in its prohibition and the vow of celibacy. When the Buddha learns that the initial transgressor, the monk Sudinna, had acceded to his mother's plea to produce an heir by making love to the wife he had abandoned, the Buddha says, "Worthless man, it would be better that your penis be stuck into the mouth of a poisonous snake than into a woman's vagina. It would be better that your penis be stuck into the mouth of a black viper than into a woman's vagina. It would be better that your penis be stuck into a pit of burning embers, blazing and glowing, than into a woman's vagina. Why is that? For that reason you would undergo death or death-like suffering, but you would not on that account, at the break-up of the body, after death, fall into deprivation, the bad destination, the abyss, hell."[10] Although the Buddha would be falsely accused of breaking the vow himself, he is represented as remaining celibate from the time that he leaves the palace. (We shall not consider here his later representation in Buddhist tantra. Perhaps the most famous of those texts, the *Guhyasamāja Tantra,* begins, "Thus did I hear. At one time the Bhagavat was dwelling in the vagina of the vajra consort of the essence of the body, speech, and mind of all the tathāgatas.")

But what sexual experience, if any, did Prince Siddhārtha have before he left the palace? He obviously fathered a child. But was there more? He was married at the age of sixteen but his son was not born (or conceived) until more than a decade later. He is described as ravishingly handsome, lusted after by women, possessing a harem of beautiful women skilled in the arts of love, arts he himself is said to possess. In the *Mahāvastu,* the Buddha tells his monks that he was "most delicately brought up," with his father providing "the means of enjoying the five varieties of sensual pleasures, namely dance, song, music, orchestra, and women, that I might divert, enjoy and amuse myself."[11] In his biography, Aśvaghoṣa reports that the king had special palaces built for his son, "like divine mansions erected on earth" where he was "ensnared by women skilled in the erotic arts, / who were tireless in providing sexual delights." The prince "did not come to earth from that heavenly mansion."[12]

As we have noted, the body of a buddha is said to have the thirty-two marks of a superman (*mahāpuruṣa*), one of which is a penis that is hidden inside his pelvis (*vastiguhya*). Compared to the penis of a horse or an elephant, it can be retracted inside his body, where it is "hidden" or invisible. According to the monastic code that the Buddha would later establish, only a male could become a monk; a physical examination was required to confirm the applicant's sex before he could be ordained. Yet the Buddha's sex seems ambiguous; his hidden attribute required for the physical act of procreation marks spiritual detachment from the world. We have noted that Aśvaghoṣa's *Deeds of the*

Buddha is the more sensual and erotic of the accounts of the years in the palace; it is only here that it is implied that the prince succumbed to the courtesans. And so the question must be asked: Did the future buddha employ the arts of love during his long days and nights confined to his palace of pleasures? Was his retractable penis also functional?[13]

When the modern reader surveys the hundreds of infractions that constitute the Buddhist monastic code, one is immediately struck by how few of them have to do with what we might regard as morality and how many of them have to do with what appear to be minor, even trivial, matters of etiquette and comportment. Each of these vows has its own creation story, and in a great many of those stories, the formulation of the vow follows a complaint from the laity of something that a monk or nun did that they somehow found to be offensive. This is perhaps not surprising, since the respect and support of the laity was essential to the survival of the saṅgha. This sensitivity may even extend to the Buddha's penis. For in the monastic code of the Mūlasarvāstivāda school, we find the Buddha having the following thought, "Lest others say that the prince Śākyamuni was not a man, and that he wandered forth without paying attention to Yaśodharā, Gopikā, Mṛgajā, and his other sixty thousand wives, let me now make love to Yaśodharā."[14] And so the prince's last act before he escapes the palace and renounces the world is to make love to his wife. Rather than father a thousand sons as a *cakravartin,* he fathers one as a (future) buddha. As we shall see, that one son, Rāhula, will also become a monk, against the strong objections of his mother and grandfather, taking a vow of celibacy and thus ending the family line. In this version, then, Rāhula is not born on that fateful day. He is conceived on that fateful night.

In this version, after making love, the prince and princess fall asleep. Each has dreams. The precise content of the dreams varies in the several versions that tell this story. However, in each, the dreams of the prince are auspicious. In each version, in the final dream he traverses a mountain of excrement without being tainted by it; we recall that in Freud, excrement can represent gold. In all but one version, the dreams of the princess are frightening. In one, the prince makes love to his wife not before her dreams but after them, in an effort to comfort her after she has had seven frightening dreams. We might note here that the Victorian translator of the *Great Renunciation,* where this version occurs, says only that "the prince reposed by her side." In a footnote he adds, "The original is more explicit. Sufficient at any rate to show that up to this time the prince was not weaned from gratification of the senses."[15]

We might consider one version of her dreams, and the prince's response, here. This version comes from a text called the *Section on the Schism in the Saṅgha* (*Saṅghabhedavastu*), a section of the monastic code of the Mūlasarvāstivāda school. Here Yaśodharā dreams that her maternal line has been cut off, that the couch on which she sleeps has collapsed, that her bracelets are broken, her teeth have fallen out, the braid in her hair is undone, that happiness has left her home, that there has been an eclipse of the moon, and that the sun has risen and then set in the east. In the version of the story in the *Play in Full,* when the prince comforts her after she tells him about similar dreams, he acts as an analyst, interpreting the dreams as prophecies of her future attainments: "When you dream that the legs of your bed break off / And the precious handle of the parasol is broken, / It shows that you, Gopā, shall quickly cross the four rivers / And see me as the single parasol bearer in the triple universe."[16] But even here, there is more than a hint of misogyny: "When you dream that your pearl necklace is torn / And that you are naked and your body is mutilated, / It shows that you, Gopā, can soon leave your female body / And swiftly attain a male body."[17]

His attempt to calm her in *Section on the Schism in the Saṅgha* is very different. Here, the prince speaks as one would to a child who has had a bad dream: "You say your couch was broken, but it is not broken; it is right here. You say your bracelets were broken, but see for yourself, they are not. . . . You say that 'happiness has left my house,' but for a woman, a husband is happiness, and I am right here. You say the moon was eclipsed by Rāhu, but is that not the moon over there?" This seems to calm her. Then she asks, "Lord, wherever you go, take me there with you."[18] He promises that he will. Yet he leaves her, that very night, and in the *Section on the Schism in the Saṅgha,* he leaves her not with a day-old son, but pregnant with a child that will not be born ten lunar months hence. For in this version of the story, Rāhula is born six years hence, on the very night that his father becomes the Buddha. We will return to how she endures those years.

The time has now come for the prince to make his escape. He rouses his charioteer and tells him to saddle a horse. Chandaka selects the magnificent horse named Kaṇṭhaka. The prince mounts the horse and rides toward the gates of the palace. Fearing that the sound of his hoofbeats will rouse the king, *yakṣas* appear who hold out their hands to cushion each step of the steed. However, fearing that the prince will seek to escape that night, the king has had his soldiers barricade the gates. So great is the strength of Kaṇṭhaka that he is prepared to leap over the city walls, the prince on his back, Chandaka holding on to his tail. But the gods silently open the gates and the prince rides out, undetected. After they have traveled some distance, the prince wishes to look at the city one last time and pulls the reins for Kaṇṭhaka to stop. This is a second backward gaze; there will be a third.

Although not listed among the thirty-two major marks and eighty secondary marks of a buddha, it is said that the vertebrae in the neck of a buddha are fused so that he is unable to turn his head. Instead, to see what is behind him, he has to turn his entire body, as an elephant does, performing what the texts call the "elephant gaze." Thus, to see the city, it would have been necessary for him to turn Kaṇṭhaka around. Knowing the prince's intention, the gods cause the spot where the steed is standing to break loose from the earth and pivot 180 degrees. Having looked back as he left his family, the prince now looks back as he leaves the world that the astrologers predicted he would one day rule.

We see here once again the role of the gods. Rather than being portrayed as we might imagine it, a man sneaking out of the house undetected in the dead of night, the departure from the palace is depicted as a momentous event in human history, with the gods in the various heavens there to witness, rejoice, and offer all manner of unsolicited aid. The gods, all with long lives, know the true identity of Prince Siddhārtha from his time in the Joyous Heaven; they know that he is the bodhisattva, the person who will discover the state beyond birth and death and will then teach the path which leads to that state. As the texts often say, he does so for the benefit of "gods and humans." For as we must always recall, the gods, despite their powers, are bound in the realm of rebirth, just as we are. And so they rejoice, carrying torches in the sky to light the way and playing heavenly music. But their assistance is not always helpful. It is said that they were showering the prince with so many garlands that the flowers piled up as high as Kaṇṭhaka's flanks, impeding his progress.

Eventually, they arrive at the banks of a wide river. Kaṇṭhaka easily leaps across. Here, the prince alights from his horse and removes his royal jewelry. As a prince, Siddhārtha has long locks, piled high on his head. Knowing that these will be a hindrance as he sets out alone, he draws his sword and cuts them off, leaving the hair on his head curling to the right (one of the thirty-two marks) and two inches long. It is said that the Buddha's hair remained that length for the rest of his life. And yet, we do not find this remarkable attribute—never needing a haircut—among the miraculous marks of a buddha. As we shall see, the hair of a buddha is considered a sacred relic, so the long locks of the future buddha are not to be discarded. The prince throws them up in the air, saying that if he is to become a buddha, let them remain in the sky. If he is to fail, let them fall. The prince's topknot ascends eight miles high, where, suspended in the air, it is caught by the god Indra (called Śakra in Buddhist sources), who enshrines it in his domain, the Heaven of the Thirty-three on the summit of Mount Meru.

The prince's royal raiment is not suited for the life of a mendicant. In one version, he exchanges clothes with Chandaka; in another he exchanges clothes with a god who has disguised himself as a hunter. In the Pāli version, the god Brahmā descends from his heaven to present the prince with the eight requisites of a monk: three robes (an inner robe, an upper robe, and a shawl), a belt, a begging bowl, a water filter, a sewing needle, and a razor. Now ready to set out alone, the prince hands his royal jewelry to Chandaka and instructs him to return to the palace and inform his father and stepmother that he is alive. He tells him to take his loyal steed with him. But before they depart, Kaṇṭhaka, knowing that he will never see the prince again, dies of a broken heart. For his devotion and service, he is reborn as a god in the Heaven of the Thirty-three.

We might pause here to consider the narrative of the Buddha's life. At least to the modern reader, despite, or perhaps because of, all the baroque resplendence, there is a certain tedium, an utter lack of tension. The prince always wins, he already seems to know what is going to happen, with armies of gods always watching, ready to provide their subservient service. He seems never to suffer a moment of doubt, a moment of despair, a moment of existential crisis so often associated with the spiritual quest.

The only exception seems to be in the famous four sights, where the prince is depicted as shocked to learn of the existence of aging, sickness, and death, and the existence of those who seek to escape them. Here, the reader must wonder: If the future Buddha had vowed eons ago to achieve buddhahood, perfecting himself over billions of lifetimes in order to reach that goal, how could he have forgotten over the brief twenty-nine years of his life as Prince Siddhārtha that beings grow old, get sick, and die? How could he forget aging, sickness, and death, the very afflictions from which he had vowed to free the world? When Buddhists are asked why we do not remember our past lives, it is often said that, in fact, we do, but the trauma of birth and the labor of learning to inhabit a new body and learn a new language causes us to forget. But the prince escaped the trauma of the journey through the birth canal by emerging from his mother's right side. And not only could he walk and talk from the moment of his birth, his first words were to announce that this was his last lifetime, that he would never be reborn again. Did he somehow forget all this during his years of pleasure in the palace?

Some of the accounts of the prince's youth seem to be aware of this problem and seek to explain his amnesia. In the five biographies considered here, the four sights are apparitions created by the gods, meant to spur the prince to leave the palace to find the path to salvation, a path that the gods themselves do not know. Only the prince has the power to find it; they can only set him on his way. In the *Buddhacarita,* the corpse is an apparition that can be seen only by the prince and his charioteer. As noted above, before the prince becomes the Buddha, there are no Buddhist monks in the world to serve as the fourth of the four sights, the sight that finally inspires him to leave the palace. In the Pāli biography, a god who had such a long life that he had seen the previous buddhas took the form of one of their monks in order to inspire the prince.

Thus, there is little drama in the story of the founder of a great religion, no agony in the garden, no doubt of prophethood. But if there is no drama, there is play, both play in the sense of performance and play in the sense of delight. The Sanskrit title of the work that Flaubert read in French is *Lalitavistara*. The word *lalita* means "play," "sport," "dalliance." The word *vistara* means "expansive," "extensive," "elaborate," a title thus translated by some as the "Extensive Sport," by others as the "Play in Full." Here, and in later incidents in other texts, we see the evidence of what might be called Buddhist docetism, borrowing the term from the early Christian heresy that claimed that God could not have suffered and died on the cross; the passion of Jesus had been an illusion. In the fifteenth chapter of the *Lotus Sūtra*, the Buddha declares, "The devas, humans, and asuras in all the worlds all think that the present Buddha, Śākyamuni, left the palace of the Śākyas, sat on the terrace of enlightenment not far from the city of Gayā, and attained highest, complete enlightenment. However, O sons of a virtuous family, immeasurable, limitless, hundreds of thousands of myriads of *koṭis* of *nayutas* of *kalpas* have passed since I actually attained buddhahood."[19] He goes on to say that although he appears to pass into nirvāṇa, his lifespan is in fact immeasurable.

In the *Play in Full*, it is the gods who create the four sights of the old man, the sick man, the corpse, and the monk, but they do so "through the power of the Bodhisattva." That is, the future Buddha causes them to do so. It is all a performance. Yet, even here, there is a moment of amnesia when the prince seems to forget his destiny, or at least pretends to. In the thirteenth chapter, called "Encouragement," before he goes on the chariot rides, the prince is deep in his dalliance with the women of the inner chamber when the buddhas of the ten directions turn the music that the women are playing into a song, over one hundred stanzas long, reminding him of his vow to achieve buddhahood, of who he was in his past lives as a bodhisattva, that the time has come for him to fulfill his promised destiny, telling him, "Now remember your supreme vow from the past: / 'I will leave behind this beautiful town, / Quickly attain the state without death or sorrow, / And satisfy those who suffer from thirst with the nectar of immortality.' "[20]

Were the life of the Buddha to lack the story of the four sights, as the canonical versions seem to, if we knew that the Buddha remembered everything from the moment of his birth and proceeded in a straight line toward enlightenment, there would be no dramatic tension, there would be no turning point for us, the reader, the audience of the play. If the prince did not pretend to forget, then he could not pretend to remember. Flaubert was not the only great modern writer to read the *Lalitavistara.* In an essay called "Forms of a Legend," Jorge Luis Borges describes it as a work in whose "pages the history of the Redeemer is inflated to the point of oppression and vertigo."[21] He describes the four sights as "powerful but unbelievable." But perhaps believability is beside the point. In the *Play in Full,* the Buddha is both playwright and protagonist, writing the play and then playing his part in order to inspire the world, understanding the power of drama to move the human heart.

5
Six Years of Austerities

I begged my way upon the high roads, clad myself in rags gathered within the sepulchres;—and, hearing of a most learned hermit, I chose to become his slave. I guarded his gate! I washed his feet. Thus I annihilated all sensation, all joy, all languor. Then, concentrating my thoughts within vaster meditation, I learned to know the essence of things, the illusion of forms.[1]

The prince is now a pauper. He enters the city of Rājagṛha, the capital of the kingdom of Magadha, a city he would come to visit often and where on Vulture Peak, a mountain outside the city, he would deliver some of his most famous teachings. But now, he is merely a beggar, albeit a healthy and handsome beggar, so much so that he creates a stir, with people wondering whether he is a human or a god. Soldiers report his presence to the king, Bimbisāra, destined to be a friend and patron of the Buddha. The king tells his soldiers to watch the beggar eat; if he swallows what is put into his begging bowl, the being is a human. Now, for the first time in his twenty-nine years, the prince is not offered the finest cuisine, food prepared for his enjoyment. He must beg from door to door, taking whatever scraps that are offered to him and eating them. At his first bite, he almost vomits, so foul is the food. It is only when he reminds himself that this is the path he has chosen that he is able to eat. The king observes all this and is so impressed by the dignity and demeanor of the stranger that he offers him half of his kingdom. Having refused rulership of the four continents, the prince politely declines, explaining that he seeks enlightenment. Bimbisāra invites him to return when he has reached his goal.

And now the prince must pursue the path in earnest, seeking a goal whose path has been long forgotten. Thus, there is no one to teach him how to get there. The religious world of ancient India was in some ways not unlike that of the modern world. There were professional priests who performed rituals, promising to bring about various boons, for a fee. And there were all manner of gurus with their own circles of devotees, to whom they taught a variety of self-help techniques based on eccentric theories, some involving meditation, others involving lifestyle, including various forms of self-mortification. Later Buddhist texts would seek to enumerate the number of such "schools" that existed at the time of the Buddha, with one text counting as many as three hundred and sixty-three.

Prince Siddhārtha seeks out a meditation teacher. To understand what he learned, we must briefly describe the Buddhist cosmos and the role of meditation in its structure. The Buddhist cosmos is divided into three realms: the Realm of Desire, the Realm of Form, and the Formless Realm. The Realm of Desire, so named because we, its inhabitants, desire the objects of the five senses, is the most extensive and variegated, with a system of six heavens, two located on the central mountain, Mount Meru, and four in the sky above. On the lower slopes of Mount Meru live the demigods (*asura*), who possess a range of magical capabilities but are inferior to the gods in their powers, enjoyments, and lifespans. In the vast ocean surrounding Mount Meru are four island continents, the abodes of humans and animals. There is also a realm of ghosts (*preta*). Located underground in the southern continent is an elaborate series of hells, stacked one atop the other, the sufferings more horrific the deeper one descends.

Located above the heavens of the Realm of Desire is the Realm of Form, so called because the beings there, also counted as gods, are free from desire for the objects of the senses but maintain some attachment to form through their senses of sight, hearing, and touch; because they have no need for food, the gods here lack the senses of smell and taste. The Realm of Form has four levels, each simply called "concentration" (*dhyāna*), hence the "first concentration," "second concentration," and so forth. Although, as its name suggests, it has no physical location, the third of the three realms, called the Formless Realm, is ranked higher than the Realm of Form. It also has four levels: Infinite Consciousness, Infinite Space, Nothingness, and the Peak of Existence (also known as the state of Neither Perception nor Non-Perception). Again, as the name suggests, the beings reborn there have no physical form, existing only as individual streams of consciousness, with the first three levels named after the object of that consciousness.

The Realm of Desire differs from the Realm of Form and the Formless Realm in several ways, the most important of which is that one is reborn into the Realm of Desire based on one's past actions, with virtuous actions leading to rebirth as a human or a god, and non-virtuous actions leading to rebirth as an animal, ghost, or denizen of hell, all of this through the workings of the "law of karma" as it is typically understood.

Rebirth as a god in the Realm of Form and the Formless Realm is different. One can only be reborn into one of the four levels of the Realm of Form or the four levels of the Formless Realm by achieving the meditative state of that level in the immediately preceding lifetime as a human in the Realm of Desire. Thus, one who achieves the second concentration of the Realm of Form through meditation practice in this life will be reborn as a god in the second concentration in the next life. One who achieves the state of Infinite Consciousness through meditation practice in this life will be reborn as a god of Infinite Consciousness in the next life. The lifespans in the Realm of Form and the Formless Realm are measured in millions of years. However, they are not eternal; when the karmic force that impelled rebirth into one of the levels of the two higher realms is exhausted, one is typically reborn in the Realm of Desire.

We recall that as a young boy meditating under the rose apple tree while his father plowed the fields, Prince Siddhārtha had achieved the first concentration of the Realm of Form. Now, he sought higher states. He would study with two meditation teachers. The first, Ārāḍa Kālāma, was a master meditator who had achieved the state of Nothingness, the penultimate level of the Formless Realm. In the realm of Infinite Space, the object of the meditator's mind is empty space. In the realm of Infinite Consciousness, the mind, in a sense, is absorbed in itself, with consciousness perceived as omnipresent. More subtle than that is Nothingness, the state achieved by Ārāḍa Kālāma, in which the mind does not perceive anything. The prince, now a mendicant, became his disciple. (Despite Flaubert's statement, the *Play in Full* does not say that he became Ārāḍa Kālāma's slave or guarded the gate.) Guided by his teacher's instructions, Prince Siddhārtha quickly achieved the state. Impressed by his student's attainment, Ārāḍa Kālāma invited the prince to join him as the other teacher in his school, but the prince politely declined, knowing that the state of Nothingness was not the final goal.

The prince next became a disciple of Udraka Rāmaputra, who had achieved the highest level of the Formless Realm, called Neither Perception nor Non-Perception. In this state, as the name suggests, consciousness perceives nothing (not even Nothingness) and yet it cannot be said that there is an utter absence of perception. Again, the prince quickly achieved the state. He was offered the position of teacher and, again, declined. It is the prince's excursions in the upper reaches of the Formless Realm to which Flaubert alludes when he writes, "Then, concentrating my thoughts within vaster meditation, I learned to know the essence of things, the illusion of forms."

Udraka Rāmaputra is said to have initially regarded the state of Neither Perception nor Non-Perception as liberation from rebirth. However, when he emerged from that state, he saw that his dreadlocks, so long that they touched the ground as he sat in meditation, were being nibbled by a mouse. He was bothered by this, immediately understanding that the fact that his mind was disturbed by something so minor was a sign that he had not achieved liberation. Indeed, as noted, this highest level of the Formless Realm is also called the Peak of Existence, where "existence" means saṃsāra, the cycle of rebirth. That is, despite the fact that it is an immaterial state, a state so subtle that it cannot be said to be either perception or non-perception, despite the fact that the lifetime there is eighty thousand eons, it is not liberation. Prince Siddhārtha realized this and bade his teacher farewell.

It is Buddhist doctrine that only the teachings of the Buddha lead to liberation from the cycle of birth, aging, and death. All other religions and philosophies can only lead to temporary happiness within the realm of rebirth, whether through virtuous deeds that will lead to a lifetime as a human or as a god in the Realm of Desire, or through the practice of meditation, which will lead to a longer lifetime in either the Realm of Form or the Formless Realm. It is noteworthy that this point is implied so early in the story of the prince's six-year quest. He immediately encounters teachers who have achieved the penultimate and then the ultimate states within the Formless Realm. Following their instructions, he quickly reaches those hard-won states himself, immediately realizing that this is not the state of liberation that they imagine. Liberation is a state he must find without a teacher. The various teachers of the day, teachers who would become his competitors for alms when he became the Buddha, had not reached it. We find such polemics implied throughout the biographies of the Buddha.

> Soon I exhausted the science of the Brahmans. They are gnawed by covetousness and desire under their outward aspect of austerity; they daub themselves with filth, they live upon thorns,—hoping to arrive at happiness by the path of death! I also accomplished wondrous things,—eating but one grain of rice each day (and the grains of rice in those times were no larger than at present)—my hair fell off; my body became black; my eyes receding within their sockets, seemed even as stars beheld at the bottom of a well. During six years I kept myself motionless, exposed to the flies, the lions and the serpents; and the great summer suns, the torrential rains, lightnings and snows, hails and tempests,—all of these I endured without even the shelter of my lifted hand. The travellers who passed by, believing me dead, cast clods of earth upon me![2]

And so, abandoning the search for a teacher, he departed, joined by a group of five mendicants who had also been disciples of Udraka Rāmaputra. They were Kauṇḍinya—the young priest who had held up one finger thirty years earlier when asked to foretell the future of the infant prince—and the sons of four of the seven other priests who had been present that day. They are known in Buddhist literature as the "group of five." Having found that deep meditative states were not liberation, they began to practice various forms of self-mortification. The Buddha would eventually reject self-mortification as the path to enlightenment, but only after Prince Siddhārtha had practiced it for six years.

In one of the more horrifying passages in the canon, the Buddha describes his practice. He recalls that he would eat only fruit that had fallen from a tree, and would clothe himself in burial shrouds, tree bark, wool made from human hair, or owls' wings. Rather than shaving, he would pull out his hair and beard. He endured all manner of painful postures, such as never sitting down and sleeping on a bed of nails. He became such a recluse that he avoided all human contact. As the text says, "Such was my seclusion, Sāriputta, that I would plunge into some forest and dwell there. And when I saw a cowherd or a shepherd or someone gathering grass or sticks, or a woodsman, I would flee from grove to grove, from thicket to thicket, from hollow to hollow, from hillock to hillock. Why was that? So that they should not see me or I see them. Just as a forest-bred deer, on seeing human beings, flees from grove to grove, from thicket to thicket, from hollow to hollow, from hillock to hillock, so too, when I saw a cowherd or a shepherd . . . Such was my seclusion."

He ate the dung of calves and, as long as it lasted, his own excrement, and drank his own urine. He slept in charnel grounds, using the bones of the dead as his pillow. "And cowherd boys came up and spat on me, urinated on me, threw dirt at me, and poked sticks into my ears." He eventually restricted his diet to a single grain of rice a day. "Because of eating so little my limbs became like the jointed segments of vine stems or bamboo stems. Because of eating so little my backside became like a camel's hoof. Because of eating so little the projections on my spine stood forth like corded beads. Because of eating so little my ribs jutted out as gaunt as the crazy rafters of an old roofless barn. Because of eating so little the gleam of my eyes sank far down in their sockets, looking like a gleam of water which has sunk far down in a deep well. Because of eating so little my scalp shriveled and withered as a green bitter gourd shrivels and withers in the wind and sun. Because of eating so little my belly skin adhered to my backbone; thus if I touched my belly skin I encountered my backbone, and if I touched my backbone I encountered my belly skin."[3]

The prince is famously depicted in this form in a genre of statues called "Fasting Siddhārtha." The *Play in Full* describes similar austerities, so extreme that "Those who passed by the Bodhisattva, such as village boys or girls, ox herders, cowherders, grass collectors, wood collectors, and those looking for dung, all thought he was a demon made of dust." However, here again in the *Play in Full,* the prince is not engaging in these practices because he believes they lead to enlightenment. Again, engaged in play, all of this is a performance intended to show the world that such extreme acts of asceticism do not work, despite the claim of false prophets, referred to in the Sanskrit text as *tīrthika,* the standard term in Buddhist texts for non-Buddhist teachers.

Eventually, he stops eating altogether and practices extreme forms of breath control. In this weakened state, he passes out and is taken for dead. In one of the Pāli accounts, the *Great Discourse to Saccaka* (*Mahāsaccaka Sutta*), the gods who observe this descend and offer to infuse heavenly nourishment through his pores. He declines. In the *Play in Full,* the Buddha's mother, now a god in heaven, is informed that her son is dead and descends to earth to see for herself. Shedding tears over his body, she is overjoyed when he awakes and assures her that the predictions of his buddhahood will come true.

When he regains consciousness, he has demonstrated that self-mortification does not lead to enlightenment, that hunger, thirst, and fatigue are impediments, not paths. After bathing, he sits down under a tree, where a young woman named Sujātā, mistaking him for a *yakṣa,* the deity of that tree, offers him a golden bowl of milk rice. Eating it (according to the Pāli version, in the form of forty-nine rice balls), he is immediately fortified, the luster returning to his body. It is the last meal he will eat for the next forty-nine days.

Seeing this, the group of five is appalled that he has surrendered to his hunger and broken his fast. Denouncing him, they depart for a game preserve outside Vāraṇāsī. Now the prince is alone. He seeks another sign. Just as he had thrown his hair up into the sky, saying that if he is to become a buddha, may it not descend, now, six years later, he casts the golden bowl into the river, saying that if he is to become a buddha, may it float upstream. Of course, it does, moving against the current for a distance of eighty cubits (about forty yards) before descending to the bottom. It makes a clicking sound, because it has come to rest on a stack of three identical golden bowls that had belonged to three previous buddhas who had done the same thing in the same river many millennia ago.

The six years of asceticism, or more accurately, ascetic practices preceded by a brief period of meditation with Ārāḍa Kālāma and Udraka Rāmaputra, are not described in the various biographies in much more detail than appears here. Among the biographies of the Buddha, the lengthiest description is found in the *Play in Full,* where the prince lists the various forms of asceticism vainly practiced by those who falsely believe in their efficacy. In this account, we see what is implied in other accounts: As was the case of the meditative states achieved by Ārāḍa Kālāma and Udraka Rāmaputra, the central point is to demonstrate the fallacy of the other religious groups in ancient India. A number of the practices described are attested in other sources; the eating of fallen fruit and the plucking out of the hair and beard were practices of the Jains, among the chief critics and competitors of the Buddhists.

There might be another motivation, for both his practice of meditation and his practice of asceticism. In the account of his practice of meditation in the *Play in Full,* we read that the prince studies meditation with Udraka Rāmaputra not because he has something to learn from him but because if he does not display his meditative prowess to his teacher, it will be more difficult to convert him after he achieves buddhahood. The ability to convert others might also be seen as the motivation for his subsequent years of strict ascetic practice. As we shall see, the Buddha does not have a chance to convert his meditation teachers, but the point is an important one. Many of the Buddha's disciples would come from the ranks of the various meditators and ascetics of the day. By demonstrating to them that he has done what they do, matching their attainments, he shows that he is one of them, someone who has shared in their experience and, importantly, has found that experience to be inadequate to the task of liberation from rebirth.

His miraculous meal consumed, his friends departed, Prince Siddhārtha, now alone, goes in search of another tree.

6

The Attack of Māra

> Only the temptation of the Devil remained! I summoned him. His sons came,—hideous, scale-covered, nauseous as charnel-houses,—shrieking, hissing, bellowing; interclashing their panoplies, rattling together the bones of dead men. Some belched flame through their nostrils; some made darkness about me with their wings; some wore chaplets of severed fingers; some drank serpent-venom from the hollows of their hands;—they were swine-headed; they were rhinoceros-headed or toad-headed; they assumed all forms that inspire loathing and affright.[1]

The prince is determined to achieve enlightenment before a new day dawns. He accepts a bundle of grass from a grass cutter and then goes into the forest to find the appropriate tree to sit under in meditation. Eventually selecting an appropriate tree, he decides to sit on its southern side, but before he can do so, in a cartoonish moment, the entire (flat) earth tilts up sharply to the north. Concluding that this may not be the right spot, the prince proceeds clockwise around the tree. When he stops at the western and northern sides of the tree, the same thing happens: the earth tilts to the east and then to the south. When he continues to the eastern side, nothing happens, causing the prince to conclude that he should sit on the eastern side of the tree. In an equally dramatic version of the selection of the tree, the prince is unsure about which of the many trees in the forest is destined to become the holy of holies of the Buddhist world. Knowing of the tree's miraculous qualities, he shoots a bolt of flame from his mouth that incinerates all the trees in the forest except the true tree.[2] So much for Buddhist environmentalism.

Having chosen the tree and determined the proper direction, the prince spreads the grass at its foot and sits down to meditate, vowing not to rise again until he finds the state beyond birth and death. As he says in the Pāli version, "Let only my skin, sinews, and bones remain and let the flesh and blood in my body dry up; but not until I attain the supreme enlightenment will I give up the seat of meditation."[3] But before he can begin to meditate, he is attacked. This is the scene that Flaubert describes, one of the most famous, and certainly the most dramatic, scenes in the life of the Buddha: the attack of Māra.

Flaubert says, "Only the temptation of the Devil remained! I summoned him." He is accurate here. Although in other versions the attack of Māra is not welcomed, in the *Play in Full,* the bodhisattva summons him: "Māra is the supreme lord who holds sway over the desire realm, the most powerful and evil demon. There is no way that I could attain unsurpassed and complete awakening without his knowledge. So I will now arouse that evil Māra. Once I have conquered him, all the gods in the desire realm will also be restrained."[4]

However, although Māra will eventually try to tempt the prince, Māra is not the devil. His name means "maker of death," but he is not the lord of death who rules the hells; that god is

Yama in the Buddhist pantheon. Māra is a god, specifically a god of the heaven called "Controlling Others' Emanations," the highest of the six heavens in the Realm of Desire. Thus, like all beings in saṃsāra, he is not an eternal being, but rather someone who has been reborn as Māra. When his lifespan as Māra is expended, he will die and be reborn elsewhere and another being in the realm of rebirth will be reborn as Māra.

Although his name means death, he is also a god of desire, seeking always to cause those who seek to escape from the world of suffering to remain bound in it. Thus, in Buddhist scholastic literature, death itself is also called Māra; the afflictions of desire, hatred, and ignorance are called Māra; the constituents of the body and mind are called Māra.

But Flaubert is right about temptation; there are many stories of Māra appearing, sometimes in disguise, to meditators, seeking to dissuade them from their quest. He appears often, for example, in a work called *Songs of the Sisters* (*Therīgāthā;* or, more literally but less euphoniously, "Songs of the Female Elders"). And as we saw above, he tried to convince the prince to rule the world as a *cakravartin* rather than escape the world as a buddha. But he failed at that and now, as the prince is on the brink of buddhahood, the defeat of death, he must be stopped. As has been discussed, the life of the Buddha is relatively free from drama. It is almost entirely free of violence, making the attack of Māra one of the most widely depicted—in both word and image—moments in the biography, allowing the artist to depict all manner of monsters. Flaubert must have delighted in their long description in the *Play in Full,* where we read, for example:

> Such an army had never been seen before, or even heard of, in the realms of gods and humans. The soldiers were able to transform their faces in a trillion ways. On their arms and legs slithered hun-

> dreds of thousands of snakes, and in their hands they brandished swords, bows, arrows, darts, lances, axes, tridents, clubs, staffs, bludgeons, lassos, cudgels, discuses, vajras, and spears. Their bodies were covered in finest cuirasses and armor.
>
> Some had their heads, hands, or feet turned backward, or their eyes facing backward. Their heads, eyes, and faces were ablaze. Their bellies, hands, and feet were deformed, and their faces brimmed with vehement ardor. Their mouths, with protruding ugly fangs, appeared contorted in the extreme, and their thick and broad tongues, rough like a turtle's neck or a straw mat, dangled from their mouths. Like the eyes of a black snake, which are flush with poison, their eyes were blazing red, as if on fire. Some of them were vomiting poisonous snakes, while others, like garuḍas emerging from the ocean, grasped these poisonous snakes in their hands and ate them. Some ate human flesh and drank blood, chewing on human arms, legs, heads, and livers, and slurping entrails, feces, and vomit.[5]

Māra's army is said to extend for miles in every direction, led by Māra himself, mounted on a huge elephant, transforming himself into a being with a thousand hands, each wielding a different weapon. Anticipating that his enlightenment is near, the good gods of the pantheon, including such famous figures as Indra and Brahmā, are attending the Buddha. Yet when they see Māra and his minions approaching, they take flight, leaving the prince, alone and unarmed, seated beneath the tree. He is unfazed.

Māra and his hosts launch a hail of weapons at him, raining down flaming balls of coal, an avalanche of rocks, sandstorms, mud storms, and ash storms. As the various projectiles approach the prince, they turn into flower petals and sandalwood powder, settling harmlessly around his feet. Māra sends down torrential rains to wash him away, causing floodwaters that rise to the treetops. He remains dry. Māra unleashes hurricane-force winds to blow him away. The hem of his robe does not flutter. In one of the accounts of the Buddha's enlightenment in the *Mahāvastu*, he routs the army of Māra with a cough.[6]

Seeing that the prince cannot be defeated with weapons, Māra turns to words, making a legalistic claim about property rights. Māra asks the prince what right he has to occupy that particular place under the tree. The prince replies that he has earned the right to sit there because he has practiced the perfections over the course of many lifetimes. The perfections (*pāramitā*) are sometimes referred to as the "bodhisattva deeds," the virtues that the bodhisattva practices and perfects over millions of lifetimes in order to be able to achieve buddhahood in his final lifetime without the benefit of a teacher. In the Sanskrit tradition there are six: giving, ethics, patience, effort, concentration, and wisdom. In the Pāli tradition, there are ten, adding renunciation, truthfulness, determination, and equanimity. Māra rejects his claim because the prince has no witness to testify to the truth of his statement, saying instead that he, Māra, has the right to sit beneath the tree; a chorus of his monsters shout that they are his witness.

This sets the scene for by far the most famous depiction of the Buddha in Asian art. The prince has his hands in his lap in the standard posture of meditation, his right hand resting on his left. Now, he extends his right hand and reaches down to touch the earth with his fingertips. This is known in Buddhist iconography as the "earth-touching" (*bhūmisparṣa*) posture. He is calling upon the goddess of the earth, who has lived long, to testify that the prince has indeed practiced the perfections over many lifetimes. She testifies with a tremor.

This image is so familiar to us that we tend to forget how odd it is. Given that the Buddha achieved enlightenment in the posture of meditation, the posture that Buddhists would emulate for millennia, why would he not be depicted in that way? Why is he touching the earth, and at a point before, not after, his buddhahood? It may be because it depicts his defeat of Māra, the god of death. But it also may be because it connects him to the cult of the earth goddess, that just as the birth of the Buddha is associated with a tree goddess, so is the enlightenment of the Buddha associated with an earth goddess, named Sthāvarā. That goddess is particularly important in the Buddhist traditions of Thailand and Laos, where she is called Thorani. In their version of the story, rather than simply causing a tremor, she appears on the scene and begins wringing water out of her hair. This is all the water from the libations that the prince had offered in a past life. She wrings so much water from her hair that it causes a flood, which sweeps away Māra and his hideous horde.

The attack of Māra, so famous in art and literature, has presented a challenge to European biographers of the Buddha who, following the lead of New Testament scholars, felt the need to explain away the miraculous. We can imagine, for example, that David Strauss would categorize this, and many other stories in the life of the Buddha, as what he called "poetical mythi," which he defined as "historical and philosophical mythi partly blended together, and partly embellished by the creations of the imagination, in which the original fact or idea is almost obscured by the veil which the fancy of the poet has woven around it."[7] The baby Buddha's birth from under his mother's armpit is obviously a problem, but one that could be explained away by appealing to some notion of purity, with the future Buddha avoiding the months of uterine horror described so gruesomely in Buddhist texts. The feats of strength are standard elements of myth, easily seen as interpolations. The childhood meditation under the tree seems unlikely but perhaps plausible, as are the chariot rides. The problem with Māra's attack is that it is described in such detail and that it occurs at such a crucial moment in the narrative. It has to be interpreted.

The obvious strategy for the modern European interpreter is to psychologize it. And thus in the entry on "Buddhism" in the famous ninth edition of the *Encyclopedia Britannica,* published in 1878 and written by Thomas W. Rhys Davids, a former colonial officer and Pāli scholar, we read, "All his old temptations came back upon him with renewed force. For years he had looked at all earthly good through the medium of a philosophy which had taught him that it, without exception, carried within itself the seeds of bitterness and was altogether worthless and impermanent; but now to his wavering faith the sweet delights of home and love, the charms of wealth and power, began to show themselves in a different light and glow again with attractive colours. He doubted, and agonized in his doubt; but as the sun set, the religious side of his nature had won the victory and seems to have come out even purified from the struggle."[8] Thus, the prince is not the confident and courageous figure portrayed in the texts, but a man who had long suppressed his human emotions and now is wracked with doubt. Rhys Davids would not be the last to offer this "psychological" interpretation. Others, writing after Freud, would see the Attack of Māra as the Attack of the Id, in which repressed forms of aggression are externalized as hideous demons. They must be faced and defeated, brought fully into consciousness and then conquered. But the attack of Māra's army was not the last foe that the future Buddha had to face. There was another element of the Id to be tamed. The next attack would take a sexual form. It is usually referred to as the attack of Māra's daughters.

> Then did he send me his daughters—beautiful with daintily painted faces, and wearing girdles of gold. Their teeth were whiter than the jasmine-flower; their thighs round as the trunk of an elephant. Some extended their arms and yawned, that they might so display the dimples of their elbows; some winked their eyes; some laughed; some half-opened their garments. There were blushing virgins, matrons replete with dignity, queens who came with great trains of baggage and of slaves.[9]

With his demonic army defeated, Māra's three daughters now approach the prince (in some versions at their father's request, in others by their own choice) seeking to rouse him from his seat by arousing his lust. They have different names in different sources; in the Pāli account they are named Tanhā, Aratī, and Rāga: Craving, Discontent, and Lust. In the *Play in Full,* Flaubert's source (where they are called Tṛṣṇā, Rati, and Arati—Craving, Passion, and Discontent), they begin by displaying the thirty-two wiles of a woman, which the sūtra enumerates. Flaubert draws from these in the passage above. The prince remains unmoved, using the opportunity to provide his own list, in his case, a list of the faults of the female form: "From the crotch, awful smells are leaked; / The thighs, the calves, and the feet are joined together like a mechanical contraption. / When I examine you, I see that you are like an illusion, / Which has deceptively emerged from causes and conditions."[10]

In the version that appears in Buddhaghosa's *Account of Origins,* Māra's daughters seek to determine what kind of woman will arouse the lust of the prince. First, each of the daughters turns into one hundred girls who stand before him. When he remains unmoved, they turn into one hundred young women who have not yet given birth, then one hundred women who have given birth once, then one hundred women who have given birth twice, then one hundred middle-aged women, then one hundred old women. In some versions, they take on this last form in order to arouse his pity; in others, to arouse his lust. In the *Buddhacarita,* the Buddha remains unmoved, but he uses his magical powers to lock the daughters of Māra into the last of their transformations. "Bending their feet, with decrepit limbs, they addressed their father: 'O father . . . the lord of the world of Desire, restore us to our own forms.' "[11] However, despite Māra's great powers, he does not have the power to restore them to their youthful forms. At his suggestion, his daughters then seek refuge in the Buddha, as Buddhists would do for centuries when they declared, "I go for refuge to the Buddha." The daughters do not mention the second and third of the three jewels, the dharma and the saṅgha, because the dharma has yet to be discovered and the saṅgha has not been formed. Thus, although it is often said that Trapuṣa and Bhallika, who would offer the new Buddha his first meal seven weeks later, were the first to take refuge, it seems that that honor belongs to Māra's daughters.[12] As soon as they do so, the prince restores them to their youthful forms.

Māra's daughters appear at different points in the enlightenment narrative. In the *Great Renunciation,* they attempt to seduce the prince before their father's army attacks. In the *Play in Full,* they arrive following the attack and return after he has achieved enlightenment. In the *Account of Origins,* they appear in the fifth week after his enlightenment. Here, as in so many other instances in the biography, there seems to have been a set of stock scenes that could be inserted into the drama at the discretion of the author. This meeting with Māra's daughters is one scene that is rarely omitted, demonstrating once again that Buddhist authors—who in many cases were celibate monks—rarely missed an opportunity to write about sex.

7
The Night of Enlightenment

Having vanquished the Demon, I nourished myself for twelve years with perfumes only;—and as I had acquired the five virtues, the five faculties, the ten forces, the eighteen substances, and had entered into the four spheres of the invisible world, Intelligence became mine! I became the Buddha.[1]

We have now come to the central moment in the drama. Māra, his minions, and his daughters have exited the stage. The prince is left alone.

In the Pāli nikāyas, there are two "autobiographical" accounts of the Buddha's enlightenment. The first occurs in a text called *The Noble Search* (*Ariyapariyesana*) found in the Majjhima Nikāya. Here the Buddha recounts his departure from home in search of the truth, his training by other teachers, his enlightenment, his first sermon, ending with instructions on the various levels of deep concentration. One notes immediately the understated tone of the narrative, devoid of the rich detail so familiar from the biographies. There is no mention of the opulence of his youth, no mention of his wife, no mention of the chariot rides, no description of the departure from the palace in the dead of night. Instead, he simply says, "Later, while still young, a black-haired young man endowed with the blessing of youth, in the prime of life, though my mother and father wished otherwise and wept with tearful faces, I shaved off my hair and beard, put on the yellow robe, and went forth from the home life into homelessness."[2] He recalls his days as a disciple of Āḷāra Kālāma and Uddaka Rāmaputta and his attainment of profound meditative states under their tutelage, but he does not specify what these are.[3] And his account of the most momentous event in the history of Buddhism, his enlightenment, is set forth in sober tones, portrayed as the outcome of long reflection rather than as an ecstatic moment of revelation:

> Then, bhikkhus, being myself subject to birth, having understood the danger in what is subject to birth, seeking the unborn supreme security from bondage, nibbāna, I attained the unborn supreme security from bondage, nibbāna; being myself subject to ageing, having understood the danger in what is subject to ageing, seeking the unageing supreme security from bondage, nibbāna, I attained the unageing supreme security from bondage, nibbāna; being myself subject to sickness, having understood the danger in what is subject to sickness, seeking the unailing supreme security from bondage, nibbāna, I attained the unailing supreme security from bondage, nibbāna; being myself subject to death, having understood the danger in what is subject to death, seeking the deathless supreme security from bondage, nibbāna, I attained the

> deathless supreme security from bondage, nibbāna; being myself subject to sorrow, having understood the danger in what is subject to sorrow, seeking the sorrowless supreme security from bondage, nibbāna, I attained the sorrowless supreme security from bondage, nibbāna; being myself subject to defilement, having understood the danger in what is subject to defilement, seeking the undefiled supreme security from bondage, nibbāna, I attained the undefiled supreme security from bondage, nibbāna. The knowledge and vision arose in me: "My deliverance is unshakeable; this is my last birth; now there is no renewal of being."[4]

This account seems to have been less popular than a longer version of Gotama's achievement of buddhahood that appears in a text called the *Discourse on Fear and Dread* (*Bhayabherava Sutta*). Here we find the more famous account of the night of the enlightenment reprised in later works like the *Buddhacarita* and the *Play in Full.* The prince becomes the Buddha by gaining the three knowledges (*tevijjā*) over the course of three periods of meditation.[5]

He meditates all night. In ancient India, the night was divided into three "watches" of four hours. During the first watch of the night, the prince has a vision of all of his past lives, in precise detail. As the Pāli passage says, "There I was so named, of such a clan, with such an appearance, such was my nutriment, such my experience of pleasure and pain, such a life-term; and passing away from there, I reappeared elsewhere; and there too I was so named, of such a clan, of such an appearance, such was my nutriment, such my experience of pleasure and pain, such a life-term; and passing away from there, I reappeared here."[6] As Aśvaghoṣa says in the *Buddhacarita,* "In this way he recalled thousands of births, / as if he were living through them again."[7] The ability to remember past lives is common in Indian religions, and is often listed as one of the five forms of supersensory knowledge (*abhijñā*, discussed in more detail in the final chapter) that come as something of a side effect of achieving deep states of meditation, regardless of one's religious or doctrinal affiliation. Buddhist texts provide instructions on how to develop this skill; the process is quite prosaic, beginning with remembering what you had for breakfast. And thus, there is nothing particularly Buddhist about the prince's achievement.

Two things seem noteworthy. The first is the number of lives he can remember: all of them. When we pause to consider this for a moment, we realize that this first phase of the night of enlightenment is impossible for the simple reason that the number of past lives of the prince, and of all beings, is infinite. And yet he claims to be able to remember each in precise detail, and during a four-hour period. One might assume that given his high level of expertise in meditation, he might have somehow seen them all simultaneously. But that would not have taken four hours, and the texts do not suggest that he did. As he says, "I recollected my manifold past lives, that is, one birth, two births, three births, four births, five births, ten births, twenty births, thirty births, forty births, fifty births, a hundred births, a thousand births, a hundred thousand births, and many aeons of world-contraction, many aeons of world expansion, and many aeons of world-contraction and expansion."[8] It is his knowledge of all of his past lives that has provided the material for perhaps the most popular genre of Buddhist literature, the *jātaka* tales, or "birth stories"—that is, the stories of the Buddha's past lives, sometimes as a human, sometimes as an animal.

The second thing that is noteworthy is that the instructions for remembering one's past lives that occur in works such as the *Path of Purification* (*Visuddhimagga*) instruct the meditator to remember in a reverse chronology, beginning with the most recent past and moving sequentially to the more distant. In the case of the Buddha, however, he seems to begin at the beginning and move forward lifetime by lifetime to the present: "Passing away there, I appeared here." And yet it is standard Buddhist doctrine that there is no beginning to the cycle of birth and death and thus nowhere to begin.

There is no particular doctrinal content to the vision of the first watch. Almost all of the philosophical schools of ancient India accepted the doctrine of rebirth. Yet although no doctrinal point is stated, several might be implied, at least for the modern reader. The first is the centrality of rebirth to Buddhism. Beginning in the twentieth century, some (especially Europeans and Americans) began to argue that one could "be a Buddhist" (whatever that phrase might mean) without "believing" in rebirth. That the accounts of the Buddha's enlightenment consistently include his vision of his past lives suggests that their existence is essential. The scene also seems to at least imply an answer to a question that has been asked in Buddhism for two millennia, from a text called the *Questions of Milinda* to the twenty-first-century undergraduate classroom: if there is no self, how can there be rebirth? The vision of the first watch of the night does not provide an answer to that question, but it affirms that there can be rebirth, and, as the prince's repeated use of the first-person singular suggests, some semblance of personal continuity, without a self. This, however, is just an implication. As we will soon see, there is nothing particularly "Buddhist" about the prince's first two visions.

We find in Indian Buddhist thought something of an aversion to origins and end times. Creation myths abound in the Hindu tradition, from the *Ṛg Veda* to Dharmaśāstras to the Purāṇas. In Buddhism, there are, of course, many stories of the past, most obviously the hundreds of stories of past lives of the Buddha and of so many others, the subject of entire genres called *jātaka* and *avadāna*. There is the story of how individual worlds come into existence in the *Agañña Sutta*. And Buddhists have long feared the future, with the disappearance of the dharma and the decline in civilization, when the human lifespan will fall to ten years, before rising again to eighty thousand. However, these narratives do not carry particular theological weight. Indeed, when asked about the origin of the world, the Buddha maintains his famous "noble silence." Among the ten (or fourteen) "unanswered questions" (*avyākṛtavastu*) that the Buddha declines to answer are: Is the world eternal?, Is the world not eternal?, Is the world both eternal and not eternal?, Is the world neither eternal nor not eternal?; Is the world endless?, Is the world not endless?, Is the world both endless and not endless? The Buddha says that the theory that the world is eternal is "a thicket of views, a wilderness of views, a contortion of views, a vacillation of views, a fetter of views. It is beset by suffering, by vexation, by despair, and by fever, and it does not lead to disenchantment, to dispassion, to cessation, to peace, to direct knowledge, to enlightenment, to Nibbāna."[9]

Such a warning may derive from the fact that Indian Buddhist philosophy is above all a theory of causation, showing how all things are constructed in the process of cause and effect, that behind this tenuous and transient construction there is no essence, no identity. For there to be a first cause, an origin, there must be that which is unconstructed; for the Buddhists the unconstructed occurs not at the beginning but at the end, at nirvāṇa, at the destruction of all causes. When Buddhist doctrine was condemned by the Jesuit missionary Ippolito Desideri in eighteenth-century Tibet, it was because of its refusal to posit a first cause, an unmoved mover, a pristine identity prior to the forging of the chains of causation, before the beginning of movement, when all movement was movement toward loss and all liberation was a return to the origin. To say that saṃsāra has no beginning is to declare that there is no primordial essence of things, behind and before the world.

The Buddha does, however, engage in retrogressive reflection to discover an origin, and, according to some accounts, this reflection constitutes his enlightenment. It is his tracing of aging and death back through their preceding causes that substitutes for cosmogony in Buddhism. The origin he discovers, however, is not God. The origin is ignorance at the beginning of a twelvefold process of dependent origination. And it is not a primal ignorance but one produced from an earlier causal chain, a specific cause which is itself an effect, rather than some first cause. Memory becomes here the history that writes the individual, the narrative that creates the continuity called the person. If memory comprises the person, then to remember what was is to be aware of who is, and to remember everything is to see the person in its manifest fullness. Thus, for the prince, to see all of his past lives was to see who he was, both in its plenitude and its paucity. The persistence of the person is multiplied through its continuity over time, through eons of evolution and dissolution as, grasping the rope of memory, he rises to the karmic present.

And what he remembers is significant. For contained in the formula of the memory of former abodes are all of the constituents of Indian social identity: place, name, caste, food. But it is this very identity which the Indian renunciate abandons when he goes forth into the forest in search of an identity that is not defined in terms of social hierarchy. The renunciate goes forth from the house and the responsibilities of the householder, giving up a permanent dwelling place, renouncing his former abode. In the case of the Buddha, the vision of his past lives amounts to an insight into his personal identity as it is found in the beginningless round of rebirth. He sees, in their entirety, those constituents from which the presence of the person can be deduced.

This vision, encompassing the entire past, will provide the potency of the vision of the third watch of the night, when he sees, in the instantaneous present, that this person who seems so present is a mere projection, that before and behind the chain of rebirth there is no agent, no person: the liberating identity beyond saṃsāra is "no self." The prince thus sees the past and present order of the world in the first two watches of the night. When he sees that that ordered world has no essence, he is awakened.

The Buddha's memories show a levelling of experience into an affectless formula. We find in his description of his past a devaluation of the world into a sphere of repetition, where each lifetime serves only as a duplication, without specificity, with only "such a clan, of such an appearance, such was my nutriment, such my experience of pleasure and pain." Here, the person becomes another constituent of the scene, another element in the process of cause and effect. The content of the Buddha's memory of his former abodes is, like all memory, a construction of the past, a remolding of the past for the purposes of the present.

In this sense, the Buddha's formulaic memory of his earlier existence destroys the past as a source of both identity and attachment and replaces it with the memory of an existence that is happily abandoned. All worldly experience comes to be subsumed under the formula of the Buddha's memory, revealing the tedium of saṃsāra. As an experience of the Buddha, indeed as a constituent of his enlightenment, this memory is invested with the power and authority of the origin, demonstrating that the Buddhist view of the world has always been the case; the Buddha's understanding of the human condition, though yet to occur in the third watch of the night, is dramatized and projected retroactively into the measureless past as the setting against which all experience is to be observed. This tension between personal identity and no identity, between saṃsāra and nirvāṇa, between continuity and cessation, between the historical and ahistorical, plays out throughout Buddhist philosophy.

As already noted, in the *Account of Origins*, the Pāli biography of the Buddha, the prince crept into his wife's chamber to look upon his infant son. He resisted the urge to hold him, knowing that to do so would awaken Yaśodharā and prevent his departure from the world. It is this last look, looking at but not touching what he was to leave behind, that forms one of the most poignant moments in the narrative. The meditation during the first watch of the night is a backward glance, not with the eyes but with the mind, a backward glance that recurs six years later beneath a tree. The prince looks back one last time at what he had been and thus at who he is, looking at but not being touched by that person made of memory. He then declares, "Birth is finished."[10]

It could be said that in the first watch of the night the prince anticipated by more than two millennia Kierkegaard's famous adage that life can only be understood backwards, but it must be lived forwards. In the second watch of that full-moon night, the prince "saw beings passing away and reappearing, inferior and superior, fair and ugly, fortunate and unfortunate. I understood how beings pass on according to their actions."[11] That is, he witnessed the workings of the law of karma. Again, there is nothing particularly "Buddhist" here; the fact that virtuous deeds (however defined) lead to happiness in the future and non-virtuous deeds (however defined) lead to suffering in the future was a widely shared view in ancient India, first appearing in its well-known form in the Upaniṣads. There are at least two points to be made here. The first is that the second watch confirms that the doctrine of karma is central to Buddhism, taking pride of place as part of the content of the Buddha's enlightenment.

The second is that it endows the Buddha with a knowledge that few share. Knowledge of one's own past lives is one of the supersensory forms of knowledge available to master meditators; knowledge of the past lives of others is not. And here, it is not simply that the Buddha knows the events of the lives of others—he knows the specific acts that they performed in the past that produced some effect of pleasure or pain in the future. This skill is apparently not unique to the Buddha. Especially in the stories of the ordination of particular monks, we have cases of arhats (usually Śāriputra) doing something of a cosmic criminal background check on the applicant to see if they have sufficient "roots of virtue," that is, good karma, to be ordained. However, it seems that an arhat's ability to read those records only goes back so many lifetimes. In these stories, when ordination is denied by a particular monk, the Buddha will do his own investigation, finding something sufficient to allow ordination. A famous case of this is when the Buddha sees that in a past life the postulant had been an ant perched on a pile of cow dung. During a torrential rain, the pile of dung began to float, driven by the rushing water in such a way that it circled the stūpa of a previous buddha. Because the ant had therefore circumambulated a sacred site, the Buddha deemed the former ant to be acceptable for ordination.

Perhaps the most important point, however, is that the visions of the first two watches of the night are not, in fact, revelations. They are not liberating insights, but rather are personal confirmations of two foundational doctrines, foundational not only to what would become what we call "Buddhism" but to many of the most important philosophical systems of ancient India: rebirth and karma. That is, there is nothing particularly "Buddhist" about these visions; instead, they place the prince among the respected teachers of the day, despite the fact that he is teaching something new. What is new will come in the third watch, the period between 2 a.m. and 6 a.m., the period that will end when the new day dawns, the period that will end when the prince becomes awakened (*buddha*).

Surprisingly, or perhaps not surprisingly, the accounts tend to say the least about this, the most important four hours in the history of Buddhism. One might say that this is because the content of the Buddha's enlightenment is inexpressible, either inexpressible because it is beyond language or inexpressible because there is too much to express. We might say that the vast canons of Buddhist literature, the sūtras, the tantras, and the commentaries in the canonical languages of Sanskrit, Pāli, Chinese, and Tibetan, as well as the works in dozens of languages across Asia, and today around the world, are all attempts to articulate the content of the Buddha's enlightenment, to recover the unrecoverable, a quest that has continued for more than two millennia.

When the insight of the third watch of the night is identified, it is often said to be dependent origination (*pratītyasamutpāda*), a rather complicated twelvefold sequence that describes the process of rebirth, not as something to be remembered, as in the first watch of the night, but as the engine of saṃsāra. We will attempt to describe it here briefly, according to one of several systems of interpretation. In this version, the sequence takes place over three lifetimes.

It begins with (1) *ignorance,* in this case, a moment of ignorance in a past life (and not necessarily the immediately preceding past life) that motivates a particular (2) *action.* That action serves as the cause for (3) a *consciousness* to be reborn—in the case of a human, in a womb—where the mind and body, called (4) *name and form*, will develop into (5) *sources*, referring here to the six sense organs, that is, the five senses and the mind. Upon birth, those sense organs have (6) *contact* with the objects of the world, producing (7) *feeling*, said to be either pleasurable, painful, or neutral. This feeling is the result of past karma and therefore beyond our control. The first point of control comes with the response to the feeling, which can be (8) *attachment*, and this can become intensified into (9) *grasping*. This then leads to the production of the cause of the next rebirth, called (10) *existence*, leading to (11) *birth* and then (12) *aging and death* in the immediately following lifetime. For those familiar with the famous Tibetan Buddhist paintings of the "wheel of life," the twelve links are depicted in a clockwise sequence around the edge of the circle. Among the points that might be noted is that ignorance is represented by a blind man, contact is represented by a couple making love, and feeling is represented by a man with an arrow in his eye.

In the *Play in Full*, the Buddha comes to understand the twelvefold sequence in reverse order, inferring the cause from its effect. Hence, aging and death are the effect of birth, birth is the effect of existence, existence is the effect of grasping, grasping is the effect of attachment, and so on. Moving backward in this way, ignorance is seen as the first cause for the cycle of birth and death. This rather technical and complicated sequence is not what is typically evoked by the word "enlightenment," especially in the case of the Buddha, where the modern reader might expect something considerably more mystical. Still, there are a number of lessons, and here specifically Buddhist lessons, to be drawn. The first is the pride of place given to ignorance as the first of the twelve links. Although this does not become clear until the Buddha's first teachings after his enlightenment, it is a specific ignorance, the belief in self. It is his doctrine of no self (*anātman*) that will distinguish the Buddha from the other teachers of the day. Ignorance serves as the cause of desire and hatred, which in turn motivate deeds that produce experiences of pleasure and pain. Once ignorance exists, there is no place to try to stop the process until one reaches the seventh and eighth links, feeling and attachment. According to Buddhist doctrine, our feelings of physical and mental pleasure and pain are the result of particular past actions, without the possibility of our intervention. That intervention comes in our response to the pleasure or the pain; we can become attached to it, leading then to grasping and then to the causes of the next lifetime, or we can respond without attachment. Thus, to the perennial question of whether there is free will in Buddhism, the answer is in the affirmative; our experience is given, but our response to that experience is free. One is able to cease attachment by seeing that, because there is no self, there is no one to be aroused by desire and protected by hatred; there is nothing to be attached to.

Elsewhere in the canon, the Buddha's enlightenment is described in terms of the famous four truths: suffering, origin, cessation, path. And so, he explains, "I directly know as it actually is: 'This is suffering'; I directly know as it actually is: 'This is origin of suffering'; I directly know as it actually is: 'This is the cessation of suffering'; I directly know as it actually is: 'This is the path leading to the cessation of suffering.' "[12]

Regardless of what the various canonical sources say about what the prince sees during the third watch, they often agree about what he says when it is over: "Through many a birth in samsara have I wandered in vain, seeking the builder of this house. Repeated birth is indeed suffering. O builder of the house, you are seen. You will not build this house again. For your rafters are broken and your ridgepole shattered. My mind has reached the unconditioned; I have attained the destruction of craving."[13]

We might pause for a moment to ponder what a strange moment this is in the history of religions. The most important moment in the history of Buddhism, the cosmic moment, the salvific moment, occurs at night, in silence, and in solitude. Nothing is spoken, nothing is heard. Like Moses on the mountaintop and Muhammad in the cave, the prince, in his solitude, is unwitnessed by human eyes. But unlike them, he receives no command to recite, no commandments carved on tablets of stone. There is no God, or his messenger, there is no witness. And there is no drama, no burning bush, no empty tomb. There is simply a man sitting cross-legged under a tree in a forest as a new day dawns. What he has experienced had not been preserved to be uncovered; it had not been hidden to be revealed. The enlightenment of the Buddha is said to be the same enlightenment achieved by the buddhas of the past, a truth that had been forgotten.

The enlightenment of a buddha is accompanied by a host of qualities. This is Flaubert's reference when he has the Buddha say, "I had acquired the five virtues, the five faculties, the ten forces, the eighteen substances, and had entered into the four spheres of the invisible world, Intelligence became mine!" His reference for "the five virtues" is unclear. The *Play in Full* mentions six perfections (giving, ethics, patience, effort, concentration, and wisdom) and the four immeasurables (love, compassion, joy, and equanimity). The other lists are accurate. There is much that could be said about each; we can only list them here. The five faculties (*indriya*) are faith, effort, mindfulness, concentration, and wisdom. The ten forces (*bāla*) are ten powers of a buddha: (1) the power of knowing the positive and negative contingencies of things; (2) the power of knowing the maturation of deeds; (3) the power of knowing diverse aspirations; (4) the power of knowing diverse dispositions; (5) the power of knowing those who possess sharp faculties and those who do not; (6) the power of knowing the paths going everywhere; (7) the power of knowing concentration, liberation, absorption, affliction, purification, and acquisition; (8) the power of recollecting past lives; (9) the power of knowing death and rebirth; (10) the power of knowing the cessation of the contaminants. What Flaubert calls "the eighteen substances" are likely the eighteen unshared qualities (*āvenikadharma*) of a buddha, which are alluded to often in the *Play in Full.* They are discussed in the final chapter.

Before closing this chapter, we need to return for a moment to the palace. We recall that in one version of the great departure, the prince makes love to his wife, perhaps for the first time in their thirteen-year marriage on the night that he renounces the world and escapes from the palace. According to this version, his son Rāhula is conceived that night. In this version, the period that Rāhula spends in his mother's womb is not ten lunar months, but six years, precisely the six years between the night of his father's departure from the palace and the night of his father's enlightenment. There is much that we might say about the symbolism of this coincidence. However, as we seek to retrieve the human from the super-human, we might note that upon the birth of Rāhula, Yaśodharā must endure rumors that the Buddha is not her son's father, that she has been unfaithful to the prince during his absence. It is only when the Buddha and his monks eventually return to Kapilavastu that, at her request, the Buddha acknowledges that he is the child's father.[14] Even in the versions of the story in which Rāhula is born on the night of the prince's departure, Yaśodharā's very human sufferings are not forgotten. In a Thai version of the story called *Bimbā's Lament* (Bimbā is another name for Yaśodharā) in which Rāhula is born on the day of the Buddha's departure, she says to the Buddha upon his return:

> I am unlucky and ashamed before you, O Lord of Jambudvīpa. You abandoned me and our child without any compassion. In the old days I never considered myself unlucky. You never gave any indication that you would leave me alone for such a long time. Prince Rāhula was just born, but you left without any concern for me. You made your departure at midnight on your bejeweled horse, Kaṇṭhaka.
>
> Even though you were married to me, Bimbā, I was left deserted. O, my lord, you are a person of merit with a father, mother, family and friends in a large palace. An astrologer had once predicted that in the future Bimbā would experience suffering. O, my Lord, when I heard this ancient wisdom I knew that it was foolhardy to think that mother, father, or king could escape from suffering. As the astrologer foretold, I suffered when you abandoned me for six years. I thought of you every day, morning and night.[15]

Later, she asks that her husband at least bestow his birthright to their son, meaning that he acknowledge that Rāhula will succeed Śuddhodana as king. Instead, the Buddha has the boy ordained as a monk, to the great despair of his mother and grandfather. But we have moved too far ahead in the story. We must return to the newly enlightened Buddha sitting beneath the tree at dawn.

Now the prince Siddhārtha is a buddha, the buddha of our age, called Gotama Buddha in the Pāli tradition, Śākyamuni ("sage of the Śākya clan") in the Sanskrit tradition. What now? What does one do when the quest for enlightenment, six years in this life, billions of lifetimes in the past, is complete? The story now enters a strange phase. The Buddha remains in the vicinity of the tree, now called the Bodhi Tree, the Enlightenment Tree. As the site of the essential moment in the history of Buddhism, and thus, from the Buddhist perspective, the history of our world, it becomes the axis mundi, referred to as the *bodhimaṇḍa,* the "seat of enlightenment," the *vajrāsana,* the "diamond seat," so called because it is indestructible, surviving the conflagration caused by seven suns that will one day dawn in the sky and incinerate our world.

8

Seven Weeks in the Forest

He is now *buddha,* awakened, enlightened, free from future rebirth, and he knows it. Now what? This begins a fascinating period in the Buddha's story, and one that Flaubert does not include, despite the fact that it is described at length in the *Play in Full.* The epochal event has occurred. In many versions of the story, he spends seven weeks in the vicinity of the Bodhi Tree. It is clearly a liminal period. He does not eat, sleep, bathe, defecate, or speak, at least to any human. Yet each week something happens. The texts identify each of the seven weeks by the event that occurs, with these events appearing in different sequences in different versions; as noted, in the Pāli version, Māra's daughters, appearing before his enlightenment in some accounts, try to seduce him during the fifth week. In a text called the *Sūtra on the Fourfold Assembly* (*Catuṣpariṣat*), the Buddha receives his first meal in the second week rather than the seventh.

Most accounts agree that for the first week he remained seated under the Bodhi Tree, reliving the experience of enlightenment. After that he walked a short distance from the Bodhi

Tree and spent an entire week standing and staring at the Bodhi Tree and where he had sat beneath it, never closing his eyes or even blinking. Next, he spent a week walking back and forth between the place where he was standing and the Bodhi Tree; in some accounts his path becomes a bejeweled promenade. According to the *Mahāvastu,* during this week, Māra was nearby, sitting on the ground, writing again and again in the dirt with a stick, "Gotama the recluse has escaped from my power."[1] The new Buddha spent another week sitting in meditation, this time developing the teachings that would be known as the *abhidharma.*

Although we find many references to monasteries in the Buddhist scriptures, the oldest archaeological remains of monasteries date from the first century CE, some four centuries after the death of the Buddha, if we assume, with some caution, first, that the Buddha lived, and second, that the Buddha died around 400 BCE. This suggests that the Buddha and his monks, like other ascetic groups of the day, often lived in the forest, eating, sleeping, and meditating under trees. The forest was the abode of spirits who needed to be appeased. But just as the Buddha commanded the respect of the visible powers—kings and merchants—he also commanded the respect of the invisible: the *yakṣas* and *nāgas* who control the natural world. When the Buddha delivered a sūtra, they were often in attendance.

Thus, it is perhaps not surprising that the first earthly creature that the Buddha encounters after his enlightenment is not a human but a *nāga,* a huge serpent, the spirit of the tree that the Buddha is sitting under. His name is Mucilinda (Mucalinda in Pāli). As a torrential rain begins, he emerges from a nearby lake, coils himself around the Buddha seven times, and spreads his cobra hood above him, keeping him warm and dry during a week of rain. When we survey Buddhist stone carvings from the earliest period of Buddhist art, from the second century BCE to the second century CE, we see this scene depicted again and again. The powerful *nāga,* the feared serpent who can kill with his poisonous breath and bring rain in time of drought, is the protector of the Buddha.

For those Buddhist schools that say there is an "intermediate state" between death and rebirth (some say that rebirth is immediate), the standard length of that state is forty-nine days. Is there a connection here? Like the dead, the Buddha does not eat, he does not sleep, he does not close his eyes. He has no interaction with the human world, only the supernatural world of gods and giant snakes. It is only after this liminal period that he is reborn, in a sense, as the Buddha that we know, the compassionate teacher who sets out to teach the inhabitants of the world, human and divine, how to escape from the world of suffering.

But first he must eat. The Buddha has not eaten since the day that Sujātā, initially mistaking him for a tree spirit, a *yakṣa,* offered him a bowl of milk rice, his last meal as a bodhisattva. Now, after forty-nine days, he has his first encounter with humans and receives his first meal as a buddha. Two merchants, brothers named Trapuṣa and Bhallika, are traveling through the forest when a deity, who had been their mother in a previous lifetime, directs them to the Buddha. They offer him rice cakes and honey. However, the Buddha tells the brothers that buddhas do not receive food into their hands. (Other ascetics of ancient India, including the rival Jains, did.) But the Buddha does not have a bowl; as we recall, the bowl in which he had received his last meal, the milk rice from Sujātā, had floated upstream and sunk to the bottom of the river. At that moment, the kings of the four directions descend from their heavens on the four faces of Mount Meru, each holding a bowl made of a precious substance; in the *Play in Full,* the bowls are made of gold. The Buddha declines; a gold bowl is not appropriate for a monk. The gods then offer him bowls of various gems and precious stones; in each case he declines. Eventually the four gods offer the Buddha bowls made of stone. Apparently not wanting to favor one god over another, the Buddha takes the four bowls and compresses them into one, into which the two merchants place the honey cakes. The Buddha eats them.

Now, having eaten the food that the brothers offered, one would assume that the Buddha would teach them. However, in the Pāli account, the Buddha does not teach them anything. In the *Play in Full,* he delivers a long speech, essentially wishing them good luck. When the brothers ask him for something to remember him by, he gives them eight hairs from his head and, in some accounts, some nail parings, the first relics of the new buddha. The two brothers are said to have then taken refuge in the Buddha and the dharma, the first two of the three jewels, because the third, the saṅgha, did not yet exist. However, in the Pāli account, the Buddha does not teach them anything, so it is unclear what is meant by "dharma" in this case. The brothers then went on their way. Where they went is consequential, since according to their story, when they returned to their homeland, they enshrined the relics in a stūpa, the first stūpa of the new buddha. In Xuanzang's account, the Buddha shows them what it should look like, inverting his new bowl on top of his folded robes. For the Burmese, the brothers returned to what is today Yangon, where they erected the Shwedagon Pagoda, the most sacred site in the land. Xuanzang explains that the two merchants (who do not seem to be brothers in this version) divided the relics between them and returned to their homeland in what is now Afghanistan, each building a stūpa in his home city.[2]

Why did the Buddha not teach the dharma to the two merchants, the first humans that he encountered after his enlightenment? In the Pāli account, after his achievement of enlightenment, the Buddha concludes that what he has understood is too profound for others to understand, saying, "Those dyed in lust, wrapped in darkness will never discern this abstruse Dhamma, which goes against the worldly stream, subtle, deep, and difficult to see."[3] There is no point in trying to teach it to others. Knowing his thoughts, the god Brahmā quickly descends from his heaven to beg the Buddha to teach, knowing that the world will be in peril if he does not do so. He explains that the gods—who in Buddhism are not immortal but are also subject to rebirth—have been long awaiting his advent and that the teachings in India up until this time are impure, taught by those still stained by ignorance. Brahmā does not dispute that what the Buddha has understood will be difficult to understand. He concedes that, indeed, some have much dust in their eyes. However, there are others with little dust in their eyes who will understand. The Buddha makes the momentous decision to teach.

This is obviously an odd moment. We recall that four incalculable eons and one hundred thousand eons in the past, the ascetic Sumedha had vowed to forgo liberation from rebirth in that lifetime by becoming a disciple of the buddha Dīpaṅkara, instead vowing to follow the long path of the bodhisattva in order to become a buddha when there was no buddha so that he could teach the path to liberation to the bereft world. That he would now, having completed the long path, decide not to do so seems preposterous. The more likely reason for this story is to demonstrate that the most famous of the Vedic gods knows that the competing philosophies of the day are inferior to what the Buddha will teach. And the story demonstrates that the gods do not know how to escape from the realm of rebirth. It is only the Buddha who knows the path to liberation from suffering.

There is much to say about each of these first weeks after the enlightenment. From one perspective, there is a mercenary motivation, for when Bodh Gayā became a pilgrimage site, which happened early on, the scene of each of the events of the seven weeks became its own shrine, another place for the faithful to make offerings; the place where the Buddha spent a week staring at the Bodhi Tree is called the Shrine of the Steadfast Gaze. From another perspective, the story provides an opportunity to demonstrate his superiority to the local gods. Ancient India, like so many traditional cultures, had an animated landscape, with all manner of spirits and sprites. Buddhist texts list eight types of non-humans, none of which are animals. The most common of these were the *yakṣa* and *nāga,* two names that are difficult to translate. A *yakṣa* is often the spirit that inhabits a tree, easily offended and able to both cause harm and bestow benefit. A *nāga* is a serpentine creature, not quite a snake, sometimes depicted in Buddhist art as a huge, multiheaded serpent, with hoods like a cobra, sometimes with the head and torso of a human and the tail of a snake. The Sanskrit term was translated into Chinese as "dragon." *Nāgas* live beneath the waters of lakes and rivers in bejeweled palaces. They have magical powers, and their breath is poisonous to humans, yet they have the all-important power to bring rain. Much of ancient Indian religion was concerned with pleasing, or at least not offending, these spirits. If *nāgas* are subservient to the Buddha, then the Buddha is worthy of worship.

That the Buddha did not teach Trapuṣa and Bhallika the truth that he had discovered seven weeks earlier suggests that they had much dust in their eyes. Having decided that he will teach, the Buddha now must determine who has little dust in their eyes, who is the most deserving recipient of his first teaching. He thinks first of his own teachers, the meditation masters Ārāḍa Kālāma and Udraka Rāmaputra, but he is informed by the gods that they both have recently died, to be reborn in the Formless Realm. He thinks next of the "group of five," despite the fact that they had disdainfully abandoned him seven weeks earlier. He saw that they were living in a royal game preserve called the Deer Park outside the city of Vārāṇāsī.

Before he arrives there, we might pause, at least metaphorically, beneath a tree. In the accounts of the Buddha's birth and the years leading to this first teaching, we are struck by the importance of trees. Prince Siddhārtha is born when his mother, en route to the home of her parents, stops in Lumbinī Garden, where, feeling birth pangs, she grasps the branch of a tree and the child emerges from under her right arm. In a stone carving of the scene from Gandhāra, dated to the late second or third century CE in the collection of the National Museum of Asian Art, Queen Māyā seems to become the tree, leaves growing from the top of her head, her right arm a branch. As noted, excavations at Lumbinī have revealed a tree shrine that predates the Aśokan monuments there, read by some as evidence that Lumbinī is indeed the site of the Buddha's birth, read by others as an attempt by early Buddhists to create a place of pilgrimage by associating the Buddha's birth with an existing shrine.[4] As already discussed, in the stories of the Buddha's youth, there is the famous moment when his father, the king, participates in an annual plowing festival to inaugurate the planting season, leaving his young son under a rose apple tree, a *jambu* tree in Sanskrit. His nurses leave him to watch the festival, eventually noticing that the shadow shading him has not moved. Returning to the tree, they find the young prince seated in meditation, the shadow having stopped so that the tree may continue to shade him from the sun.

On the day before his enlightenment, he sits down under a tree believed by the villagers to be the abode of a *yakṣa,* a tree spirit. A young woman named Sujātā had prayed to the *yakṣa* to give her a son, and after her son was born she made regular offerings of milk rice to the *yakṣa.* When her servant saw the emaciated prince seated under the tree, she assumed he was the *yakṣa,* leading Sujātā to bring him a bowl of milk rice on a golden platter. Consuming this meal, the prince immediately both regained his strength and alienated his five companions, who abandoned him for abandoning their ascetic practices. As described above, it was this meal that sustained the prince for the next forty-nine days. Later that day, he chose the tree where he would sit all night in meditation, becoming enlightened (*buddha*) at dawn. He remained seated under that tree for the next seven days, before, according to some versions of the story, moving to another tree, a banyan tree, for another seven days. He later sat beneath yet another tree, protected by the *nāga* Mucilinda. When a storm broke out, the great serpent emerged from a nearby lake, coiled his body around the Buddha and spread his hood above him to protect him from the storm. And in the seventh week, again seated under a tree, the Buddha had his first encounter with humans when the merchants Trapuṣa and Bhallika offered him his first meal.

The supposed sites of several of these trees became shrines in the vicinity of the Bodhi Tree, the Buddhist sanctum sanctorum. As just noted, one might certainly argue that these shrines were created to generate offerings from pilgrims to Bodh Gayā. However, more important than this commercial motive, they provide evidence of the importance of the forest, the earth from which it grows, and the spirits who inhabit it, in Indian religion. It is the respect that he inspires among the spirits in the forest, more than among the monks in the monastery, that made him a figure worthy of worship in ancient India. In aniconic Buddhist art, the presence of the Buddha is often represented by a tree, sometimes festooned with garlands, sometimes with a pair of footprints at its foot. The naturally growing tree would eventually be replaced by a human construction, the stūpa.

After the Buddha declares, "I became the Buddha," Flaubert adds two sentences, a stage direction, in parentheses: "All the gods bow themselves down. Those having several heads, bend them simultaneously." This is the only time that the long parade of pagan deities pays homage to a foreign figure, perhaps a sign of Flaubert's own homage to the Buddha. In response, the Buddha "lifts his mighty hand aloft and resumes." So let us return to our story.

9
To the Deer Park

The new Buddha has now set out to find his five friends, a journey of about one hundred and fifty miles. During this journey, one of the stranger encounters in the biography occurs. In Buddhist literature, people sometimes comment on another person's skin tone, even that of a stranger. It is usually the skin tone of the Buddha, but not always. Before becoming a disciple of the Buddha, the famous monk Śāriputra compliments the monk Aśvajit, one of the group of five, on his skin tone. In the Buddhist monastic code, one monk asks another the secret of his beautiful skin and the monk replies that he has been masturbating. Shortly thereafter, the Buddha makes masturbation a violation of the code.

Not long after he sets out from the Bodhi Tree the Buddha encounters an ascetic named Upaka, a member of the Ājīvika sect, one of the many sects of ancient India, sufficiently important to be mentioned in the Aśokan inscriptions (where the emperor reports granting them caves). The sect no longer exists. The Ājīvikas are traditionally counted as one of the six sects who are opponents of the Buddhists. None of their own texts survive, so knowledge of them derives from descriptions by their Buddhist and Jain opponents. There, they are described as strict fatalists, rejecting entirely the law of karma, believing that all cases of both happiness and sorrow are the result of fate (*niyata*). After a vast number of lifetimes, however, all beings will enter a state of purification. Despite this, they are described as strict ascetics, going naked and having few possessions.

Upaka, struck by the Buddha's demeanor, stops to comment on his clear and bright complexion. Seeing this as a sign of spiritual attainment, he asks him who his teacher is. The Buddha replies, "I have no teacher, and one like me exists nowhere in all the world with all its gods because I have no person for my counterpart. I am the Accomplished One in the world, I am the Teacher Supreme. I alone am a Fully Enlightened One whose fires are quenched and extinguished."[1] When Upaka asks the Buddha if he is the *anantajina*, or "eternal conqueror," the Buddha answers in the affirmative. To this, Upaka shakes his head, says what might be roughly translated as "Whatever," and goes on his way.

It is unclear exactly why this story appears. That the story is somehow important is confirmed by Buddhaghosa. In his commentary on the Dīgha Nikāya, he says that the only reason the Buddha walked from the Bodhi Tree to the Deer Park was so that he could encounter Upaka; otherwise, he would have flown.[2] One might suggest that Upaka is meant to represent the early struggles of the Buddhist community to gain recognition among the many philosophical groups of the day. Or, it could simply be one of many condemnations of the Ājīvikas found in Buddhist literature: an Ājīvika was the first ascetic to meet the Buddha after his enlightenment, yet he failed to recognize him, despite being told exactly who the Buddha was, and by the Buddha himself.

Soon, the Buddha arrives in the Deer Park. Seeing him approach, the group of five, still regarding the prince as a slacker, decides that they will ignore him when he arrives. Yet, as he draws closer, they are struck by his charisma, and rise to greet him, addressing him, as they always had, as "friend" and "Siddhārtha." The Buddha says they should not call him that anymore, referring to himself as the Tathāgata. The exact meaning of this term that is so commonly used to refer to the Buddha remains unclear. It can be translated as either "one who has thus gone" or "one who has thus come," with "thus" perhaps referring to the way that the buddhas of the past had come and gone. The Buddha then, as the texts say, "set the wheel of the dharma in motion," or, as it is often described in English, gave his "first sermon." It is impossible to know exactly what he said; there are several versions in the various canons, which differ in important ways.

The most well-known version contains three of the most famous terms for the tradition: the middle way, the eightfold path, and the four noble truths. Alluding to his own life, he says that both self-indulgence and self-mortification are extremes to be avoided, that it is by following a middle way between those extremes that he has achieved enlightenment. More specifically, that middle way consists of eight elements: right view, right intention, right speech, right action, right livelihood, right effort, right mindfulness, and right concentration. He does not elaborate on these terms, but turns next to the four noble truths. First is the truth of suffering. He says that birth, aging, sickness, death, encountering the unwanted, and not encountering the wanted are all suffering, that, in brief, the "five aggregates"—the various physical and mental elements that constitute the person—are suffering. The second truth is the origin, or cause, of suffering, which the Buddha identifies here as craving, and enumerates as craving for sensual pleasure, craving for existence, and craving for non-existence. These last two are the subject of much commentary. The third truth is cessation, the declaration of a permanent end to suffering. Although he does not specify it here, this cessation is nirvāṇa. And fourth, there is a path leading to the cessation of suffering, the eightfold path that he has already enumerated.

Rendering the Buddhist language of "setting the wheel of the dharma into motion" into the Christian language of the "first sermon" is unfortunate, because it occludes the allusion to the magical wheel of the *cakravartin,* which rolls across the worlds, bringing them under his command. Here, the wheel of the Buddha begins to roll, showing the path to freedom. We recall that when the king summoned the court astrologers to predict the future of his infant son, all but one said that he would become either a *cakravartin* or a buddha. The imagery of the wheel recalls that moment. And it certifies the prediction of the lone dissenter, the young Kauṇḍinya, who said that there was no doubt that the prince would become a buddha. This Kauṇḍinya, now thirty-five years older, is one of the group of five. The text states that at the conclusion of the Buddha's discourse, Kauṇḍinya had a stainless vision of the dharma, understanding that whatever is caused can also cease, that if there is a cause of suffering, there must also be an end to suffering.

The commentators identify Kauṇḍinya's attainment as that of a stream-enterer, the first of the four stages of enlightenment: stream-enterer, once returner, never returner, and arhat. The first has entered the stream flowing to liberation and will achieve nirvāṇa in seven lifetimes or less; the second will be reborn in the Realm of Desire one more time at most; the third will never return to the Realm of Desire but will achieve nirvāṇa from the highest heaven of the Realm of Form, and the fourth is fully liberated from rebirth and will enter nirvāṇa at death. These four are called the four "noble persons" in Buddhism. And indeed, the standard English translation "four noble truths" is a mistranslation. The term should be translated, admittedly less euphoniously, as the "four truths for the noble ones," making the important point that suffering, origin, cessation, and path are not true for the benighted, they are true for those who, like Kauṇḍinya, have a stainless vision of the dharma.

Five days later, the Buddha turned the wheel of the doctrine for the second time, setting forth the central philosophical insight of the tradition: that among the constituents of mind and body, there is no self. Here, the Buddha goes through each of the five aggregates—form, feeling, discrimination (in the sense of the ability to distinguish between objects), compositional factors, and consciousness—declaring that each is not the self; if it were, we would have control over our feelings of pleasure and pain, for example, but we do not. He goes on to describe each of the constituents of the person to be impermanent, suffering, and not self and instructs that, for each one, we should think, "This is not mine; this is not me; this is not my self." At the conclusion of this second discourse, called "The Sign of No Self" (*Anattalakkhana*), the group of five were all arhats.

One night shortly thereafter, the Buddha encountered the son of a wealthy merchant named Yaśas who, like Prince Siddhārtha, had become discouraged by the vapidity of worldly life and had left his home and parents behind. The Buddha set forth what is called a "graduated discourse," one that begins with generosity and morality and ends with the four truths, after which Yaśas became a stream-enterer and soon after that an arhat. The Buddha next converted Yaśas's parents, who became lay disciples. Next, fifty-four of Yaśas's friends became disciples of the Buddha and quickly became arhats. Now, with sixty arhats (not counting the Buddha himself) in the world—the group of five and Yaśas and his friends—the Buddha sent them out to teach, famously instructing them to "Go forth for the good of the many, for the happiness of the many, out of compassion for the world, for the welfare, the good and the happiness of gods and humans. Let no two of you go in the same direction."

The ministry of Jesus was short: three years from baptism to crucifixion. The ministry of the Buddha was long, some forty-five years. But not that much happens. There are some narrative loose ends that need to be tied up; much of this occurs when he eventually returns to the palace to see his father, stepmother, wife, and son. At the urging of his stepmother, he establishes an order of nuns. He converts some more ascetics and wins the patronage of kings, but much of this is rather formulaic. He survives some assassination attempts by his evil cousin Devadatta. With three of the four great moments in his life—his birth, his enlightenment, and his first turning of the wheel of the dharma—now done, all that remains is his death, his passage into nirvāṇa, discussed in the next chapter. This last is a story that the tradition tells at length. And then, although there is much to say about doctrine, in biography there is nothing left to tell. The tradition would seek to remedy this narrative deficit by turning to the past. And so does Flaubert, without really saying so.

> That I might effect the deliverance of beings, I have made hundreds of thousands of sacrifices! To the poor I gave robes of silk, beds, chariots, houses, heaps of gold and of diamonds. I gave my hands to the one-handed, my legs to the lame, my eyes to the blind;—even my head I severed for the sake of the decapitated. In the day that I was King, I gave away provinces;—when I was a Brahman I despised no one. When I was a solitary, I spake kindly words to the robber who slew me. When I was a tiger I allowed myself to die of hunger.[3]

As we have noted, in Buddhism, the cycle of birth and death has no beginning. As we have noted, during the first watch of the night of his enlightenment, the Buddha had precise memories of all of his past lives. And as we have noted, four incalculable eons and one hundred thousand eons in the past he made a vow to become a buddha in the distant future, using those eons as a time to "accumulate merit," to do the good deeds that would eventually empower him to become a buddha in a world where there was no one who knew the path to nirvāṇa. The Buddha therefore has many edifying tales to tell. These are the stories to which Flaubert alludes, paraphrasing the *Play in Full,* where we read: "You, Benefactor of the World, delight in the qualities of the victorious ones. / In your past lives you gave away your wealth, jewels, and gold; / Your beloved wife and children; your land, cities, and villages; / And even your own head, eyes, hands, and feet. / O Best of Men, in former times you were a virtuous king. / When a person came before you and said, / 'Please give me this land with its cities and villages,' / You gave it away with a happy and undisturbed mind."[4]

The stories themselves do not appear in the *Play in Full.* It is likely that Flaubert found them instead in a book by the great translator Stanislas Julien (1797–1873), holder of the chair in Chinese that had been founded at the Collège de France in 1814. In 1853, he had published *Histoire de la vie de Hiouen-Thsang et de ses voyages dans l'Inde, despuis l'an 629 jusqu'en 645,* a translation of the travel account of the monk Xuanzang (602–664), the most famous of the Chinese pilgrims to India. Many of the pilgrimage sites in India are represented as the site of a deed, often a particularly grisly deed, of the Buddha in a past life. In his description of his visit to the site, Xuanzang often tells the story. For example, when the bodhisattva was King Śibi he gave away his eyes. When he was an elephant, the bodhisattva killed himself to feed some hungry travelers lost in the jungle. When he was Prince Mahādeva, he killed himself to feed a starving tigress who was about to devour her own cubs.

These stories appear across the Buddhist world, often portrayed in painting and stone, sometimes providing a narrative background to the central figure of the seated buddha. In the Pāli version of the life of the Buddha, one or more stories are listed for each of the ten perfections that the bodhisattva must master in order to become a buddha. Thus, for the perfection of patience, the text provides the name Khantivāda, a sage who, falsely accused by a drunken king of trying to seduce his courtesans, simply said, "I practice patience," as the king methodically lopped off his ears, nose, and limbs, screaming with each blow, "Tell me what you teach."

These stories are known as *jātaka* (or "birth," meaning here "previous births") in Pāli and Sanskrit, and it is noteworthy that in English-language scholarship they are known as the "Jataka Tales," implying that for the Buddhologist they are simply stories and not histories. Indeed, much of the focus on the *jātaka* collection since the nineteenth century has been in the field of folklore studies, where scholars have identified versions of many of these stories in Hindu literature as well as various twice-told tales in Persian, Arabic, and European sources, suggesting the existence of a floating corpus of folklore employed in different times, in different places, and for different purposes across history.

The Buddha's ability to remember every moment of millions of past lives provides a doctrinal justification to transform folklore into sacred canon. The *jātaka* stories, of which there are five hundred and forty-seven in the Pāli version, are transformed from children's stories into the word of the Buddha with the addition of a few sentences at the end in which the Buddha identifies the story as the account of one of his past lives, identifying the dramatis personae, regardless of whether the hero is human, mammal, fish, or foul: "In that existence the otter was Ānanda, the jackal was Moggallāna, the monkey was Sāriputta, and I was the wise hare." As Walter Benjamin says of the storyteller, "His gift is the ability to relate his life: his distinction, to be able to tell his entire life. The storyteller: he is the man who could let the wick of his life be consumed completely by the gentle flame of his story."[5]

We see here something that we see throughout the history of Buddhism, both in India and abroad. Just as long-locked Hindu ascetics are converted to shaven-headed Buddhist monks; just as the Hindu cosmos becomes the Buddhist cosmos, with the axis mundi shifted from Mount Meru to Bodh Gayā; just as the immortal Hindu gods become deities still bound in the realm of rebirth, all subservient to the Buddha, so the narrative imagination of ancient India is appropriated by the Buddhists, simply by having the Buddha tell a children's tale and end by saying, "I was the deer."

> And having, in this last existence, preached the law, nothing now remains for me to do. The great period is accomplished! Men, animals, the gods, the bamboos, the oceans, the mountains, the sand-grains of the Ganges, together with the myriad myriads of the stars,—all shall die;—and until the time of the new births, a flame shall dance upon the wrecks of worlds destroyed![6]

Flaubert here speaks of things that do not appear in the *Play in Full*. It is the case that after the Buddha has achieved enlightenment and preached the dharma, nothing remained for him to do. Just after his enlightenment, Māra had told the new Buddha that he should now pass into nirvāṇa. The Buddha had replied, "Evil One, I will not take final Nibbāna till I have monks and disciples who are accomplished, trained, skilled, learned, knowers of the Dhamma, trained in conformity with the Dhamma, correctly trained and walking in the path of the Dhamma, who will pass on what they have gained from their Teacher, teach it, declare it, establish it, expound it, analyze it, make it clear; till they shall be able by means of the Dhamma to refute false teachings that have arisen, and teach the Dhamma of wondrous effect." He made the same promise regarding nuns, laymen, and laywomen, going on to say, "Evil One, I will not take final Nibbāna till this holy life has been successfully established and flourishes, is widespread, well-known far and wide, well-proclaimed among mankind everywhere."[7] Forty-five years later, Māra returned and reminded him of his vow, a vow that was now fulfilled. The Buddha agreed, saying, in effect, "I preached the law, nothing now remains for me to do. The great period is accomplished."

However, that does not mean that the world will come to an end when the Buddha passes into nirvāṇa. According to Buddhist cosmology, the world and its inhabitants will abide for billions of years, during which Maitreya, the next buddha, will come. It is only when what is called the period of abiding comes to an end that what is called the period of destruction will begin. It is only then that our world system, but not all world systems, will indeed be incinerated by seven suns. However, thanks to the workings of karma, all of the beings of our world will have been evacuated by then, reborn in one of the realms of other worlds, where they will wander, awaiting the advent of a buddha.

10

Passage to Nirvāṇa

(Then a great dizziness comes upon the gods. They stagger, fall into convulsions, and vomit forth their existences. Their crowns burst apart; their banners fly away. They tear off their attributes, their sexes, fling over their shoulders the cups from which they quaffed immortality, strangle themselves with their serpents, vanish in smoke;—and when all have disappeared . . .)[1]

This scene does not appear in the lives of the Buddha. In the *Play in Full,* when King Śuddhodana takes his infant son into the temple, the statues of the gods there rise from their seats and prostrate at the feet of the child, singing in unison: "Mount Meru, the greatest and best of mountains, would never bow down to a mustard seed; / The great ocean, the *nāga* king's abode, would never bow down to a puddle; / The brilliant sun and moon would never bow down before a firefly. / So how could the Noble One, with merit and wisdom, bow down before the gods?"[2] But the gods do not die.

This passage may have reminded Flaubert of a scene from the twenty-second chapter of the Gospel of Pseudo-Matthew, likely composed in the early seventh century, a scene that does not appear in the Synoptic Gospels. During the flight into Egypt, when Mary and Joseph are fleeing from Nazareth with their infant son to escape Herod's slaughter of the innocents, they stop in the city of Sotinen in Egypt. There, Mary takes the Christ child into a temple that contains three hundred and fifty-five idols, one for each day of the Egyptian year. The idols all prostrate before the infant, shattering to pieces in the process. Or, Flaubert may have seen Tommaso Laureti's painting of 1582 on the ceiling of the Constantine Room in the Vatican. Called *The Fall of the Idols and the Triumph of Christianity,* it shows a smashed statue of Mercury at the feet of a crucifix.

But Flaubert's idols are not statues that smash themselves into cold stone. They are living deities compelled to commit gruesome forms of suicide upon hearing the words of the most famous of idols, the Buddha. What might this mean?

We can note that the chapter continues with the appearance of a host of gods, often in gruesome guise, from Babylonia, Ethiopia, Greece, and Rome. But before they appear, Hilarion, always seeking to undermine Anthony's Christian faith, says, "Thou hast even now beheld the belief of many hundreds of millions of men."[3] We can only speculate about what he means by this, but it may be that the idols of the distant past no longer have believers; without their sacrifices, the idols commit suicide. The Buddha and his teachings remain the truth for a huge portion of humanity.

Few of the works that are considered biographies of the Buddha take him to the end of his life and his passage into nirvāṇa. The Pāli biography ends with the gift to him of Jetavana monastery in the third year after his enlightenment. The *Play in Full* ends with his first teaching to the group of five in the

Deer Park at Sarnath. This may be due in part to the fact that in the Pāli canon there is an entire text devoted to the Buddha's final days, death, and cremation, called the *Great Discourse on the Final Nirvāṇa* (*Mahāparinibbāna Sutta*). In the Sanskrit tradition, these events are recounted most famously in the *Buddhacarita.* A great deal has been said and can be said about the account in the *Great Discourse on the Final Nirvāṇa.* This is perhaps to be expected, since many matters must be settled and questions must be answered before the Buddha passes away forever.

It is important to note that there is a Mahāyāna sūtra with the same title, but in Sanskrit: *Great Discourse on the Final Nirvāṇa* (*Mahāparinirvāṇa Sūtra*), a much longer text, and a very different text. Here, the Buddha is lying on his right side, the posture in which he is so often depicted in Buddhist art, the posture from which he is to pass away. Yet, in the Sanskrit version, the Buddha does not die, he does not pass into nirvāṇa, his body is not cremated, and his relics are not enshrined in stūpas. Instead, the Buddha, the great teacher of impermanence, declares that his body is permanent (*nityakāya*). The Buddha explains, "At times, I show [myself entering into] parinirvāṇa in the Jambudvīpas of a billion worlds, and yet, ultimately, I do not take parinirvāṇa."[4] In other words, he lives forever. Thus, at the end of this text, there is no distribution of the relics. Instead, a number of miracles occur, concluding with two million billion women turning into men.[5]

We might see the two accounts as further evidence of the difference between the caricatures of the Theravāda and the Mahāyāna, the one spare, sober, and realistic; the other baroque, extravagant, and hyperbolic to the point of heresy. And yet there is an odd moment in the Pāli account that gives us pause.

Not long before his death, the Buddha and Ānanda go to a forest shrine to meditate so that the Buddha, now eighty years old, can regain his strength. At one point, the Buddha mentions that, if he is asked to do so, a buddha can live "for an eon or until the end of an eon."[6] Ānanda does not respond, even though the Buddha repeats the same statement twice. Not long after, Māra appears and reminds the Buddha that shortly after his enlightenment, the Buddha had told him that he would not enter nirvāṇa until he had established a community of monks, nuns, laymen, and laywomen, who were wise, disciplined, and could preserve his teachings. Māra points out that that time has now come. The Buddha rather grudgingly agrees, saying that he will pass into nirvāṇa three months later. He then "relinquishes his life force," causing the earth to quake.

Ānanda feels the tremor and asks the Buddha what has happened. The Buddha enumerates eight reasons for an earthquake, including a buddha's relinquishment of his life force. It is only then that Ānanda realizes his oversight, begging the Buddha to live for an eon or until the end of the eon: "May the Blessed One remain, O Lord! May the Happy One remain, O Lord, throughout the world-period, for the welfare and happiness of the multitude, out of compassion for the world, for the benefit, well being, and happiness of gods and humans."

But the Buddha tells him that it is too late, reminding Ānanda that he has missed his chance, not only on these recent three occasions, but fifteen other times in the past, which the Buddha goes on to enumerate, concluding, "But you, Ananda, were unable to grasp the plain suggestion, the significant prompting, given you by the Tathagata, and you did not entreat the Tathagata to remain. For if you had done so, Ananda, twice the Tathagata might have declined, but the third time he would have consented. Therefore, Ananda, the fault is yours; herein you have failed."[7]

And the fault is great, because *kalpa,* the term translated as "eon" here, is a very long time, so long that when the Buddha describes it in the Pāli canon, it is not measured in years. The relevant unit here is the *yojana*, a traditional measure of distance in ancient India, often said to derive from the word for "yoke" and thus the distance a yoked team of oxen could plod in one day. There is a wide range of opinion on how far that is, with the figure of 7.2 kilometers often calculated. The Buddha asks us to imagine a castle that is one cubic *yojana* in size, filled with mustard seeds. A *kalpa* is the amount of time it would take to empty the castle if one removed one mustard seed every century. Elsewhere, he describes a block of stone one cubic *yojana* in size. A *kalpa* is the amount of time it would take to wear away the stone if one stroked it with a soft piece of cotton cloth once every century. In other words, when the Buddha tells Ānanda that if asked to do so, a buddha can live for an eon or to the end of an eon, he is essentially saying that a buddha can live forever.[8] The difference between the Pāli version and the Sanskrit version of the Buddha's final days is that in the Sanskrit version, someone must have asked him to do so.

II

Did the Buddha Exist?

11

Times and Teachings

In Chapter 5 of *The Temptation of Saint Anthony*, statues of the ancient idols of world history suddenly appear. First to come are those from before the Flood, their heads covered in seaweed and their bellies filled with sand, causing Anthony and Hilarion to roll with laughter. Next come animal-headed idols and then statues of demons; at their feet are humans slaughtered on stone altars and the bones of devoured children. This gruesome scene is replaced by a valley where a herdsman calls out to a passing cloud, praying for rain. The valley then turns into a sea of milk, where a god lies sleeping on a coiled serpent. A lotus emerges from his belly. It blossoms to reveal a god with three faces. Three goddesses then appear, followed by all manner of gods, one with the head of an elephant, another with fourteen arms, one riding a crocodile. Next the god of the sun and the goddess of the moon. "And among these gods are the Genii of the winds, of the planets, of the months, of the days,—a hundred thousand others;—multiple are their aspects, rapid their transformations. Behold, there is one who changes from a fish into a tortoise: he assumes the form of a boar, the shape of a dwarf."[1] And then the Buddha appears.

There seems to be some kind of chronology here, beginning with antediluvian idols followed by idols demanding human sacrifice. After a pastoral animist interlude, Flaubert moves to theism and a creator god. Here, he turns to Hindu mythology, where Viṣṇu, sleeping on a serpent in a sea of milk, a lotus growing from his navel, gives birth to the three-faced Brahmā, who in turn transforms into three gods—Brahmā the creator, Viṣṇu the sustainer, and Śiva, the destroyer—and then their consorts, Sarasvatī, Lakṣmī, and Pārvatī, and then a host of other gods, ending with the first, second, third, and fifth of the ten avatars of Viṣṇu: Matsya the fish, Kūrma the tortoise, Varāha the boar, and Vāmana the dwarf. When Anthony asks, "Pour quoi faire?" Hilarion replies, "That he may preserve the equilibrium of the universe, and combat the works of evil. But life exhausts itself; forms wear away; and they must achieve progression in their metamorphoses."[2]

Flaubert does not describe the next three incarnations, the sixth, seventh, and eighth avatars: Paraśurāma, Rāma, and Kṛṣṇa. He turns instead to the Buddha. And the Buddha is counted as the ninth avatar of Viṣṇu, at least by Hindus. His incorporation, some might say his kidnapping, occurs in a number of Hindu scriptures called *purāṇas,* with the earliest versions appearing around the fourth century CE and thus centuries after the death of the Buddha. As Hilarion correctly notes, the incarnations appear in age after age to right a particular wrong, with the avatars following something of an evolutionary sequence, from fish to animal; to half-human, half-animal; to short human to tall human. The renowned Rāma and Kṛṣṇa are the seventh and eighth. The Buddha is the ninth and the most recent. The tenth avatar, Kalki, harbinger of the apocalypse, has yet to arrive.

In one of the Hindu versions of the Buddha's story, demons begin reciting the sacred Veda and practicing asceticism, causing them to gain powers that threaten the supremacy of the gods, who beg Viṣṇu to destroy the demons. To deprive them of their power, Viṣṇu appears as the Buddha. He teaches the demons to reject Vedic sacrifice, to ignore caste distinction, and to deny the existence of a creator deity. The demons become the Buddha's disciples and embrace his teachings. As a result, they lose their power and are reborn in hell. Viṣṇu's purpose in appearing as the Buddha was deception. He convinced the demons that things which according to Hindu doctrine are true—Vedic sacrifice, caste distinction, and a creator god—are in fact false.

Among the several ironies here is that, according to Buddhism, the Buddha did in fact condemn Vedic sacrifice and the existence of a creator deity. Although his attitude toward caste is more complicated than is often portrayed in nineteenth-century European scholarship, members of all four castes are listed among his disciples. It likely goes without saying that this story of the Hindu god Viṣṇu appearing as the Buddha in order to defend Vedic sacrifice is not accepted by any of the several schools of Buddhism that have appeared over the centuries, nor is it reported (at least approvingly) in any Buddhist text. But let us return to Flaubert, for this is not the Buddha he portrays.

None of the gods who appear before him, including the Hindu gods, speak. Yet Flaubert has the Buddha speak, and his speech is potent. Halfway through it, the gods all bow down to him. And, as we have seen, when he concludes his speech, "They stagger, fall into convulsions, and vomit forth their existences. Their crowns burst apart; their banners fly away. They tear off their attributes, their sexes, fling over their shoulders the cups from which they quaffed immortality, strangle themselves with their serpents, vanish in smoke."[3]

What are we to make of this? Is the appearance of the Buddha—depicted, as we have seen, with admirable accuracy by Flaubert—meant to mark the twilight of the idols? Does the

Buddha mark for Flaubert, as he did for some of his compatriots, the end of Indian myth and the advent of Indian history? There is much in his positive and detailed portrayal of the Buddha to suggest that this is the case. But there is something further to consider. Chapter 5 of *The Temptation of Saint Anthony* does not end with the discourse of the Buddha and the immolation of the idols. Flaubert goes on to introduce a host of other gods, gods of Babylonia, Persia, Ephesus, Anatolia, Egypt, Greece, and Rome, moving from Orient to Occident, until he comes to Yahweh himself. When Anthony's long night of often nightmarish visions finally ends, the face of Jesus appears on the rising sun. Does the Buddha therefore represent merely the greatest of the Oriental idols before Flaubert turns to the Occidental idols? Or does the Buddha stand alone, at the midpoint of the chapter, representing the apex of the human and of history before Flaubert plunges back into myth, dispelled only when the true savior arrives? These are important questions, but they are questions for the literary critic. Our question is: did the Buddha exist?

Historians of ancient India speculate that as increased trade led to the growth of cities and city-states, there were those who rejected life in the city and retreated into the forest, rejecting the world of Vedic sacrifice for an otherworldly goal. These ascetics were the authors of the Upaniṣads, which declared the identity of *ātman,* the eternal self, and *brahman,* the eternal reality, and which introduced the doctrines of rebirth and liberation from rebirth. The Jains, said to follow the teachings of Mahāvīra, a contemporary of the Buddha, taught their own path to liberation from rebirth, again postulating an eternal self, called the *jīva.* From both historical and philosophical perspectives, it seems entirely plausible that another teacher, also asserting the existence of a cycle of rebirth, would make a different claim, that liberation lay in the realization that the self is an illusion. But when did he live and what did he teach?

In 1879, the British journalist Edwin Arnold (1832–1904) published his famous life of the Buddha in verse, *The Light of Asia.* In 1891, he published a second, and far less popular, work about Jesus, called *The Light of the World,* trying to appease the Anglican critics of his bestseller and hoping, in vain, that it might improve his chances of succeeding Tennyson as poet laureate. Thus, as we ponder dates and historical markers, we might begin with Arnold's "light of the world."

Based on Roman records and Jewish chronicles, scholars have confirmed the existence of a rabbi named Jesus of Nazareth who was probably born between 6 BCE and 4 BCE (Roman sources say that Herod died in 4 BCE) and who was executed during the rule of Pontius Pilate, the governor of Judaea from 26 CE to 36 CE. As for his teachings, the consensus among scholars is that the earliest books of the New Testament are Paul's letters, with Galatians and First Thessalonians dated to around 50 CE, within two decades of the crucifixion, with churches to receive those letters established as far away as Galatia in Turkey and Thessalonica in Greece. Although Paul's encounter with Jesus was of the supernatural variety, he knew several of his direct disciples, including Peter. The Gospel of Mark, the earliest of the Synoptic Gospels, is dated to 66–74 CE, and thus composed during the lifetime of contemporaries of Jesus. The *Antiquities of the Jews,* composed in Latin by the Jewish historian Josephus, dated to 93 CE, mentions both Jesus and John the Baptist.

Many questions remain about the life and teachings of Jesus. The events of his life, for example, during the so-called lost years between the Disputation—when his parents found him debating with the elders in the temple at age twelve—and his baptism by John at age thirty are not recounted. Beginning in the nineteenth century, some claimed that he was in India studying Buddhism during those years. Still, there is sufficient textual and archaeological evidence to conclude that Jesus was a historical figure who lived during the first decades of the years that would be named after him (Anno Domini); today his existence is so widely accepted that those years are simply called the Common Era.

Buddhists also measure history based on the life of their founder. We find the initials A.N., for "After Nirvāṇa," in some English-language works on Buddhism. We immediately note that Christians and Buddhists differ here, one measuring time from the arrival of their savior on earth, the other measuring time from his departure, despite the fact that the deaths of the two founders are the events described in the greatest detail in the canons of the two religions. There is much to ponder here, both historically and theologically, but we can note that the Buddhist measurement of time from the disappearance of their founder into nirvāṇa came to play a central role in theories of the disappearance of his teachings and in predictions of the advent of what is sometimes called the degenerate age. Thus, for Buddhists, it is important to know when he died; in some East Asian schools, the date of the Buddha's death, and our distance from it, would determine whether enlightenment is still possible.

The date of his death is almost as consequential for scholars, since so many events, from the dates of the councils that codified the canon to the birth of famous philosophers, are dated from the death of the Buddha. For that reason, Eugène Burnouf described the death of the Buddha as "the major fact that sets the foundation for the entire historical development of Buddhism."[4]

A single text, a very important text, the *Great Discourse on the Final Nirvāṇa* (*Mahāparinibbāna Sutta*), states that the Buddha died when he was eighty. Although there are always reasons to doubt round numbers, this figure is generally accepted. The question, then, is when that eightieth year occurred.

In Chinese Buddhist works, one of the most widely accepted dates for his death is 949 BCE. According to the *Kālacakra Tantra,* a work of great importance in Tibet, composed in the eleventh century, the passing of the Buddha took place in 878 BCE. The Theravāda tradition of Sri Lanka and Southeast Asia places the death of the Buddha in 544 BCE. Tibetan Buddhist sources give dates as early as 2420 BCE. What is called the "long chronology" gives his life dates as 624–544 BCE. The "corrected long chronology" gives them as 566–486 BCE. The "short chronology" gives them as 448–368 BCE.

Contemporary scholars continue to argue for death dates ranging from 544 BCE to 368 BCE. In his influential *A History of Indian Buddhism: From Śākyamuni to Early Mahāyāna,* the Japanese scholar Hirakawa Akira, following Nakamura Hajime, uses 463–383 BCE as the dates of the Buddha. Today, the scholarly consensus is that the Buddha likely died in the period between 420 BCE and 350 BCE, a remarkable, some might say shockingly vague, calculation for one of the most famous figures in human history.[5] And this, despite the fact that in the great sweep of history, the Buddha lived, or—perhaps more accurately—Buddhism began, fairly recently. The pyramids of Egypt were built around 2500 BCE; the *Epic of Gilgamesh* was composed around 2100 BCE, with copies surviving from the seventh century BCE; Hesiod composed his *Theogony* around 730 BCE; and Rome was founded, and the first Olympiad took place, in the eighth century BCE. Many of the poems in the Chinese classic the *Book of Songs* (*Shijing*) date from the Western Chou period (1046–771 BCE). In India, the Indus Valley city of Mohenjo-daro dates to around 2500 BCE. The inscriptions on the clay seals found there have yet to be deciphered.

The first mention of the Buddha is found on a stone inscription discovered in a cave in what is today the state of Bihar in northern India. That this was, or would become, an important center of Buddhism can be deduced from the fact that the name Bihar comes from *vihāra,* a standard term for a Buddhist monastery. The inscription is one of the renowned "rock edicts" of the Indian emperor Aśoka. Scholars refer to it as Minor Rock Edict I. The inscription says that it was composed in the eleventh year of his reign; his ascent to the throne is generally placed in 268 BCE. Aśoka was clearly a historical figure. Indeed, he is the most famous king in Buddhist history, renowned especially in Sanskrit Buddhist sources for establishing eighty-four thousand stūpas containing relics of the Buddha and in Pāli Buddhism for sending his son (a monk) and his daughter (a nun) to establish the orders of monks and nuns in Sri Lanka. The Sanskrit and Pāli accounts, however, differ in many ways, and in the view of modern scholarship they overstate the depth of his devotion to Buddhism. His promotion of the dharma, mentioned so often in his edicts, seems to mean not the teachings of the Buddha but a more general moral rectitude.

The discovery of an inscription mentioning the Buddha from the third century BCE provides at least a *terminus ad quem* for his death. However, the Sanskrit and Pāli accounts of the life of Aśoka disagree with each other. Like that of all great events in Buddhist history, the coronation of Aśoka is dated from the time of the Buddha's passage into nirvāṇa. The *Legend of Aśoka* (*Aśokāvadāna*), the most important Sanskrit source, says that Aśoka will appear (which presumably means will be crowned) one hundred years after the death of the Buddha. The *Great Chronicle* (*Mahāvaṃsa*), the most famous Pāli source, says that Aśoka was crowned two hundred and eighteen years after the death of the Buddha. Hence, we have a gap of more than a century from sources containing content regarded largely as legend.[6]

The dates of the Buddha are, therefore, a problem yet to be solved. To the frustration of many, it may in fact be insoluble. We may take some comfort in the fact that at least one Buddhist text acknowledges the issue. In a text called *Introduction to the Domain of the Inconceivable Qualities and Wisdom of the Tathāgatas* (*Tathāgataguṇajñānācintyaviṣayāvatāranirdeśa*), we read:

> Some know the essence of the teaching of the Blessed One, while others know the Blessed One's teaching in a state of decline. Some know that ten, twenty, thirty, forty, or fifty years have elapsed since the Blessed One taught the dharma. Some know that ten, twenty, thirty, forty, or fifty years have elapsed since the Blessed One passed into nirvāṇa. Some know that a hundred or a thousand years have elapsed since the Blessed One attained perfect awakening. Others know that a hundred or a thousand years have elapsed since the Blessed One passed into nirvāṇa. Some know that ten, twenty, thirty, forty, or fifty thousand years have elapsed since the Blessed One attained perfect awakening. Others know that ten, twenty, thirty, forty, or fifty thousand years have elapsed since the Blessed One passed into nirvāṇa. Some know that ten, twenty, thirty, forty, or fifty hundred thousand million eons have elapsed since the Blessed One attained perfect awakening, while others know that ten, twenty, thirty, forty, or fifty hundred thousand million eons have elapsed since the Blessed One passed into nirvāṇa. . . . The complete and perfect Buddha, in order to break the pride, conceit, and arrogance of sentient beings who have previously accumulated roots of virtue, in order to ripen their previously accumulated roots of virtue, and in order to guide them to the teaching of the Tathāgata—displays the decline and disappearance of the authentic dharma of the Tathāgata.[7]

In addition to the question of when the Buddha lived, we are faced with another question: what did the Buddha teach? New Testament scholars, armed with sophisticated tools of textual analysis and contemporary or near-contemporary documents, have sought for centuries to answer the question of what Jesus taught. Yet that question remains to be settled. The earliest Buddhist texts that survive are manuscripts discovered in Pakistan that can be carbon-dated to the first century BCE, likely several centuries after the death of the Buddha, depending on which of the many dates of his death one favors. We know that the teachings of the Buddha were preserved orally for centuries, but that does not mean that we can say with certainty that those teachings were the words of a historical Buddha. Much of what is preserved in the canon is clearly "later." As Étienne Lamotte wrote, "By being transmitted via so many spokesmen, the Saddharma [true dharma] ran the greatest of dangers. From the beginning, it should have been enclosed in a code of authentic writings, recognized by all the members of the Community unanimously; however, the Buddhists only belatedly perceived the necessity of a codification of the Dharma; moreover, the oral transmission of the Doctrine rendered such a task, if not impossible, at least very difficult."[8]

Over the centuries and continuing to the present day, there have been debates about which texts are indeed the word of the Buddha; the Sanskrit term is *buddhavacana; vacana* is derived from the Sanskrit term for "voice." We know that prominent proponents of the Mahāyāna sūtras—which include such famous texts as the *Lotus Sūtra,* the *Diamond Sūtra,* and the *Heart Sūtra*—argued for centuries that these works were the word of the Buddha. The duration of their earnest defense makes it clear that there were many who disagreed, regarding the Mahāyāna sūtras as apocryphal. The same can be said for the still later tantras, including those that begin with "Thus did I hear," the traditional imprimatur of authenticity. Modern scholars do not regard the Mahāyāna sūtras or the Buddhist tantras as the word of the Buddha.

The charge of apocrypha entails the assumption of orthodoxy. Here, the various Buddhist traditions have agreed that the discourses and monastic code preserved today in the Pāli canon (and in similar versions in various other Indic languages, many of which were translated into Chinese) represent the word of the Buddha. They part company on the question of whether they are his final word. But even here we find some anxiety. In one text, prior to the passing of the Buddha, his disciple Śāriputra, claiming that the rival Jains had fallen into disharmony and dispute after the death of their founder, preemptively summarizes the Buddha's teaching under ten headings, which the monks then memorize and recite. The title of that text, *Saṅgītisutta,* might be rendered *Recitation Sūtra.* Shortly before his last meal, anticipating the problem of controlling the canon after his passing, the Buddha sets forth criteria for authenticating his word after he is gone, providing four "great authorities" (*mahāpadeśa*). To be considered authentic, a teaching must be the words (1) of the Buddha, (2) of a community (*saṅgha*) of elders, (3) of a smaller group of learned elders, or (4) of a single learned monk. When a monk claims to have heard a teaching directly from one of these four sources, the saṅgha must determine whether it is the word of the Buddha by seeing whether it fits into the sūtras and accords with the vinaya. There are, in fact, sūtras in the canon that are spoken by others, often a learned monk, with the Buddha's sanction. These four criteria seem to go further, opening the possibility for sūtras spoken after the death of the Buddha to become canonical.

That canon is traditionally called the *tripiṭaka,* the "three baskets": the *sūtra,* or discourses of the Buddha; the *vinaya,* or discipline, which includes the monastic code and the stories of its formulation; and the *abhidharma,* sometimes translated as the "higher dharma," the more technical expositions of epistemology and ontology. Scholars regard the abhidharma as being formulated after the Buddha, a position held by some Indian Buddhist schools. Some elements of the monastic code, especially the stories of the individual proscriptions, are considered to post-date the Buddha. For example, much of the vinaya is concerned with the myriad details of monastery life. Yet there is no archaeological evidence of monasteries until centuries after the Buddha's death, if we knew when he died. This leaves the sūtras.

Nineteenth-century scholars inherited, without much dispute, the Theravāda view (held in the British colonies of Ceylon and Burma, for example) that the Pāli canon represents what they would call "primitive Buddhism" (with "primitive" being used here in a positive sense, as in "primitive Christianity") or "original Buddhism," with the Mahāyāna and tantra dismissed as later accretions. However, they did not stop there, eventually seeking to identify which parts of that canon could be traced back to the Buddha himself and which parts had been added after his death. That story is too long to tell here, but it did result in a phenomenon that we might call the "Good Buddha, Bad Monk" theory.

In recent decades, this theory has been used in an attempt to extricate the Buddha from the dense misogyny found throughout the canon. In this case—setting aside the question of whether the Buddha was good and the monks were bad—there are reasons to accept the theory. For example, there is evidence to support the claim that the order of nuns—and hence the degrading account of its founding—came into existence after the death of the Buddha.[9] A more radical use of the theory occurred a century ago in the works of the first important female scholar of Pāli Buddhism outside Asia, Caroline Rhys Davids (1857–1942), the wife of Thomas W. Rhys Davids, a former British colonial officer in Sri Lanka and founder of the Pali Text Society. Like so many European scholars and artists of her day, Caroline Rhys Davids was a proponent of Spiritualism, believing in the ability of the living to contact the spirits of the dead. One of its leading proponents was Arthur Conan Doyle, the creator of the hyper-rationalist Sherlock Holmes. Like so many European women, Rhys Davids had lost a son, Arthur Rhys Davids, an RAF ace, in the Great War. After his death (and the death of her husband in 1922), her scholarly views of Buddhism began to change. She was unable to accept that, as a soldier who killed others in a war that was not fought to defend the dharma, her son had been reborn in hell. More consequentially, she could not accept the foundational doctrine of Buddhism, that there is no self or soul that travels from one lifetime to the next. If there was no self, it would be impossible to contact her son's spirit.

She did not stop at the rejection of this, the fundamental insight of Buddhist philosophy; in one of the earliest manifestations of the "Good Buddha, Bad Monk" theory, she claimed that the Buddha did not teach *anatta,* no self. In fact, she believed, he taught self, *atta* (*ātman* in Sanskrit). After the Buddha passed into nirvāṇa, the monks added the negative prefix. One might imagine a Buddhist version of Dostoevsky's Grand Inquisitor, in which the Buddha returns at the time of the Third Council where, because he teaches that there is a self, he is condemned as a heretic. Such a scene would make clear that the question of who is, in fact, good and who is bad in a Good Buddha, Bad Monk theory is subject to debate.[10]

Although generally lacking the trappings of Spiritualism, scholars today continue to try to identify the Buddha's original teachings, using philological analysis to identify chronological strata in the language of the Pāli canon, strata that clearly exist. This allows us to have some sense of which texts (and which passages within texts) are earlier and which are later. The question is whether they allow us to find the Buddha, especially a good Buddha, who would always be innocent of whatever it was that the subsequent generations of bad monks attributed to him.

If we can use the dates of Aśoka to determine the dates of the Buddha, do Aśoka's inscriptions provide any insight into the Buddha's teachings? In a minor edict referred to by scholars as the "Schism Edict," the emperor warns monks and nuns against causing a schism in the saṅgha, declaring that a monk or nun who causes a division will be returned to lay life. It is found at three sites, including Sarnath, the site of the Buddha's first teaching. In that edict, he lists seven "expositions of the dharma" by name, recommending them to monks, nuns, laymen, and laywomen.[11] Sūtras by those names are not found in the current canon, but scholars have identified portions of as many as six texts that seem to correspond to the works enumerated by Aśoka.[12] Here, we find praise for the *muni,* the sage, the person who lives a celibate life in solitude, living on alms, unattached to the world, free of anger and greed. Other texts describe the sage as always ethical, never angry or arrogant, living the life of the ascetic, while also describing the dangers of living in the forest. In another, the Buddha instructs his son, the monk Rāhula, in the importance of telling the truth and how to consider the consequences before engaging in an action of body, speech, or mind.

The content of the sūtras recommended by the emperor to the Buddhist monks and nuns of his realm are therefore ethical instructions and admonitions to asceticism. Such teachings were common to the various renunciant groups of ancient India. There is little here that one might consider distinctively

Buddhist. When we turn to Aśoka's instructions to his subjects more broadly, we find a similarly simple morality, extending to refraining from killing animals. In the edict in which he recommends the seven sūtras, he says that he has been a lay follower of the Buddha for two and a half years. In another edict he declares, "Whatever was spoken by the Buddha was well spoken." And yet, in his many edicts he makes no mention of karma, rebirth, or the several realms of saṃsāra. For Aśoka, there seem only to be heaven and earth.

What we do find throughout his edicts is the word *dharma*, referring most often in Buddhism to the Buddha's teachings, the second of the three jewels. Yet for Aśoka, this multivalent Sanskrit term seems simply to mean "morality" or "righteousness." In Second Pillar Edict, he defines *dharma* as having few faults and many good deeds, and being endowed with mercy, charity, truthfulness, and purity. In the rock edicts in Greek, *dharma* is translated as *eusebeia*, meaning reverence to parents and gods; in the edicts in Aramaic, it is *qyst*, or "truth."

Thus, Aśoka provides little assistance in identifying what the Buddha taught. The Buddhism that he promotes enjoins social virtues common to many traditions. In defining *dharma* as he did, was Aśoka drawing selectively from a larger corpus of Buddhist doctrine in order to promote virtues that would contribute to the peace of his realm? Was there more that was known to monks and nuns, and this is simply what he, as a layman, knew? Or was this the extent of the Buddhist doctrine of his day?

In his inscriptions, Aśoka sometimes uses the term *śramaṇa brāḥmaṇa*. The second term refers to brahmin priests. The former is more difficult to translate, sometimes rendered as "renunciant," "mendicant," or "ascetic." This term is generally thought to refer to those who have renounced family life to practice various forms of religious devotions in the forest. It seems to have originally included what would come to be called Hindus, Buddhists, and Jains, as well as members of other ascetic groups that no longer survive. The brahmins are the household priests who perform life cycle rituals in the village and the city. The ascetics are those, including those not of the brahmin caste, who have renounced life in the world. The two groups were sometimes antagonists, Buddhist monks and brahmin priests being but one example.

Aśoka, however, does not distinguish between them in his edicts, seeming to use the term *śramaṇa brāhmaṇa* to include religious practitioners of all stripes, urging his subjects to treat them with generosity and respect. This again raises the question of whether Aśoka was in fact a devout Buddhist, or whether, like other kings of other ages, he was something of an equal-opportunity patron of the several religions of his realm. His admonitions to his subjects to support *śramaṇa brāhmaṇa* would favor the latter view. Another edict says that he donated caves for the use of the Ājīvikas, one of the many *śramaṇa* groups that has not survived, rivals of the Buddhists, and a group that his father had supported. It is the case, however, that the only *śramaṇa* group that he identifies with are the Buddhists. As noted, in Minor Rock Edict I, dated from the eleventh year of his reign, we find Aśoka declaring that he had been a lay disciple (*upāsaka*) of the Buddha for more than two and a half years, and that in the past year he had become more pious and visited the saṅgha, warning against schism in the saṅgha and recommending the reading of those seven specific "expositions of the dharma." But if nothing can be said with certainty about the life or the teachings of the Buddha, can we say that he existed?

12

Stūpas and Sūtras

Unlike the Buddha, in Aśoka we have what is clearly a historical figure. And we have his words, recorded during his lifetime. It is thus difficult to overstate the importance of Aśoka and his edicts for the question of the historicity of the Buddha. There are Aśokan pillars or inscriptions at a number of sites associated with the life of the Buddha, including the four main places of pilgrimages—the place of his birth, enlightenment, first teaching, and passage into nirvāṇa—with indications that he personally visited Bodh Gayā, the site of the Buddha's enlightenment, and Lumbinī, the place of the Buddha's birth, where he had a pillar erected and exempted its town from some taxes. It is clear that the Buddha was sufficiently famous by the time of Aśoka that places of pilgrimage associated with the events of his life had been established and were considered sufficiently important to be honored by the emperor. However, no Buddhist monasteries dating from Aśoka's reign have been excavated, suggesting that the Buddhist community of monks and nuns was originally peripatetic, as Buddhist texts themselves state. A final Aśokan inscription provides a further important piece of evidence. Evidence of what is more difficult to say.

It is a standard element of Buddhist doctrine that prior to "our buddha," known either as Gotama Buddha or Śākyamuni Buddha, there have been previous buddhas, variously enumerated going back over millennia and eons. They lived similar lives and taught the same dharma. Significantly, the teachings of each previous buddha must disappear from the world before a new buddha comes to teach the dharma again, revealing the path to liberation that had been forgotten. They are, therefore, unknown to human history, their existence revealed by the Buddha, that is, our buddha, through his comprehensive knowledge of the past, both near and distant. The most recent of these buddhas before our own, Kāśyapa, is said to have lived for sixteen thousand years. A historicist reading of this particular, and particularly important, Buddhist doctrine is that in order for the newly founded Buddhist community to establish its legitimacy, it had to establish its antiquity. Like the eternal Vedas of the Buddhists' brahmin opponents, the teachings of the buddhas, and hence the Buddha, must be eternal, not simply the musings of a minor prince after a single night spent sitting under a tree.

There are various lists of previous buddhas; one of the most famous is a list of the five buddhas of the present era. In this list, our buddha, Gautama Buddha, is the fourth, and Maitreya, the future buddha, is the fifth. The second of these five is named Kanakamuni (Konāgamana in Pāli); he also appears in the lists of twenty-nine buddhas and seven buddhas. In 1895, two fragments of a pillar were discovered at Nigali Sagar in Nepal, about six miles from Lumbinī, the site of the Buddha's birth. The inscription states that in the fourteenth year of Aśoka's reign, the emperor visited the stūpa of Kanakamuni, which he doubled in size.

The mention of the stūpa of a previous buddha in an Aśokan inscription suggests that the cult of the previous buddhas was already well enough established during Aśoka's reign for there to be a stūpa for Kanakamuni, a stūpa that was sufficiently famous that the emperor would visit it. Of even greater interest is that that stūpa was sufficiently old that it needed to be enlarged. Archaeological research does not reveal the presence of a stūpa at Nigali Sagar, only the fragments of the pillar. Those fragments, however, seem to have been moved from another site seven miles away, where there is indeed a brick stūpa. When excavated, it was found to contain animal bones.[1] This inscription is the only time that Aśoka mentions a stūpa; in the legends later composed about him, he creates eighty-four thousand.

What should we make of all this? If this inscription is authentic, it means that the cult of the previous buddhas was in existence and widely known during the reign of Aśoka. From one perspective, this can be seen as evidence that the Buddha was a historical figure. In order to establish the legitimacy of their founder and his teachings, the Buddhist community, or the Buddha himself, proclaimed the existence of his predecessors, names that were sufficiently well known by the time of Aśoka that a stūpa had been erected to commemorate a previous buddha, not Kāśyapa (Pāli: Kassapa), the immediate predecessor of our buddha, but Kāśyapa's predecessor. The famous Boudhanath Stūpa in Kathmandu is said to enshrine the relics of Kāśyapa; it dates from the fifth or sixth century CE.

At the same time, Aśoka's reference to Kanakamuni could be seen as evidence that the Buddha was not a historical figure. In order for the Buddhist community to gain legitimacy in the religious milieu of ancient India, one founding sage was not enough; a series of sages needed to be projected back in time. We have noted that Mahāvīra, the founder of Jainism and generally presented as an older contemporary of the Buddha, is counted as the twenty-fourth *tīrthaṅkara* ("ford maker") of Jainism. The biographies of the two founders share much in common, from their kṣatriya caste to their departure from the palace to their practice of asceticism prior to their achievement of enlightenment while sitting in meditation under a tree. In the Buddhist chronologies, Kanakamuni is projected far back in time to a period when the human lifespan was twenty thousand years; according to Buddhist cosmology, the human lifespan is declining. Was this the name of a historical or mythological sage whose name was known in the early centuries BCE and which was appropriated by the Buddhists? In Hinduism, the name Kāśyapa appears often, most importantly in this context as one of the "seven sages" (*saptarṣi*) of the Vedas.

The doctrine of previous buddhas suggests that Śākyamuni Buddha was less the individual that modern biographies portray him to be and more a generic figure, more similar than distinct from his predecessors. It is said that all of the buddhas who have come in the past and who will come in the future sit cross-legged in their mother's womb; they are all born in the "middle country" of our continent, the southern continent of Jambudvīpa; immediately after birth they all take seven steps to the north; they all renounce the world after seeing the four sights (an old man, a sick man, a dead man, and a mendicant) and after the birth of a son; they all achieve enlightenment seated on a bed of grass; they stride first with their right foot when they walk; they never stoop to pass through a door; they all found a monastic order; they all can live for an eon; they never die before their teaching is complete; and they all die after eating meat. Four sites on the earth are identical for all buddhas: the place of enlightenment, the place of the first sermon, the place of descending from the Heaven of the Thirty-three atop Mount Meru, and the place of their bed in Jetavana monastery.

Indeed, buddhas can differ from each other in only eight ways: in lifespan, height, caste (either brahmin or kṣatriya), the conveyance in which they go forth from the world, the period of time spent in the practice of asceticism prior to their enlightenment, the species of tree they sit under on the night of their enlightenment, the size of their seat there, and the circumference of their aura.[2] As will be discussed in the final chapter, the Buddha, a buddha, is essentially a composite of qualities (*dharma*).

The permanent, or more permanent, embodiment of those qualities is the stūpa. When the Buddha achieved enlightenment at the age of thirty-five, he achieved what is called the nirvāṇa with remainder, that is, with the remainder of the mind and body that were the effects of the karma that produced his final lifetime. He could have entered nirvāṇa at that time—and Māra, the deity of death and desire, implored him to do so—but he remained in the world for another forty-five years in order to teach. At the age of eighty, he entered what is called final nirvāṇa, or the nirvāṇa without remainder, with no remnant of mind or body. From a certain perspective, he ceased to exist at that time. But two things did remain, one invisible and one visible: his teachings in the form of sound and his relics, the bits of bone and teeth found among the ashes of his funeral pyre. The teachings were known by those who memorized and chanted them, the monks and nuns. The relics are what remained for the rest of us, remaining for our commemoration of the person they once were. As we will see, before he died, the Buddha said that anyone who dies while on pilgrimage to the four sacred sites—of his birth, enlightenment, first teaching, and death—will be reborn as a god. Thus, for those who regard these passages as the final instructions of the Buddha, the motivation for much Buddhist practice over the centuries has been there from the beginning, a motivation found in so many religions: to be rewarded with an afterlife of happiness. Some scholars have assumed, however, that this recommendation was something included in an account composed after the Buddha's death, at a time when those four sites were already places of pilgrimage, with the words of the Buddha providing a celebrity endorsement enticing people to visit them.

As we have noted, archaeological evidence suggests that Lumbinī, the site of the Buddha's birth, was originally the site of a tree shrine that predates the monuments erected by Aśoka there.[3] This pilgrimage site may have later been connected to the story of the Buddha's mother, who, en route to her parents to give birth to her first child, stopped in the forest and grasped the branch of a tree. Her child emerged from under her right arm, taking seven steps, a lotus blossoming under each foot, declaring that he was the best of bipeds. Bodh Gayā, the site of his enlightenment, is a short distance from Gayā, long a place of Hindu pilgrimage. Sarnath, where he gave his first teaching, is on the outskirts of the sacred city of Vārāṇsī on the banks of the Ganges. Archaeological evidence suggests the presence of an ancient burial ground at Kuśinagara, the place of the Buddha's death and cremation. Thus, each of the four places seems to have been put to some form of religious use prior to achieving Buddhist prominence. As Buddhism spread southward, stories were told about the Buddha's presence in cities there. Thus, it was at Sāṃkāśya that the Buddha descended from the Heaven of the Thirty-three on a magnificent staircase, where, according to the Theravāda account, he had taught the abhidharma to his mother, who had been reborn in the Tuṣita heaven after her death. Xuanzang reports that the original staircase had sunk underground but that pious kings had later built a seventy-foot reproduction.[4] Stūpas were erected at each of these sites.

What evidence might stūpas provide for the historicity of the Buddha? The Gṛhyasūtras, the Vedic texts that provide life-cycle rituals, explain that the dead should be cremated, the bones gathered in a basket and then placed in a covered urn and buried in a pit. One should then "go away without looking back, should bathe in water, and perform a *śrāddha* ritual for the deceased."[5] There are also references to burying the corpse in an earthen mound or a brick tomb in an uninhabited area. We do not find a cult of the dead or the veneration of relics, until we come to Buddhism. Indeed, the great Hindu epic the *Mahābhārata,* apparently mocking the Buddhists, predicts that in the impending dark age, humans will not build temples and worship the gods; they will worship an *eḍūka,* a structure for rubbish or bones. *Eḍūka* is another word for a stūpa.[6]

This is what we know from ancient texts. Archaeology provides a further twist. Excavations of Buddhist stūpa complexes in India have revealed the presence of more ancient megalithic mounds. These appear in many cases to be burial sites, although the bones they preserve are not always human; sometimes they are the bones of horses, oxen, and birds. The precise purpose of these burial grounds is not known, but it seems that when Buddhists built stūpas, they often did so at sites already associated with the dead. As one scholar has concluded, "The Buddhist deposits, then, would probably best be explained as a reflection of the incorporation or continuation of elements of local megalithic practice."[7] Such tumuli have been discovered, for example, at Kuśinagara, the site of the Buddha's cremation and the site of one of the eight original stūpas. What was different is that the Buddhists turned the burial grounds of their teacher into marvelous monuments, adorned with garlands and scented with sandalwood, decorated with elaborately carved stone panels, a place of pilgrimage, a place not of pollution but of purity and of purification.

With all this in mind, let us turn to the account of the death of the Buddha that appears in the *Great Discourse on the*

Final Nirvāṇa. The Buddha must conduct much business in his final hours, including giving detailed instructions on how his body should be cremated and what should be done with his remains. He says that his relics should be buried in a mound at a crossroads. The word for "mound" here is *stūpa* (*thūpa* in Pāli). The Buddha explains to Ānanda that his cremation and burial should be that of a *cakravartin,* a universal monarch, one of the two destinies that the astrologers had predicted for the infant Prince Siddhārtha eighty years before. It is noteworthy that Ānanda does not know what such a funeral is, requiring the Buddha to explain it to him in some detail. This may be because the last *cakravartin* is said to have lived when the human lifespan was eighty thousand years. All of this suggests that the authors of the *Great Discourse on the Final Nirvāṇa,* composing their account long after the death of the Buddha, needed to signal that the Buddhist method for disposing of their sacred dead was new or, in the Buddhist sense, so old that it had been forgotten. The Buddha goes on to explain that, far from a domain of the dead to be avoided, this will be a site of pilgrimage. Indeed, anyone who reverently honors his stūpa with garlands, incense, or sandalwood paste will find happiness in the future: "And whosoever lays wreaths or puts sweet perfumes and colours there with a devout heart, will reap benefit and happiness for a long time . . . and, then, at the breaking-up of the body after death, they go to a good destiny and rearise in a heavenly world."[8]

The *Great Discourse on the Final Nirvāṇa* relates that the Buddha's relics were not, however, entombed in a mound at a crossroads. Various groups of his followers came to Kuśinagara to claim them, almost going to war before a brahmin named Droṇa proposed that he divide the relics into eight shares to be distributed to each group. These eight shares were thus given to eight groups from different regions of northern India, who each took them home and built a stūpa. It is from seven of these eight stūpas that Aśoka is said to have made eighty-four thousand. The eighth stūpa was not broken open by Aśoka; it was preserved at Rāmagrama beneath the waters by the *nāgas*, the feared and revered snake deities of ancient India.[9] This stūpa, wrapped in the coils of huge snakes, would become the most depicted stūpa in early Buddhist art. These depictions appeared most often on elaborately carved stone panels around the base of stūpas, often with inscriptions that gave the name of the donor. Most of these inscriptions are not from royalty; they are from laypeople, including merchants and merchant guilds, as well as monks, nuns, and their families, including many women.[10] And what the early decorative panels depicted was often not the Buddha. As we will see, for centuries, the Buddha himself was absent, at least in the form that we now know him.

As we debate the historicity of the Buddha, so much seems to hinge on Aśoka, and especially the very different dates that the two Buddhist sources—the Pāli and the Sanskrit—provide for his coronation, measured, of course, like so many Buddhist dates, from the Buddha's passage into nirvāṇa. How long after the death of the possibly historical Buddha did the certainly historical Aśoka ascend the Mauryan throne? The date of his ascension is placed circa 268 BCE. Buddhist sources say that he was initially passed over for the crown, becoming king only after he had killed his brothers. The year of his birth is not known, but is estimated as 302 BCE. If, as the Sanskrit biography states, a king named Aśoka appeared (which likely means "was crowned") one hundred years after the death of the Buddha, then the Buddha would have died in 368 BCE, a mere sixty-six years before the birth of Aśoka. If, as the Pāli biography of Aśoka states, he became king two hundred and eighteen years after the death of the Buddha, then the Buddha would have died in 486 BCE, one hundred and eighty-four years before the birth of

Aśoka. The Sanskrit source—if we suspend suspicion of its round number of one hundred—would seem to support the historicity of the Buddha; if a generation is about thirty years, sixty-six years would be about two generations. The Pāli source would seem to support, or at least allow for, legend; two hundred and eighteen years would be more than seven generations.

Adherents of a religion believe that their founder's life and the accounts of that life found in their sacred scriptures are true, at least in some sense of that term. This great weight of tradition means that those who question the historicity of the Buddha bear the burden of proof and must challenge the views of not only millennia of Buddhists but centuries of Buddhist scholarship. Perhaps the greatest European scholar of Buddhism of the twentieth century, Msgr. Étienne Lamotte, consistently searching for history and finding myth in his 870-page *History of Indian Buddhism from the Origins to the Śaka Era,* writes about the life of the Buddha, "The various interpretations given to it by our religionist schools have obscured a problem already complicated enough in itself. It remains nonetheless a fact that Buddhism could not be explained if it were not based on a personality powerful enough to give it the necessary impetus and to have marked it with its essential features which will persist through all history."[11] This is the argument that there must have been a Buddha. Among the advocates for his existence, we encounter it again and again.

Lamotte was writing in 1958 in the wake of Karl Jaspers's proclamation, now largely discredited, of what he called the "Axial Age." This was an age when, in cultures around the world between the eighth and third centuries BCE, figures emerged whose teachings would have a profound effect on civilization, including Confucius, Laozi, the Buddha, Zoroaster, Homer, Elijah, and Jeremiah. He was also writing in a time when scholars had renounced the old European division of the nations of the world into Christians, Jews, Muslims, and Idolaters. Through the efforts of Burnouf and others, Buddhists had been released from the category of idol worshippers, and the Buddha was no longer an idol. Buddhism had been granted the status of a religion, even a philosophy, and the Buddha was its founder. Indeed, as already noted, for Burnouf, the Buddha marked the moment when India moved from myth to history. Burnouf would go on to argue for the importance of establishing the date of the Buddha's death, since all subsequent time in Buddhism is measured from that date. Almost two hundred years after he made this important directive, the date remains unknown.

The first Buddhist relics to be identified by the British—sadly, belatedly—had been found in Sarnath, the site of the Buddha's first teaching, commemorated by a stūpa built by Aśoka. In 1794, one of the ministers of the King of Benares had the stūpa torn down so that its bricks could be used for a housing project. In the course of doing so, eight meters below the surface the workers discovered a stone box that contained a jade casket. Upon opening the casket, what appeared to be human bones and ashes were found among pearls, gold leaves, and semi-precious stones. Some suggested that they were the bones of the consort of a former prince who had committed *sati* upon the death of her husband. Following Hindu custom, the bones were thrown into the sacred, and nearby, Ganges River. Five years later, Jonathan Duncan, the East India Company's commissioner for Benares, offered his own opinion in *Asiatic Researches, or Transactions of the Society Instituted in Bengal, for Inquiring into the History and Antiquities, the Arts, Sciences, and Literature of Asia* "that the bones found in these urns must belong to one of the worshippers of BUDDHA, a sect of Indian heretics, who, having no reverence for the *Ganges,* used to deposit their remains in the earth, instead of committing them to the river; a surmise that seems strongly corroborated by the circumstance of a statue or idol of BUDDHA having been found in the same place under ground."[12]

Other Buddhist relics avoided this watery fate but were also misidentified. Seeking a strategy for an invasion of Afghanistan, the British sought archaeological evidence of Alexander the Great's successful conquest in 330 BCE. The famous stūpa of Manikyala, said to venerate Prince Mahāsattva—a previous incarnation of the Buddha who committed suicide in order to feed a starving tigress who was about to devour her cubs—was initially identified as the tomb of Bucephalus, Alexander's beloved steed.[13] The disastrous Anglo-Afghan War of 1838–1842 did not duplicate Alexander's success. In 1838, when James Prinsep of the East India Company announced to the Asiatic Society of Bengal that he had deciphered the inscriptions of Aśoka, he wryly noted that Indian antiquities only aroused the interest of Europeans when there appeared to be "a plausible point of connection between the legends of India and the rational histories of Greece or Rome."[14] One of Aśoka's inscriptions had mentioned the Greek king Antiochus II (r. 261–246 BCE). It was the work of another officer of the East India Company, James Turnour, stationed in the colony of Ceylon, who connected the Buddha to Aśoka through his translation of the *Great Chronicle* (*Mahāvaṃsa*) of Sri Lanka, which relates the story of Aśoka sending his monk son and nun daughter to the island to establish the dharma, a story that scholars would eventually come to regard as a myth.

If an idol is the physical embodiment of a divine being, then it could be argued that Buddhists, with their elaborate rituals for animating icons, are idolaters. Today, however, *idolater* or "idol worshipper" is a term of abuse. Thus, if the Buddha is not an idol, he must be human.[15] And if he is human, he must be historical. And yet when we look at the various biographies of the Buddha, we find much myth and little history. According to a famous list, the Buddha, and all buddhas, do the same twelve things: they descend from the Tuṣita heaven, they enter their mother's womb, they are born, they are proficient in the arts, they take delight in their consorts, they renounce the world, they practice asceticism, they go to the seat of enlightenment, they subjugate Māra, they attain enlightenment, they turn the wheel of the dharma, and they pass into nirvāṇa. In the various versions of the life of the Buddha, each of these is heavily mythologized. For example, as we have noted, there are detailed descriptions of Queen Māyā's womb, not the putrid prison of flesh where ordinary beings must suffer during the ten lunar months of gestation, "hemmed in by foul-smelling filth and trapped in pitch-dark gloom,"[16] but a spacious baroque palace, "finely shaped, exquisite and beautiful to behold. It was square in form and had four pillars. At the top was a beautifully adorned upper floor scaled to fit a six-month-old fetus. Inside that upper chamber was a throne with a sitting area that was likewise scaled to fit a six-month-old fetus."[17] This is not to say that some accounts of his life are not quite so, for want of a better word, mythologized.

There are relatively few extended autobiographical passages in the Pāli canon.[18] In one, called the *Greater Discourse to Saccaka (Mahāsaccaka Sutta),* the Buddha describes to Saccaka, the son of a Jain teacher, his practice of austerities—especially stopping the breath—in some detail, going on to describe his decision to abandon these practices and eat solid food and his subsequent attainment of enlightenment, with the revelation during the third watch of the night identified as his vision of the four truths. A longer autobiographical passage is found in *The Noble Search* (*Ariyapariyesanā Sutta*), a passage that is remarkably spare. Here the Buddha explains the difference between an ignoble search (when someone who is subject to birth, aging, sickness, and death seeks what is also subject to these) and the noble search (when someone who is subject to birth, aging, sickness, and death seeks what is not subject to these). The sutta describes the famous visitation from the god Brahmā, who urges the Buddha to teach, as well as his encounter with the Ājīvika named Upaka when he is en route to Sarnath, an odd moment described in Part 1, a moment that we will return to.

However, perhaps what is most interesting about the Buddha's narration of his life story in this text is what it does not include. He explains that during his youth, he decided to set out on a noble search, going on to say, "Later, while still young, a black-haired young man endowed with the blessing of youth, in the prime of life, though my mother and father wished otherwise and wept with tearful faces, I shaved off my hair and beard, put on the yellow robe, and went forth from the home life into homelessness."[19] That is the full extent of his description of his youth. There is no mention of his mother's famous dream or of his descent from the Tuṣita heaven into her womb, no description of that resplendent womb, of his birth from his mother's right side, of his presentation to his father and the prophecies of the astrologers. His mother does not die after seven days. There is no mention of his boyhood meditation under the *jambu* tree as his father plowed the fields, there is no mention of a wife and child, no mention of four chariot rides, and no mention of a clandestine escape from the palace. The detailed drama of the twenty-nine years spent under palace-arrest, so often depicted in early Buddhist art, do not appear in the Pāli suttas. The "great departure" is reduced to one sentence.

What are we to make of this? Should it be described as demythologized or, more consequentially, as pre-mythologized and therefore perhaps "early" and even historical? Does this suggest a human original that only later became encrusted with myth? This was the position taken by the great French scholar of Buddhism André Bareau (1921–1993), who dismissed all the elements of the Buddha's biography up until the time of his departure as myth. For Bareau, the future Buddha was not a prince, but the son of a modest squire. His mother did not die shortly after his birth and he was not married at the time of his departure. He was a battle-hardened warrior who only later in life came to renounce the world, stricken with grief at the death of his mother and his wife, shaving his head and living as an ascetic. He arrived at his insights not during a single night of meditation but over months and years. Bareau's Buddha, for whom almost nothing is historically certain, is human, all too human.[20]

We note that in the five famous biographies of the Buddha that are our primary source here, all but one end not long after his enlightenment; they end with his first teaching of the four truths seven weeks after his enlightenment or with his acceptance of the gift of Jetavana monastery in the third year after his enlightenment. They do not tell the story of the three times that the Buddha's cousin, himself a monk, tried to murder the Buddha. They do not tell the story of his famous ascent to the heaven on the summit of Mount Meru to teach the dharma to his mother, who had been reborn as a god after dying seven days after the Buddha's birth. They do not tell the story of the Buddha becoming disgruntled by the petty bickering of the monks of Kauśāmbī and going off into the woods to meditate among the elephants. They do not tell the story of the miracle match at Śrāvastī, where the Buddha humiliated the teachers of other tenets, not through philosophical disputation but by rising into the sky and shooting fire and water from his body.

In the Pāli canon, by far the most detailed account of the life of the Buddha describes not his birth or even his enlightenment, but his death, his passage into nirvāṇa. This, in a sense, is the certification of his achievement, because after cycling in saṃsāra from time without beginning, he will not be reborn again. His death also provides his relics that, entombed in stūpas, will ensure his physical presence in the world, a place for the world to worship. Perhaps this is why Buddhist time is measured not from his birth—for how many times had he been born?—but from his death, his final death, his nirvāṇa.

That final birth is dwarfed by all that comes before: all the buddhas of the past, variously enumerated. A text called the *Chronicle of the Buddhas* (*Buddhavaṃsa*) describes twenty-four buddhas of the past, a past that extends over trillions of years. Our buddha's path is described in the Pāli tradition as a series of rebirths lasting four incalculable eons plus one hundred thousand (ordinary) eons. (An "incalculable" eon has been calculated by some at 10^{140} years, as we noted in Part 1. An ordinary eon has been calculated at 4.32 billion years.) Twenty-four buddhas appeared during this time. The future buddha met each of them during his long bodhisattva path, making offerings to each. What is important in his final lifetime is his completion of that long path in the form of his achievement of "complete and perfect enlightenment" (*samyaksaṃbodhi*). This is why some of the later biographies stop there. Once he is a buddha, the deeds that he does are simply the deeds that all buddhas do. The personal detail that we seek in the genre of biography is irrelevant.

Yet the fact that none of these texts, composed during the first millennium after the Buddha's death (if we knew that date), relates all of those famous elements does not mean that those stories are unimportant. It means that their Buddhist authors did not feel it necessary to gather them into a single work that we would call a biography. Perhaps this is not because there are not enough stories about the Buddha but because there are too many. We recall that, according to the tradition, the Buddha did not set forth the full code of discipline for monks and nuns in a single session. Instead, he made a rule only after a monk or nun did something that, in his view, they shouldn't have. In addition to setting down those rules, the vinaya provides the story of its origin, explaining in each case what a monk or nun did and the Buddha's declaration that it should not be done in the future. In the monastic code of the Theravāda tradition of Sri Lanka and Southeast Asia, there are two hundred and twenty-seven vows for monks and three hundred and eleven vows for nuns. Each of those has a story that involves the Buddha. Yet, as discussed in the context of the founding of the order of nuns, it is clear that many of those stories were composed long after the Buddha died, once again, if we knew when he lived, and if we knew that he lived at all. Other stories of the Buddha appear in the *avadāna* literature, a term often translated as "legend." To what extent, then, does the presence, or absence, of stories figure in the calculation of history? What do the so-called biographies as well as all the other stories of the Buddha tell us about his historicity? Here, we might turn to the "criterion of dissimilarity."

In his highly influential, and highly controversial, *The Life of Jesus, Critically Examined,* first published in 1835, the twenty-seven-year-old David Strauss wrote, "Wherever a religion, resting upon written records, prolongs and extends the sphere of its dominion, accompanying its votaries through the varied and progressive stages of mental cultivation, a discrepancy between the representations of those ancient records, referred to as sacred, and the notions of more advanced periods of mental development, will inevitably sooner or later arise. . . . As long as this discrepancy is either not in itself so considerable, or else is not so universally discerned and acknowledged, as to lead to a complete renunciation of these Scriptures as of sacred authority, so long will a system of reconciliation by means of interpretation be adopted and pursued by those who have a more or less distinct consciousness of the existing incongruity."[21]

In describing the attempts by the biblical scholars of his day to account for this incongruity, he enumerated three types of myths. The first are historical myths, which he describes as "narratives of real events coloured by the light of antiquity, which confounded [in the sense of 'confused'] the divine and the human, the natural and the supernatural." The second are philosophical myths, that "clothe in the garb of historical narrative a simple thought, a precept, or an idea of the time." The third are poetical myths, where one finds "historical and philosophical mythi partly blended together, and partly embellished by the creations of the imagination, in which the original fact or idea is almost obscured by the veil which the fancy of the poet has woven around it."[22] The question for the modern biographer of the Buddha is whether there are any historical myths to be found in the various versions of his life. That is, are there any "real events"?

In order to identify elements of the Gospels that represent, or are likely to represent, events in the life of Jesus, scholars of Early Christianity sometimes rely on the "criterion of dissimilarity," that is, elements that are somehow anomalous, in the sense that they do not conform to Jewish descriptions of the Messiah or early Christian depictions of Jesus. An often cited example is the baptism of Jesus by John the Baptist. According to the Jewish practice of the period, the person who was baptized was considered to be inferior to the person performing the baptism. Since, according to Christian doctrine, Jesus was the Messiah, he would not have been baptized by John, and because he was without sin, there was no reason for his baptism. Thus, the fact that the Gospels report the baptism suggests that it actually happened.

The Buddhist canons are filled with things that seem at first sight to be incongruous with buddhahood. The Buddha complains of headaches and backaches; a shard of a rock cast down by his evil cousin Devadatta cuts his foot; when begging for alms one day he is given no food; a woman named Ciñcamānavikā feigns pregnancy by strapping a wooden bowl to her belly and declares that the Buddha is the father. These worldly events were catalogued by the tradition and addressed in various commentaries. In the *Questions of Milinda*, the Greek king questions the monk Nāgāsena about some of them. The answers to such questions often provide an occasion to discuss the mechanisms of karma, of how something done in a distant past can have residual effects even in the final lifetime as a buddha. Mahāyāna sūtras also discuss these apparent anomalies, showing them in each case to be something that the Buddha feigned, using his skillful means (*upāya*) to teach an important lesson, explaining away things that might humanize the Buddha in the process. For example, during the three months of a particular rains retreat, the Buddha and his monks were forced to subsist on horse barley. According to a Mahāyāna text, the Buddha does this because it allows five hundred horses to offer half of their feed to the Buddha and his monks, causing the horses to be reborn as gods in the Tuṣita heaven. The text assures us that even eating "wood, clumps of earth, pebbles, and bricks" is no hardship, for the Buddha is endowed with a sense of taste that gives whatever he eats a flavor that surpasses the food of the gods.[23]

These stories are too numerous to tell, but few clearly fulfill the criterion of dissimilarity. The Buddha's headaches and backaches often provide an occasion for another monk to preach the dharma in the name of the Buddha, allowing other voices to add to the canon. The false accusation by Ciñcamānavikā is instigated by members of a competing sect who are condemned for their calumny. Devadatta may well represent a conservative faction in the early community, vilified in Buddhist history forever by having their supposed advocate attempt to assassinate the Buddha three times. He is swallowed by the earth and descends to the Avīci hell; Ciñcamānavikā suffers a similar fate. But let us consider three other scenes in more detail, important because they occur at three key moments in the story of the Buddha: immediately after his attainment of enlightenment, immediately before his passage into nirvāṇa, and immediately after it.

As discussed in Part 1, according to the standard account, after his achievement of enlightenment, the Buddha spent seven weeks in the vicinity of the Bodhi Tree, neither eating, nor sleeping, nor speaking (to humans) until the final week, when he was approached by two merchants, who offered him his first meal as a Buddha. As already noted, the seven weeks are important for a number of reasons. For example, the Buddha does not teach the two merchants; instead, he offers them eight hairs, which they eventually enshrine in a stūpa, thus foreshadowing what would become the most significant monuments in the Buddhist world.

Before allowing the seven weeks to pass, we might recall that those weeks are not about the formulation of doctrine or even about enlightenment as much as they are about demonstrating the Buddha's superiority to various gods and demigods. Just before the seven weeks begin, he is mistaken for a *yakṣa,* a tree spirit, by Sujātā, who offers him the meal that breaks his long fast, his last meal before his enlightenment. After eating it, he defies the laws of physics by causing his plate to float upstream. Then, after finding the right tree, he defeats Māra, not a demon but a god. Over the next seven weeks the *nāga* Mucilinda protects him from a storm, the divine kings of the four directions offer him a begging bowl, and Brahmā begs him to teach. Apart from the brief encounter with the two merchants, no humans appear during these seven weeks to interact with the newly enlightened Buddha, or even to see him. Everything occurs in the forest, among its spirits. When we think of other religions and their defining events, we think of the destruction of Jerusalem and the Babylonian captivity, we think of Pontius Pilate declaring *ecce homo* to the assembled crowd before the public execution, we think of Muhammad's *hijrah* from Medina to Mecca. The case of the Buddha is different; none of the events of the seven weeks seem to occur in the presence of humans, none of the events seem to occur in history.

Before humans, or at least humans that the Buddha might teach, appear in the story, there is a crucial conversation with a god. As we have discussed, according to some accounts, Brahmā, the most exalted of the gods in the Buddhist pantheon, descends from his heaven and implores the Buddha to teach the path that brings about the cessation of suffering. The Buddha declines, saying that what he has understood is too profound for others to understand. Brahmā persists, conceding that this is true for many, but there are others with "little dust in their eyes" who would understand. The Buddha eventually agrees, deciding that his two former meditation teachers would be most deserving, but he is informed by gods that they both have recently died. He then decides that the next most deserving are his five companions in asceticism. They had abandoned him in disgust seven weeks earlier on the day before he achieved enlightenment because he accepted a bowl of milk rice from Sujātā.

Discerning that they are now in a deer park outside the city of Vārāṇasī, he sets out to find them. En route, he encounters an ascetic named Upaka, a member of the Ājīvika sect, one of the many sects of ancient India. Upaka, struck by the Buddha's demeanor, stops to comment on his clear and bright complexion. Seeing this as a sign of spiritual attainment, he asks him who his teacher is. The Buddha (making it clear that no self does not mean no ego) replies, "I have no teacher, and one like me exists nowhere in all the world with all its gods because I have no person for my counterpart. I am the Accomplished One in the world, I am the Teacher Supreme. I alone am a Fully Enlightened One whose fires are quenched and extinguished."[24] Upon hearing these words, Upaka shrugs, says the Pāli equivalent of "Whatever," and continues on his way.

It has been argued that this story of the Buddha's encounter with the Ājīvika Upaka meets the criterion of dissimilarity.[25] It is not a case of two merchants offering the Buddha some food. Here, a fellow ascetic, a *śramaṇa,* encounters the Buddha and is sufficiently perceptive to discern that the Buddha has achieved an exalted state. Yet, when the Buddha rather emphatically confirms that he indeed has, the ascetic simply walks away. One would expect instead that he would have asked to become the Buddha's disciple. The fact that he does not, it is argued, suggests that this encounter actually occurred. Yet this story appears in *The Noble Search* right after the Buddha has rather grudgingly accepted Brahmā's request to teach, deciding that his first disciples will be the group of five. The story provides an opportunity to suggest that the Ājīvikas, who would become some of the Buddhists' greatest rivals, recognized the Buddha's attainment but, in the words of Brahmā, had too much "dust in their eyes," or too much pride and resentment, to become his disciples.

The next moment that might fulfill the "criterion of dissimilarity" is more difficult to explain. When the Buddha is about to die, he tells Ānanda that two meals are especially important in the life of the Buddha and that those who offer those meals therefore accrue great merit. The first is the bodhisattva's last meal before he achieves buddhahood. In the case of Śākyamuni, this is the golden bowl of milk rice offered by Sujātā, who mistook him for a *yakṣa.* By eating this meal, he immediately regained his strength after years of fasting; it was a meal so potent that it sustained him through the attack by

Māra, through the night of his enlightenment, and through the next forty-nine days. The other meal is not the first meal after enlightenment. It is a buddha's last meal before he passes into nirvāṇa. This meal was offered by a blacksmith (and thus a man of low caste) named Cunda. Much has been written about the food that was offered to the Buddha and his monks. Immediately after eating the meal, the Buddha suffers an attack of "red flow." The attack is described as so painful that the Buddha feels he is about to die. And soon thereafter he does die. How could the noble Buddha suffer such an ignoble fate?

The Buddha's final meal may be the most discussed case of intestinal indisposition in the history of religions. What was it that he ate? When did he eat it? Why did he eat it? Did it cause his death? For the carnivore monks of the Theravāda tradition, the meal, *sūkaramaddava,* literally "soft pork" in Pāli, was pork. For the vegetarian monks of China, it was something soft that pigs eat, a kind of truffle or mushroom. One scholar has suggested it was the fly-agaric mushroom (*Amanita muscaria*), known for its hallucinogenic properties.[26] It is noteworthy that both pork and mushrooms are considered unclean in the Hindu law codes and thus not to be consumed by those of the higher castes. What was the medical condition that afflicted him? The Pāli term, *lohita-pakkhandikā,* literally "red flow," is most often translated as "dysentery" or "diarrhea," although one physician, a Buddhist monk, has offered the diagnosis of mesenteric infarction, a decrease of blood flow to the small intestine resulting in severe abdominal pain.[27]

Traditional sources, however, are far more interested in the cosmic cause, that is, the karmic cause. As has been noted, over the early centuries of the tradition, Buddhist authors sought to understand those rare events in the canon in which the Buddha seemed particularly human: when he had a headache, when he had a backache, when he stepped on a thorn, and, especially, when he was afflicted with bloody flows. So we learn that he had a backache because in a previous life as a wrestler, he killed his opponent by breaking his back. He stepped on a thorn because he had once murdered someone with a spear. And we learn that he suffered from bloody flows because in a previous life as a physician, after repeatedly treating the son of a merchant without being paid, he became so angry that he gave the child a purgative that killed him.

These are acts of murder, which typically result in rebirth in one of the Buddhist hells, not a backache or a headache. But Buddhist karma theory describes something that might be called residual karma, an aftereffect of a negative deed that has already been expiated in a rebirth in the lower realms. Thus, it is often said that someone who murders a human will be reborn in hell; when they are eventually reborn as a human, their lifespan will be short. One explanation of the bloody flows, therefore, is that it is the residual effect of the angry doctor's prescription. Many other explanations are offered. For Nāgasena, for example, at the time of his enlightenment, the Buddha destroyed all of this past karma; after his enlightenment, he experienced no karmic effects, positive or negative. And thus, Nāgasena must explain why the Buddha got sick and died: it was because he was old.[28]

However, a reading of the sūtra suggests that the Buddha does not die of dysentery. Long before the last meal, the Buddha had told Ānanda that if asked to do so, a buddha can live for an eon or until the end of the eon; Ānanda does not take the hint and is later put on trial for his negligence. The Buddha then has a conversation with Māra, conceding that he has done what he set out to do and declares that he will pass into nirvāṇa three months hence, which he does. After the bout of dysentery, the Buddha walks with Ānanda to Kuśinagara, stopping along the way to have an extended conversation with a local man named

Pukkusa, who gives the Buddha two robes of gold cloth. When Ānanda puts one of the robes on the Buddha, the gold robes are outshone by the luster of the Buddha's skin. He tells Ānanda that the skin of a buddha becomes especially radiant on the night of his enlightenment and the night that he passes into nirvāṇa. In an account of his postprandial journey that does not appear in the *Mahāparinibbāna Sutta*, the Buddha and Ānanda come across a group of young men trying unsuccessfully to move a massive boulder embedded in the road. The Buddha dislodges the boulder with his toe, flips it into his hand and then casts it into the sky. When it reaches the heaven of the god Brahmā, it descends again, sending the young men fleeing in fear. The Buddha deftly catches it and turns it into dust.[29]

Arriving in a grove of trees, the Buddha lies down on his right side and spends several hours giving teachings, instructing Ānanda to tell Cunda that he is not responsible for his death and instead gained great merit by the gift of the last meal; he ordains a passing mendicant, explains to Ānanda how to cremate his body, and gives a range of final instructions to the assembled monks.

And then, in the third watch of the night, the same time he achieved the nirvāṇa with remainder forty-five years earlier, he achieves the nirvāṇa without remainder, but only after a final display of his meditative prowess, his mind moving up and down and then up again among the various levels of absorption before exiting the world forever from the fourth concentration. At no time is there a mention of dysentery or of the Buddha experiencing any discomfort. Yet the last meal and its ignoble effects remain a mystery. Like other moments of discomfort suffered by the Buddha, his bout of dysentery must be explained. Several explanations appear in the Pāli tradition. As noted above, (1) it was a result of a negative deed by the Buddha in his past life as a doctor; (2) it was the revenge of a demon who caused himself to be reborn as a poisonous pig; (3) it was simply because the Buddha was old and weak; and (4), as we will see below, the dysentery came from another cause and the "pig's delight" in fact sustained the Buddha for the short remainder of his life.[30]

Can dysentery be a criterion of dissimilarity? That is, can dysentery be proof of historicity? If not, what narrative function can it serve? After Cunda serves him the final meal and before he serves the monks, the Buddha says, "Whatever is left over of the 'pig's delight' you should bury in a pit, because, Cunda, I can see none in this world with its devas, māras, Brahmās, in this generation with its ascetics and Brahmins, its princes and people who, if they were to eat it, could thoroughly digest it except the Tāthāgata."[31] The Buddha does not explain why. However, at least for the Pāli tradition, there is a reason. In its most famous biography of the Buddha, the *Account of Origins* (*Nidānakathā*), ascribed to the great fifth-century master Buddhaghosa, we find a further link between the two meals offered to the Buddha, the one right before his achievement of nirvāṇa and the second right before his passage into nirvāṇa.

Referring to Sujātā's offering of food to the emaciated prince, food that would sustain him for the next forty-nine days, Buddhaghosa writes, "The deities by their divine power, as though they were extracting honey by squeezing out a honeycomb formed on a stick, brought together the beneficial energy of the deities and men of the four great continents and their two thousand surrounding islands and placed it there. At other times the deities infuse energy at each mouthful, but on the day of the Enlightenment and on the day of the passing into Nibbāna they infuse it into the vessel itself."[32] Thus, the tradition has a way of explaining, or at least of explaining away, the attack of dysentery, with the Buddha knowing what he is eating and what effect it would have on others. The gods infuse the two meals with energy to sustain him through the two nirvāṇas: the nirvāṇa with remainder when he is thirty-five and the nirvāṇa without remainder when he is eighty. He does indeed suffer from the latter meal, so much so that the sūtra says that he "suffered sharp pains as if about to die." Yet, unlike any other god or human, he survives. And he seems to recover quickly. He and Ānanda appear to have set out for Kuśinagara after the noon meal, the Buddha's body outshining the gold robes he is given along the way.

The third story that might fulfill the criterion of dissimilarity occurs shortly after the Buddha's death. Among the most famous scenes in Buddhist painting, especially in East Asia, is the death of the Buddha. Lying on his right side between two trees, he is surrounded by gods, monks, laity, and animals. Sometimes his mother, having been reborn as a god following her death seven days after his birth, has descended from heaven and is depicted weeping atop the tree at his feet. The gods, humans, and even the animals are in various states of despair; some, understanding the impermanence of all things, sit in stoic sadness, others wail on the ground in paroxysms of grief. This mourning continues through the Buddha's cremation and the disposition of his relics.

According to the vinaya account, shortly after the Buddha's death, Mahākāśyapa, the monk who had been given the honor of lighting the Buddha's funeral pyre, overhears a monk named Subhadra telling his fellow monks to stop grieving, that they should be happy that the Buddha is gone because he is no longer around to tell them what they can and cannot do. Now they can do whatever they want. Alarmed by this, Mahākāśyapa calls a meeting of five hundred arhats to collect and codify the Buddha's teachings "before those who speak what is not the dharma become strong and those who speak what is the dharma become feeble." This meeting is known to history as the First Council, where the monk Upāli first recited the entire vinaya and the monk Ānanda recited all the sūtras, with everything being memorized and chanted by the assembled arhats.

Subhadra's shocking statement of "good riddance" to the Buddha seems entirely out of place in the story of the monks' mourning, meeting the criterion of dissimilarity. However, it serves an important narrative function. Scholars are in agreement that the Buddhist canon, including the Pāli canon where this story is most famously found, evolved over centuries, with new texts and elements of the monastic code being added long after the Buddha's death, whenever that occurred. Although there were surely meetings of monks to decide what should and should not be included, the story of the First Council is clearly a myth. Yet it is an important myth because it claims that the Pāli canon contains only what the Buddha taught, as proven by the fact that it was assembled immediately after his death. Indeed, the Theravāda tradition holds that the sequence of the hundreds of texts that today constitute the Pāli canon is exactly the sequence in which those texts were recited by Upāli and Ānanda. The story of the First Council is thus an attempt to sanctify the texts that one sect accepted and to exclude the texts that they rejected. Yet there must have been an impetus for the monks to meet so soon after their teacher's passing. What better impetus than for an ungrateful monk being overheard rejoicing at the death of the Buddha?

And it seems clear, even from the canon, that sūtras would continue to be "remembered" long after the death of the Buddha. In a passage from the Mūlasarvāstivāda vinaya, perhaps dating from the fourth century of the Common Era, Upāli, the monk who had remembered and recited the monastic code, asks the Buddha, "Reverend One, in the future monks will appear who have imperfect memories, feeble memories. If they do not know in which place, village, or town which sūtra was taught and which rule of training was promulgated, how are they to supply them?" The Buddha replies, "Upāli, those who forget the name of the place, et cetera, must declare that it was one or another of the six great cities, or somewhere where the Tathāgata stayed many times. If he forgets the name of the king, he must declare it was Prasenajit; if the name of the householder, that it was Anāthapiṇḍada; of the lay sister, that it was Mṛgāramātā."[33] The "six great cities" are a standard list in Buddhist literature. Prasenajit was the king of one of them: Śrāvastī. A survey of the Pāli canon finds that of 1,009 texts, some 83 percent are set in one of five cities. In 70 percent of those texts, that city is Śrāvastī.[34]

13
The Forest of Theories

As we seek to apply the criterion of dissimilarity, so many elements of the biography seem to serve a polemical purpose. Indeed, the famous story of his descent into the city of Sāṃkāśya on the stairway from the Heaven of the Thirty-three, depicted so often in Buddhist art, serves at least four purposes. First, it allows the Buddha to express his filial piety by ascending to heaven to teach his mother, reborn there upon dying seven days after his birth. Second, it provides an explanation for why it is wrongly imagined that the Buddha did not teach the abhidharma; in fact, he taught it to the gods on the summit of Mount Meru, later repeating it to Śāriputra, who then shared it with the world. Third, it turns the city of Sāṃkāśya into a place of pilgrimage. And fourth, it provides the creation myth for the first Buddha image, crafted by sculptors transported to heaven at the request of King Rudrayāna, who could not bear the Buddha's absence from earth during the three months of his seventh rains retreat.[1]

Given all this, one might ponder whether we can distinguish between the Buddha and what might be called the Buddha function. We might describe the Buddha function as the necessity felt by the Buddhist tradition over the past two millennia to derive all authority from the Buddha himself. We see this most obviously in the monastic code, where every single rule, no matter how minor, is said to have been made by the Buddha. We see this most obviously in the Mahāyāna sūtras, where texts clearly composed centuries after his supposed death are ascribed to him, with all manner of stories about where those sūtras had been in the meantime. And so we see descriptions of all manner of events and teachings, composed over centuries, centered around an absent figure. Yet absence implies a previous presence. The question is: How far back in time must one go to find not the Buddha function but the Buddha himself? Is it possible that there is no Buddha, that there is only the Buddha function? In 1863, Robert Spence Hardy, a British missionary to Ceylon and no friend of the Buddha, wrote, "There is no life of Gótama Buddha by any native author, yet discovered, that is free from the extravagant pretensions with which his history has been so largely invested."[2] Over a century later, Rupert Gethin, a distinguished scholar of Pāli and a friend of the Buddha, wrote, "The historian must recognize that he has virtually no strictly historical criteria for distinguishing between history and myth in the accounts of the life of the Buddha."[3]

There was much doubt about the historicity of the Buddha among early European travelers to Asia. On January 29, 1552, Saint Francis Xavier wrote a letter from Kochi on the southwest coast of India to his companions in Europe in which he described his trip to Japan: "I tried to learn if these two, Ameda [Amitābha] and Xaca [Śākya], had been men dedicated to philosophy. I asked the Christians to make an accurate translation of their lives. I discovered from what was written in their books that they were not men, since it was written that they had lived for a thousand and two thousand years, and that Xaca will be born eight thousand times, and many other absurdities. They were thus not men, but pure inventions of the demons."[4] A little more than a century later, Simon de la Loubère, envoy of Louis XIV to the court of Siam, wrote about the Buddha (whom he called *Sommona-Codom*), saying, as "they have no reasonable Memory of him, it may be doubted, in my Opinion, that there ever was such a man. He seems to have been invented to be the Idea of a Man, whom Vertue, as they apprehend it, has rendered happy, in the times of their fables, that is to say beyond what their Histories contain certain."[5] The Carmelite missionary to Malabar in southern India, Paulinus of St. Bartholomew (1748–1806), wrote in 1796 in his *Viaggio alle Indie orientali*, "This god is said to have been the author of a great many books, and to have invented arithmetic, the art of writing, geometry, astronomy, and, in short, all those sciences which have been cultivated and improved by the industry of man. The opinion of those who consider him as having been really a writer, a king, a legislator, is ridiculous."[6] That Roman Catholic missionaries, and a French diplomat whose delegation included Roman Catholic missionaries, none of whom could read Buddhist texts, should declare the Buddha to be a myth is not particularly surprising.

As European scholars began to learn Buddhist languages and read Buddhist texts, a consensus began to emerge that the Buddha was, in fact, a historical figure. The most prominent proponent of this view was Eugène Burnouf, who argued that India emerged from the mists of myth into the light of history with the Buddha. Yet, Burnouf's most learned British contemporary disagreed. Horace Hayman Wilson (1786–1860) was the leading scholar of Sanskrit in Great Britain during the first half of the nineteenth century, a distinguished scholar and author of a still highly regarded Sanskrit-English dictionary, published in 1819. On April 8, 1854, he delivered a paper to the

Royal Asiatic Society entitled "On Buddha and Buddhism." The paper begins, "Much has been written, much has been said in various places, and amongst them in this Society, about Buddha, and the religious system which bears his name, yet it may be suspected that the notions which have been entertained and propagated, in many particulars relating to both the history and the doctrines, have been adopted upon insufficient information and somewhat prematurely disseminated."[7] Like us, Wilson was troubled by the wild differences among the dates that various Buddhist traditions gave for the death of the Buddha; he listed thirteen, ranging from 2420 BCE to 453 BCE. For Wilson, these inconsistencies "throw suspicion upon the narrative and render it very problematical whether any such person as Sákya Sinha, or Śakya Muni, or Sramana Gautama, ever actually existed."[8] Wilson found the names of the principals, King Śuddhodana, Queen Māyā, and Prince Siddhārtha, as well as that of their city, Kapilavastu, to be fanciful and unattested in the Vedic literature of the period; he describes the name of the Buddha's mother, which means "illusion," as "a manifest allegorical fiction." This and more led him to conclude that "it seems not impossible, after all, that Sákya Muni is an unreal being, and that all that is related of him is as much a fiction as is that of his preceding migrations, and the miracles that attended his birth, his life, and his departure."[9]

If our buddha was an invention of the community that took his name, then the Buddhists would have also needed to invent a lineage of previous buddhas extending back in time. As already noted, there seems to have been a precedent for this among the Jains, where the twenty-three predecessors of Mahāvīra, today referred to mostly as *tirthaṅkara,* are also called *buddha* in Jain texts. Indeed, as one might expect, there was a religious vocabulary in ancient India, largely deriving from the Vedas, that the various *śramaṇa* groups, both Hindu and non-Hindu, appropriated for their own use, in many cases changing the meaning. Standard epithets of the Buddha, including *jina* and *tathāgata,* as well as that apparently most Buddhist of all terms, *nirvāṇa,* were also used by the Jains. The term *buddha* itself was an epithet in Vedic India prior to the emergence of Buddhism.[10]

To take another famous term, in Buddhist texts *brāḥmaṇa* often refers to a member of the brahmin caste, whose claim to purity by birth the Buddha rejects; the true brahmin, the Buddha declares, is a person who gains purity through virtue and wisdom. In other cases, he appropriates and redefines Vedic terms. For example, the term *traividya* (*tevijja* in Pāli) means one who has the "threefold knowledge," that is, knowledge of the three Vedas, the *Ṛg Veda, Yajur Veda,* and *Sāma Veda.* The Buddha completely redefines this term in the *Tevijja Sutta* to mean one who has the three knowledges attained on the night of his enlightenment: the knowledge of past lives; the divine eye, or the knowledge of the workings of the law of karma; and the knowledge that the defilements have been destroyed and the cycle of rebirth has ended. The presence of a shared vocabulary among the ascetic groups of ancient India is therefore well attested, with different groups defining these terms in their own ways for their own purposes. It does not seem to be the case that there was a single historical figure, whom we call the Buddha, who inaugurated the creation of this new lexicon for a tradition that would be named after him.

As noted earlier, one could write an entire book about the biographies of the Buddha composed by European scholars, a biography of biographies. And, as noted earlier, this is not that book. However, it is important to mention the French Indologist Émile Senart (1847–1928), who offered a brilliant, one might even say solar, solution to the question of the Buddha's historicity. Most scholars, from the nineteenth century to the present day, have sought to discover the historical Buddha beneath encrustations of myth.[11] Senart proposed something very different. A student of ancient Indian mythology, he discerned its elements throughout the life of the Buddha, especially myths dealing with the sun and sunlight: at his birth, light floods the entire world, like the sun at dawn; his defeat of Māra beneath the Bodhi Tree is the sun god's conquest of the thunder demon; his turning of the wheel of the dharma is the sun god setting the solar orb in its course across the heavens. These mythological elements were fully present in ancient India before the Buddha's birth and were well known to his followers. For Senart, then, the Buddha is a solar god; the Buddha began as myth. He does not deny that there may have been a teacher called the Buddha. Rather, he contends that the teacher underwent an apotheosis that turned him into the sun god, incinerating the historical figure in the process. The authors of the Pāli canon, the works considered at Senart's time to be the earliest Buddhist scripture, then attempted to undo that apotheosis, performing their own euhemerism, their own demythologizing of the Buddha, their own attempt to turn the myth into a man. The result was the figure that is known from the Pāli canon. This surgical procedure was so successful that nothing of the original Buddha remained. A Buddha may have lived; the Buddha that is known to us never existed. Thus, Senart concedes the existence, however tentatively, of a Buddha who was outshone by the sun. "It is obvious that Buddhism has, like every doctrine, necessarily had a founder, a leader, no matter how broad an influence upon his teaching one concedes to later developments, how restricted one supposes his own role to have been, and how low the degree of his originality."[12] Senart's radical claim remains relevant; the route by which he reached it has been largely dismissed by scholars.

Among modern biographies of the Buddha, we find both proponents and skeptics of the Buddha's historicity well represented. Perhaps the most important work in the former category is *Gotama Buddha: A Biography Based on the Most Reliable Texts* by the great Japanese scholar Nakamura Hajime (1912–1999), published in English in two volumes in 2000 and 2005. Arguing that the historical Buddha is to be found in canonical sources preserved in Pāli and Chinese rather than in the later biographies, Nakamura constructs a biography from those elements, one that he considers to most accurately represent the human Buddha, as opposed to the deified Buddha. For Nakamura, the historicity of this human Buddha is not in question: "There can be no doubt concerning the existence of the person who advocated the unique thought that we attribute to him."[13] That thought then spread around the world. "That Buddhism was able in later times to reach across the world and warm people's hearts was due largely to the personality and character of its founder."[14]

More recently, the most influential proponent of the Buddha's historicity is Stephen Batchelor. In his *After Buddhism: Rethinking the Dharma for the Secular Age* (2017), he seeks "imaginatively to re-inhabit the world of fifth century BCE India in order to recover glimpses of the historical Gotama before he mutated into the quasi-divine Buddha, and the core elements of his teaching before they mutated into the various orthodoxies of Buddhism."[15] His method is to identify those passages that seem inconsistent both with later Buddhist orthodoxy and with the generic assumptions of the various ascetic movements of ancient India. In doing so, he constructs a biography of the Buddha living in a material world of intrigue, betrayal, and despair.

The skeptics of the Buddha's historicity in the present century are fewer. Here, we might mention Hans Penner's *Rediscovering the Buddha: Legends of the Buddha and Their Interpretation* (2009), a work that went largely unread because

Penner was not a scholar of Buddhism. Penner tells the story of the life of the Buddha and then interprets it as myth, drawing on Durkheim, Lévi-Strauss, and Mauss. He pauses, however, to consider claims for the historicity of the Buddha made by some of the most famous figures in the field, finding in each case that the argument for the historical Buddha is little more than a declaration of faith: "There must have been."[16] More recently, Bernard Faure has written his own life of the Buddha, drawn largely from East Asian sources. Before doing so, he surveys the history of European and American scholarship on the historicity of the Buddha, pointing out the many problems it inevitably entails, how the linear structure of biography is broken by the life of the Buddha. The various Sanskrit and Pāli biographies he describes as "a late, laborious construction, one that, barely finished, seems once again to fragment, unravel, and multiply all over again."[17] Indeed, he finds myth the more appropriate and productive model, calling the historical Buddha "one of the great myths of modern times." "Whether the Buddha existed or is only a myth," Faure concludes, "the mythological Buddha is very real—since all Buddhism derives from it."[18]

But our concern here is not the biography of Buddhology, however interesting that might be, but the biography of the Buddha. From the Buddhist perspective, was the Buddha a human being? In the final chapter we will consider the various bestial qualities of his body. Here, we can recall that he was conceived in a Buddhist version of immaculate conception, descending from the Tuṣita heaven into his mother's womb without his father's participation. He emerged from his mother's body ten lunar months later not through the birth canal but from her right side. He could walk and talk at birth, with lotuses blossoming under his feet. When his father took him to worship the statues of the gods in the temple, the statues bowed to him. The list goes on and on. His famous "twin miracle" at

Śrāvastī, in which he rose into the air and shot fire and water from his body, is called superhuman (*uttarimanuṣya*). When the Buddha descends from the summit of Mount Meru where he taught the abhidharma to his mother, flanked by the gods Indra and Brahmā, it is called *devāvatāra,* the descent of the gods. One of the epithets of the Buddha is *devātideva,* the "god surpassing the [other] gods," which is also an epithet for Viṣṇu and Śiva. Three categories of gods are enumerated in the Pāli canon: "conventional gods" (*samuttideva*), that is, humans who are called gods, such as kings; "rebirth gods" (*upapattideva*), that is, the gods of the Buddhist pantheon who reside in the various heavens; and "pure gods" (*visuddhideva*), that is, buddhas.[19] Indeed, gods and demigods are present at every major moment of the biography: his birth, his departure from the palace, his enlightenment, and his passage into nirvāṇa. It is the presence of these deities, from the good Brahmā to the evil Māra, that make those moments memorable. Indeed, it is the presence of those deities, some reverent, others hostile, that makes him worthy of worship by humans. All of this suggests that he was considered divine in ways surpassing those called *deva* in Sanskrit, a cognate of "divine." Yet European and American scholars have long sought to dispel the myth and find the history, to deny the god and find the man. And so we return to the question: is this a garden-variety case of apotheosis, or was he never a man?

What the Buddha taught is also a difficult, perhaps impossible, question to answer. The teachings of the Buddha are often named as two, the dharma and the vinaya, the doctrine and the discipline. When the Buddha is about to die, he tells Ānanda that the monks may feel that they have no master. However, he says, the dharma and the vinaya will be their master when he is gone. These, of course, are two of the famous "three baskets" (*tripiṭaka*) that constitute the Buddhist canon. Despite the famous story of the Buddha flying to the summit of Mount Meru to teach the third basket, the abhidharma, to his mother, there is strong evidence to support the view that the abhidharma as a category of Buddhist scripture came into existence after his death. What can be said about the doctrine and the discipline?

The discipline generally is taken to mean the monastic code, the elaborate set of rules: two hundred and twenty-seven for monks, three hundred and eleven for nuns, according to the Theravāda. These are divided into categories, based on the gravity of the misdeed. For a monk, four deeds result in expulsion: killing a human, stealing, sexual misconduct (defined here as penetrating the orifice of a human or animal, living or dead, to the depth of a sesame seed), and lying about spiritual attainments. Four more are added for nuns: enjoying physical contact with a male between the collarbone and the knee, concealing the expulsion offense of another nun, becoming the follower of a suspended monk, and possessing any of eight dispositions tinged with sexuality. The code is described as having developed organically, with the Buddha making a rule only after a particular misdeed had been committed. Much of the vinaya is devoted to telling the story of how each rule came about.

The story about sexual misconduct (in which a monk agrees to his mother's request to father a child to provide an heir for the family fortune) and the story about stealing (in which a monk steals some wood to make a hut) are relatively easy to imagine. The stories about killing, lying, and causing a schism are not. It is difficult to imagine sixty monks asking another monk to slit their throats because they have become overwhelmed by the thought of the foulness of the human body. One can imagine monks lying to laypeople about having spiritual powers but find it hard to accept the Buddhist claim that such powers (such as the ability to fly) exist. One can imagine dissension in the saṅgha but find it hard to imagine that the original schism was caused by a monk who tried to assassinate the Buddha, on three occasions. Much of the vinaya deals with the minutiae of monastic life from toilet etiquette to the design of cells to the materials for walls. Yet monasteries are not mentioned in the Aśokan inscriptions, and the word usually translated as "monastery" (*vihāra*) does not occur in donative inscriptions of such famous stūpa sites as Bharhut and Sanci. Indeed, there is no archaeological evidence for monasteries before the first century CE, long after the death of the Buddha by any calculation of his dates.[20]

There is a separate code for nuns. However, in the Pāli nikāyas the Buddha sometimes refers to a nun by name, but nowhere does he speak to one. In the *Mahāparinibbāna Sutta,* the lengthy account of the Buddha's final days and his passage into nirvāṇa, although laywomen are present, no nuns are mentioned. The earliest mention of nuns appears in Aśoka's Minor Rock Edict III, the "Schism Edict." This has led some to suggest that the order of nuns was established after the death of the Buddha, but before the reign of Aśoka.[21] The code for nuns, represented as having been set forth by the Buddha, therefore, would have been set forth after his death.

Is there evidence of the Buddha that we cannot see? What can we learn about the Buddha, and his historicity, from art? Here, we discover that the mystery of the Buddha extends beyond the questions of chronology and history to representation. For the sake of this discussion, we might as well place his death in 400 BCE, give or take fifty years. Aśoka mentions him in Minor Rock Edict I, which can be dated to the eleventh year of his reign, or 257 BCE. Because he also mentions a stūpa (the stūpa of a previous buddha) in another edict, one can assume that stūpas existed by then. In Buddhist legend Aśoka is renowned for opening seven of the eight "nirvāṇa stūpas" erected after the Buddha's death, removing their relics, and building eighty-four thousand stūpas throughout his kingdom, all in one day, with the assistance of *yakṣas*.

The first figural representations of the Buddha date from around 200 BCE, some two hundred years after this death, again, if we knew that he died circa 400 BCE. These are stone carvings discovered, for the most part, at stūpa sites: on panels that surround the base of the stūpa, on railings, and on gates. Yet, in one of the great mysteries of Asian art, the Buddha himself is absent. Absent is the svelte figure in the gracefully draped robe, his calm mien marked by his downcast eyes, his closed lips, his long earlobes, the circle between his eyes, his close-cropped curls turning to the right, the protrusion crowning his head. We cannot see him, but we know, we assume, we hope that he is somehow there. It is not that other figures—the Buddha's mother, his charioteer, his loyal steed, all manner of gods and devotees—are not present in their divine and human forms. Only the Buddha is absent. His presence can only be inferred by assuming, for example, that two figures flanking a large upright wheel—or an empty throne, or a pair of footprints—their hands joined at their chest in a gesture of reverence, are paying homage to the Buddha. The Buddha, or at least the Buddha as we have come to imagine him, is missing. These static scenes are later joined by narrative scenes, well-known events from his story: his mother, Queen Māyā, holds a cushion with a pair of baby footprints; gods accompany a riderless horse as it leaves a palace; Māra and his minions attack an empty throne; a giant serpent coils around a seat. Thus, we can infer that by this time these stories were well enough known to be carved in stone and recognized by those who saw them, perhaps with some instruction from a monk. Artists knew the difference between the future Buddha in his last life, that is, during his life as Prince Siddhārtha, and the future Buddha in his previous lives as a bodhisattva. For in his last lifetime, he is represented by a symbol, like a parasol on the saddle of a horse, yet in a lifetime before his last, as Prince Mūgapakkha, for example (from the *jātaka* of that name), he is depicted in his human form.

These representations of the absent Buddha, what art historians call "aniconic art," continued for some three centuries. We might pause to ponder this. It is only at the beginning of the second century CE, some five hundred years after his death, again, if we knew when he died, that the first images of the Buddha appear, the figure with the hair curling to the right, the long earlobes, the protrusion on the crown of his head, the wheels on the palms of his hands and the soles of his feet, the circle between his eyes, some of the thirty-two marks of a superman. It is only then that, as in the eleventh chapter of the *Lotus Sūtra,* the door of the stūpa opens and the Buddha appears. This means that for the first five hundred years after the Buddha's death—assuming that we knew when he died—the Buddha is not carved in stone in the form that we know him.

Perhaps coincidentally, perhaps not, the aniconic representations of the Buddha occurred during a period when orthodox Hindu priests rejected the worship of images of the Vedic gods because the Vedic gods were formless and all pervasive. Perhaps coincidentally, perhaps not, the first images of the Buddha begin to appear around the time that images of Viṣṇu and Kṛṣṇa start to appear as well, based on the argument that images of these gods should be made in order to bring joy to the worshipper.[22] Perhaps coincidentally, perhaps not, the first images of the Buddha begin to appear around the time that images are first made of Mahāvīra, the Jain founder, whose biography is so like that of the Buddha. Perhaps coincidentally, perhaps not, the first images of the Buddha begin to appear around the time that the first freestanding biographies of the Buddha are composed, such as Aśvaghoṣa's *Buddhacarita.* Those biographies rarely contain anything new. They are retellings of stories already told, stories carved in stone centuries before, yet unadorned by any carving of the Buddha.

We might compare this with the first images of Jesus, which seem to date from the late second century, some two hundred years after the crucifixion. We note here, however, that the early Christian community consisted of Jews who followed the commandment against graven images. It is perhaps noteworthy that early images of Jesus are found not in Palestine but in the catacombs of Rome. Scholars have scoured the Buddhist canon for a passage in which the Buddha prohibits the making of his image and have found none.[23] There is a rule in the monastic code that prohibits monks and nuns from making images of living beings, but this was occasioned by the Buddha's lovesick half-brother Nanda drawing pictures of the wife he had abandoned. The rule does not apply to laypeople, and the carvers of aniconic Buddhist art, though rarely named, were likely members of the laity.

In ancient India, carvings of deities, especially *yakṣas,* begin to appear in the third century BCE; the earliest surviving piece is dated to 275 BCE. In the following century, images of the aniconic Buddha start to appear, most often on the large stone panels that ring the drum of a stūpa. On the panels, *yakṣas* are often depicted around the absent Buddha. Thus, on a single panel, one often finds depictions of *yakṣas,* who from a historical perspective do not exist, worshipping the Buddha, while the Buddha, who, for the sake of argument, did exist, is absent, at least in the form that is so familiar today. The *yakṣas* are invisible but they are depicted; the Buddha is visible but is not depicted. And yet this invisible Buddha becomes an object of religious devotion long before the cults of such famous gods as Viṣṇu and Śiva emerge.

Why did the body of the Buddha remain invisible for so long? One might speculate that so many centuries after his death, no one remembered what he looked like. But this is true of all manner of religious figures of the ancient past who are widely depicted in painting and sculpture by their traditions. If one were to propose a theological reason, one might say that the Buddha was gone, passed into nirvāṇa, never to reappear in our world. Yet it is rare that we find the fine points of Buddhist philosophy represented in Buddhist art. Noting that so many of the aniconic images appear in the vicinity of stūpas, one might speculate that the devotees believed that the physical form of the Buddha was entombed within the stūpa, and thus to depict him again would be redundant. None of these explanations seems particularly compelling.

One must also then account for the appearance of figural images of the Buddha in the second century of the Common Era, with the aniconic continuing to exist alongside the figural for years before being replaced by it. This change was long attributed, with a certain European triumphalism, to Greek influence, noting that the first images appeared in Gandhāra in the far northwest of the Indian domain, a region long under the influence of Greek kings; Alexander the Great had defeated a Hindu army in the Punjab in 326 BCE, and Indo-Greek kings ruled large regions of what are today Pakistan and Afghanistan until the first decade of the Common Era. In 1905, the French art historian Alfred Foucher (1865–1952) published *L'Art Gréco-Bouddhique du Gandhâra: Étude sur les origines de l'influence classique dans l'art Bouddhique de l'Inde et de l'Extrême-Orient.* There, he argued that the images of the Buddha that appeared at the beginning of the second century of the Common Era looked a lot like Apollo. Foucher's theory of Greek origins was challenged in 1927 by the Sri Lankan art historian Ananda Kentish Coomaraswamy (1877–1947), who pointed out that figural images of the Buddha, images that did not look anything like Apollo and were dated from the same time, had been discovered in Mathura, just south of Delhi. The place of origin of the buddha image remains a topic of debate among art historians.[24]

In the stories carved on stūpas, the Buddha is visibly absent. We can only detect his presence because we already know the stories. Without knowing the reason why Buddhist artists, who carved all manner of kings and animals, gods and monsters, chose not to carve the Buddha, without even a generally accepted theory as to why they did not do so, do we have reason to believe that his absence in the solidity of stone somehow suggests his absence from the shifting sands of history? It seems a question tempting to ponder.

What of the other element of the Buddha's teaching, the dharma, referring to his discourses, or "sermons"? Philologists are able to use text-critical methods to determine some chronology of the works in the Pāli canon. Thus, based on the analysis of meter and grammar, two chapters of the *Suttanipāta* (the *Aṭṭhakavagga* and the *Pārāyanavagga*) are thought to belong to the earliest strata of surviving Pāli literature. The content of these works also suggests their antiquity, with monks depicted as living in the forest rather than in monasteries. Whether these texts represent the teachings of the Buddha himself, however, is more difficult to determine. For much of these texts is not particularly "Buddhist" (as we have come to understand the term), offering rather generic warnings against "thirst" (*taṇhā*) for sense objects and attachment to "views" (*diṭṭhi*)—this despite "right view" being the first element of the eightfold path, said to have been set forth in the Buddha's first sermon. The texts, however, are not free from mythology, with the *Aṭṭhakavagga* referring to the Buddha's descent from the Tuṣita heaven.

By the last half of the first millennium BCE, doctrines of karma and rebirth seem to have been present among many of the *śramaṇa* groups, as were various regimens of asceticism and meditation that offered a path to liberation from rebirth to those who followed them, regardless of their caste; critique or reinterpretation of the Vedic sacrifices performed by brahmin priests is a common motif. There is also a devaluation or rejection of the Vedic gods. These doctrines and practices were elaborated and refined by the Buddhists, but it is difficult to say how much of this can be traced back to an individual teacher. Among the *śramaṇa* traditions that survive to the present day, the Buddhists had most in common with the Jains; one sign of this similarity is consistent criticism of the Jains that we find in Buddhist texts. But the Buddhists and Jains were just two of many such groups during this period, most of which no longer survive. The *Brahmajāla Sutta,* the text that opens the Dīgha Nikāya, the collection of long discourses of the Buddha, lists sixty-two views held at the time. Where the Buddhists part company from the Hindu and Jain ascetics is on the question of the existence of the self, with the Upaniṣads proclaiming the primacy of the *ātman,* the Sāṅkhya seeking the separation of the person (*puruṣa*) from nature (*prakṛti*), and the Jains seeking the liberation of the soul (*jīva*) from bondage (*bandha*). The Buddhists were not alone, however, in denying the existence of a permanent self. The self (as well as rebirth) was also denied by the notorious Lokāyata (roughly translated as "Beyond the Pale") school, which, despite its excoriation in Hindu, Jain, and Buddhist texts, seems to have survived well into the Common Era. There is much more that one could say. The question here is: If the Buddha existed, what elements of his teaching were sufficiently innovative to attract the followers who eventually became the saṅgha? And why did Buddhism survive when so many of its contemporary and competing schools, schools like the Ājīvika and the Lokāyata, did not? Was it because its four truths were somehow truer than the teachings of the other schools? Was it because of its notion of nirvāṇa? Can we say that the remarkable persistence of Buddhism across India was due to the profundity of its doctrine?

All of this raises, yet again, the question of whether there ever was a Buddha. Was what we call Buddhism just a group of ascetics and philosophers propounding the kinds of views that one finds in works like the *Aṭṭhakavagga*, a text whose title may mean the "chapter on the purpose"? It extols the sage, not for any particular teaching but for his freedom from attachment to any view. Here we find no mention of the four truths and the eightfold path that are set forth in the traditional account of the Buddha's first sermon.

All of this suggests that Buddhist monks were not so different from the Vedic priests who opposed them. Perhaps that is a reason for their mutual antipathy. The *Ṛg Veda* was composed around 1500 BCE and was maintained orally for centuries. Because of the sophisticated mnemonics developed by Vedic priests, scholars are fairly confident that the *Ṛg Veda* as it exists in its written form today closely reflects the work composed millennia ago. It famously has no author, considered to have existed as sound from time immemorial, eventually being heard (*śrūti*) by the Vedic sages. The Mīmāṃsā school of Hindu philosophy argues that the Vedas are trustworthy because they are not the products of flawed humans. In many ways, the words of the Buddha are not different. The Buddha is the source of apparently limitless teachings which are heard by his audience in ways that are most appropriate for them. The Vedas had an endogamous caste of priests whose task it was to preserve the Veda. The Buddhists had a celibate saṅgha of monks, some of whom were charged with preserving the Buddha's words. And like the Vedas, those words seem to be of timeless origin, or at least lost in time.

And yet, unlike the Vedas, the sūtras will someday disappear. Thus, the measurement of time from the death of the Buddha most commonly evokes not hope for the future but longing for the past. The calculations of time in Buddhism occur most commonly in discussions of the period known as the degenerate age. A wide variety of calculations of its ominous advent are found in Buddhist texts. One of the most famous was set forth in Sri Lanka by the fifth-century CE monk Buddhaghosa. It became the chronology for the Theravāda tradition, which held that the Buddha passed into nirvāṇa in 544 BCE. According to this tradition, by the end of the first millennium no one will be capable of achieving even the state of a stream-enterer, much less that of an arhat. By the end of the second millennium, monks will not be able to maintain the monastic vows. By the end of the third millennium (which, according to the Pāli tradition, will occur in 2456), all Buddhist books will have disappeared. By the end of the fourth millennium, all monks will return to lay life. At the end of the fifth and final millennium, the last remnants of the dharma, the relics of the Buddha, will emerge from the stūpas around the world and gather under the Bodhi Tree, where they will burst into flames. This is called "the nirvāṇa of the relics."

There are many other chronologies, but all describe a process of decline and deterioration as the dharma, and the capacity to practice it, disappears. As humanity moves farther and farther from the death of the Buddha, lifespans shorten, wrong views proliferate, the afflictions grow stronger, physical and mental capacity weakens, and the environment declines. This decline becomes all the more ominous when we do not know when it begins and whether we have already entered an age where it is impossible to put the Buddha's teachings into practice. All of this suggests, at least speaking in terms of the retrieval of the past we call history, that the Buddha is irretrievable, at least by benighted beings like ourselves.

Scholars often refer to Gotama Buddha, Śākyamuni Buddha, our buddha, as the historical Buddha, with the buddhas of the past, with their detailed biographies and their improbable lifespans, sometimes referred to as prehistoric. Does this beginningless series of buddhas allow us to renounce the search for the historical Buddha? What would be lost if we did not describe our buddha as historical, instead including him in the prehistoric category, an inhabitant of a time before history, a time of myth? Yet when we use the term "prehistoric," we think of dinosaurs and fossils, we think of bones, we think of relics.

In 1898, a trench was dug through a hill near the Indian town of Piprahwa, revealing the remains of a stūpa. It contained a stone coffer containing five reliquaries, one of which held some eighteen hundred gemstones and pieces of embossed gold, as well as some bone fragments and ash. The inscription on its cover could be read to say that these were the relics of the Buddha. Newspaper headlines around the world declared, "Relics of Buddha Found." Based on its language and script, scholars have dated the inscription to the early second century BCE, with the gemstones from a period ranging a century before and after. Excavations conducted in 1971 revealed what appeared to be an earlier stūpa, where a brick enclosure was opened to reveal a soapstone container holding bone fragments as well as broken pieces of its cover. It was made of Northern Black Pottery (or NBP, as archaeologists refer to it), which can date to between 700 BCE and 200 BCE. Those who argue that these two sets of bone fragments are relics of the Buddha speculate that the fragments discovered in 1971 are the original share of the relics claimed by the Buddha's Śākya clan shortly after his death, while the relics discovered in 1898, at a higher and thus later level, were donated by Aśoka at the time of his visit to Lumbinī (some ten miles away).

Such conclusions obviously require a number of assumptions. The first is that the account of the death of the Buddha, the cremation of his body, and the distribution of the relics is a historical account, and that Aśoka really did break open seven of the eight original stūpas and redistribute the relics. That is, one must assume that these stories are histories. When stories are inconsistent with each other, one must decide which is history and which is story. In this case, there is the famous account that, not long before his death, the Buddha's entire Śākya clan was annihilated by the army of Virūḍhaka. And yet, there is also the famous account that, shortly after his death, an armed delegation of his clan arrived to claim the relics of their esteemed kinsman. Both of these stories cannot be true. If one is true, the motivation of the concoction of the other must be postulated.

In one of his edicts Aśoka says that he enlarged the stūpa of a previous buddha. He does not say that he did so at Lumbinī, although he says that he visited there. He does not say that he broke open any stūpas. That story comes from the *Aśokāvadāna,* where we read that he built eighty-four thousand stūpas from the relics that he retrieved by breaking open seven of the original eight. The *terminus ad quem* of this text falls around 300 CE, or some five centuries after Aśoka's death. Several decades later, Vasubandhu composed his *Treasury of Abhidharma,* where he states that anyone who breaks open a stūpa will be reborn in hell. To our long list of questions about the historicity of the Buddha, we must therefore add: what is the relation between the textual record and the archaeological record? The Buddha left no DNA.[25]

Perhaps all that is left is a conviction, perhaps just a feeling, the feeling that there must have been a Buddha. Buddhist philosophers famously rejected the idea of God, of an eternal deity who is the creator of the universe. With their doctrine of dependent origination and their doctrine of saṃsāra, the beginningless round of rebirth, they rejected Aquinas's arguments for the existence of God, the belief that there must be an uncaused cause, a prime mover. And yet this famous Christian argument for the existence of God is, in a sense, the argument of those who claim the Buddha was a historical figure. How could there be Buddhism without a person called the Buddha? Just as there has always been God, there has always been the Buddha. Yet Ānanda failed to ask him to live forever.

I was teaching at Middlebury College when John Macquarrie (1919–2007), best known as the translator of Heidegger's *Being and Time,* was invited to campus. After his lecture, there was a small reception with the members of the small Department of Religion, to which the local Lutheran pastor was invited. At one point in the conversation, the pastor asked Macquarrie if he believed in the resurrection. Macquarrie said that that depended on what one meant by the resurrection. The pastor replied, "The physical resuscitation of a corpse." Macquarrie, an Anglican priest and a distinguished theologian, did not reply.

What, then, does it mean to believe? What does it mean to be a Buddhist? Every Friday, in mosques, we hear, "There is no god but God. Muhammad is the messenger of God." Every Saturday, in synagogues, we hear, "Hear, O Israel: Adonai is our God, Adonai in One. Blessed is God's name; His glorious kingdom is for ever and ever. And you shall love Adonai your God with all your heart, with all your soul, and with all your might." Every Sunday in Catholic churches, we hear, "I believe in God, the Father almighty, Creator of heaven and earth, and in Jesus Christ, his only Son, our Lord, who was conceived by the Holy Spirit, born of the Virgin Mary, suffered under Pontius Pilate, was crucified, died and was buried; he descended into hell; on the third day he rose again from the dead; he ascended into heaven, and is seated at the right hand of God the Father almighty; from there he will come to judge the living and the dead." In Buddhist temples, we hear, "I go for refuge to the

Buddha. I go for refuge to the dharma. I go for refuge to the saṅgha." There is much that might be said about these and other "affirmations of faith." We can simply note here the difference between the Christian and Buddhist statements, one marked with specific events that, from the Christian perspective, occurred and will occur in history.

All three of the Abrahamic affirmations are declarations of belief. The Buddhist formula is a declaration of a destination. The Buddhist formula does not declare a doctrine, it just names the dharma. And Buddhists have debated for centuries what that dharma discloses. The most famous version of the dharma is the summary that Aśvajit, one of the "group of five," gave to a young seeker named Śāriputra, who had stopped him on the road. Aśvajit said, *ye dharma hetuprabhavā hetuṃ teṣāṃ tathāgato hy avadat teṣāṃ ca yo nirodha evaṃ vādī mahāśramaṇaḥ.* After the refuge formula, this is the most famous statement in all of Buddhism, carved in stone and entombed in stūpas around the globe and across the centuries, recited in Sanskrit or Pāli, regardless of the speaker's mother tongue. It is rarely translated, but it means, "Of those phenomena produced through causes, the Tathāgata has proclaimed their causes and also their cessation. Thus has spoken the great renunciant." It just tells us what the Tathāgata said. "Tathāgata" is a common epithet of the Buddha. Like the identity of the Buddha, its meaning remains a mystery. Uncertainty about the speaker does not mean that those words are not true.

In an essay about the Buddha that was published in 1785, Voltaire wrote, "By what fate, by what fury, did it happen that in all countries, the excellence of such a holy and necessary morality has always been disgraced by extravagant tales, by prodigies more laughable than all of the fables of Metamorphoses? Why is there not a single religion whose precepts do not come from a sage and whose dogmas are not of a madman?"

But what if Buddhism is a religion whose teachings do not come from either a sage or a madman?

Scholars of Buddhism have long sought to identify the oldest texts in the canon. As already noted, one of the candidates is the *Aṭṭhakavagga,* or "Chapter on the Purpose." It is largely free of the technical terminology and lists familiar to the tradition, suggesting to some that it was composed prior to their formulation. The sage (*muni*) and the "true brahmin" are extolled more often than the monk (*bhikkhu*). Its primary theme is non-attachment, specifically to sensual pleasure, to views, and to the belief in the self. Much of the praise for non-attachment is consistent with the admonitions to morality found in the texts recommended by Aśoka. The danger of attachment to philosophical views is stated in stark terms at several points in the text. It has been suggested that some of the more "radical" statements regarding the rejection of all views derives from an ascetic group at the time of the Buddha that came to be incorporated into the monastic community.

But what if that ascetic group was the monastic community, a group of ascetics and philosophers propounding the kind of views that one finds in the *Aṭṭhakavagga?* What if Buddhism was a tradition without origin, a passing down without a founder? At some point, did it become necessary to imagine a founder, to create a figure out of nothing, out of emptiness, out of absence, to give him weight through story, a story in which he could not be depicted materially, leading to the period of aniconism? At some point, did a figure begin to emerge out of empty space into the form that we know? As already noted, the Jains, like the Hindu schools, used the word *buddha* to describe an enlightened being. It seems a small step from self to no self. It seems a small step from *buddha* to Buddha.

Eventually, statues began to be created. Among the bodies of the Buddha is the *śilpanirmāṇakāya,* the "crafted emanation body," a buddha made by an artist. But a statue of the Buddha is not the Buddha if it is hollow, if the empty space left by its bronze cast remains unfilled. In order for the image to be animated, it must be filled. It is only when it is filled that it comes to life, it is only when it is filled that it has a life. The physical filling is sometimes relics, sometimes jewels, sometimes tiny internal organs sewn from silk, sometimes scrolls of mantras wrapped around a stick, a stick called a life stick. And sometimes it is filled with stories. It is from those stories that a biography, literally, the writing of a life, can be concocted. And once that story is told, it is locked in that statue with the mantra *jaḥ hūṃ baṃ hoḥ.*

In the Palazzo Doria Pamphilj in Rome, there is an early painting by Caravaggio, circa 1595, entitled *Rest on the Flight into Egypt.* On the right side of the painting, the Madonna and Christ child sit sleeping. In the center of the painting, with his back turned to the viewer, stands an angel, playing a violin. On the left side sits Joseph, transfixed by the angel's music. But as in so many of Caravaggio's paintings, there is something unexpected. In his hands, Joseph holds the musical score for the angel to read. Caravaggio did not paint random musical notes on his canvas; he copied a Flemish motet to the Virgin Mary. The lyrics are from the Song of Songs 7.6. They begin, "*Quam pulchra es et quam decora*" ("How beautiful you are, how fair"). The painting seems to suggest that in order to ensure immortality, even of the divine, it is we who must provide the words.

14
The Horror of Enlightenment

Give me no light, great Heaven, but such as turns
To energy of human fellowship;
No powers beyond the growing heritage
That makes completer manhood.

—*George Eliot*

The most sacred image of the Buddha in Tibet is simply called the Jowo, the Lord. He sits on the altar of the Jokhang, the House of the Lord, the temple referred to by European travelers as the Cathedral of Lhasa. According to legend, the image was carved during the Buddha's lifetime and brought to Tibet by the Chinese princess Wencheng during the seventh century. Photos taken of the statue since the reopening of Tibet to tourism in 1980 show a beautiful statue, dressed in brocades, adorned with an elaborate gold crown studded with turquoise stones. However, photos taken before the Chinese invasion of Tibet in 1950 show the brocades and the crown but depict a very different visage. Here, the face looks swollen, even bloated, the skin mottled, with none of the beauty of the statue that we see today, much less in other famous statues of the Buddha around the world.[1]

This suggests, as some have reported, that the original Jowo was destroyed during the Cultural Revolution, and that what we see today is a replica. The odd face of the original statue, however, is easily explained. One of the ways that devout Buddhists in Tibet made merit over the centuries was to offer gold leaf that would be applied to the face of this most holy of images. It is these layers of gold that changed—perhaps distorted or even defaced—the face of Śākyamuni. What the original statue might have looked like is difficult, perhaps impossible, to discern. To apply layers requires a core, something smaller than the form that now appears, and something older, more ancient. As we have seen in the preceding chapters, the greatest challenge that faces the biographer of the Buddha is the apparent absence of the original, the absence of the core around which the centuries of accretions accrued. In this chapter, we attempt to imagine what the resulting figure might be like after layer upon layer has been applied.

Despite some important regional differences, especially in the size and shape of the crown protrusion, the Buddha as depicted in art has remained relatively consistent across the long history of the tradition, that is, during the centuries after his aniconic phase. At the same time, the Buddha as depicted in texts became increasingly baroque—a term defined by Montaigne as "bizarre, inutilement compliqué"—in both body and mind. As we have seen, the Buddha from early on was but one of many buddhas who have come in the past and who will come in the future, and, according to many Mahāyāna texts, who abide in other buddha fields in the present. But apart from a distinguishing feature (often a *mudrā* or hand gesture), they are difficult to distinguish because in many ways they are so similar.

As discussed in Chapter 12, they share a long list of identical qualities, and they all perform the same twelve deeds, differing from each other in only eight ways: in lifespan, height, caste (either brahmin or kṣatriya), the conveyance in which they go forth from the world, the period of time spent in the practice of asceticism prior to their enlightenment, the kind of tree they sit under on the night of their enlightenment, the size of their seat there, and the circumference of their aura.[2] Indeed, buddhas are so similar that some texts suggest that they are all the same. In the eleventh chapter of the *Lotus Sūtra,* before the Buddha summons myriads of buddhas from other buddha fields to witness his opening of the door of the huge stūpa that has emerged from the earth, he says, "I shall now gather all my magically created forms who are teaching the dharma in the worlds of the ten directions."[3]

Yet, despite this sameness, in a certain sense, the Buddha becomes a figure who cannot be fully depicted in material form or even in narrative form. The Buddha, a buddha, comes increasingly to be depicted—whether "reduced" or "expanded" is the proper verb—as a list of qualities. Physically, and most famously, there are the thirty-two marks and eighty secondary marks as well as the eleven signs on the palms of the hand and the soles of the feet. But there are also the sixty qualities of his voice, the eight or twelve deeds (*kārya*) all buddhas perform, the three or four bodies, the ten masteries (*vaśitā*), the ten powers (*bala*), the eighteen unshared qualities (*āveṇikadharma*). These qualities seem to have been added to the Buddha, both to his body and to his mind, through a process of accretion, whether to account for points of doctrine, to exalt the Buddha above the Hindu gods, or to describe some element of his carved image. As we have observed, the term "accretion" suggests that there was something there onto which the layers were applied.

The more appropriate metaphor might be the mosaic, the pieces of colored glass and shards of mirrors, each taken from a different source where they served a different purpose, to create a pattern, at least when viewed from a particular perspective. Whether that pattern is representational or abstract is a question to ponder.

Our focus in this afterthought is not the process but the result. Our purpose is not to pass judgment, whether ethical or aesthetical, but to pause to consider what it would be like to be endowed with what are called the *buddhadharma,* a term meaning here not the teachings of the Buddha but his qualities. When all of these qualities are assembled, who would the Buddha be? When all of the pieces are considered and each has been traced to its source, what would the image look like? And what would those bits of mirror reflect?

We might begin with his body. The Buddha has several bodies. The most famous enumeration is the three—the emanation body (*nirmāṇakāya*), the enjoyment body (*saṃbhogakāya*), and the truth body (*dharmakāya*)—with some texts adding a fourth body, the nature body (*svabhāvakāya*), whose precise meaning is debated, especially in Tibet. There is much that could be said about each of these.[4] Our immediate interests here are the first and the third. As the figure of the Buddha passed through higher and higher phases of apotheosis, the tradition was left with the problem of what to do with his physical "human" body. As we have seen, in the account of his final days, the Buddha gives specific instructions on how that body is to be cremated. This instruction from the master himself solved the most immediate of the physical problems, while providing the relics that would prove so central to the spread of Buddhism across India and then across Asia. The larger issue was doctrinal. If to be a Buddhist is to go for refuge to the three jewels—the Buddha, the dharma, and the saṅgha—what is the Buddha jewel? Is it the man who grew old and died after a bout of dysentery? As he himself said, "Enough, Vakkali. Why do you want to see this foul body? One who sees the dhamma sees me."[5] The Buddha's body was, like all impermanent things, subject to decay and disintegration. In that case, how could it be a place of refuge from suffering?

The solution to this doctrinal conundrum was to say that the Buddha jewel was the Buddha's qualities: his wisdom, his compassion, his equanimity, his mind that is always in equipoise. The term for "qualities" here is *dharma.* Thus, when a Buddhist goes for refuge to the Buddha, they are seeking refuge in the corpus of his qualities, his *dharmakāya.* This is obviously not a physical body that walked the roads of northern India and preached the *dharma* (in the sense of "teaching"); another concept was needed to name that body. This seems to be the origin of the *nirmāṇakāya.* Often translated as "emanation body," the Sanskrit term *nirmāṇa* has the sense of something created, composed, or conjured. This last sense is suggested in a famous passage from the sixteenth chapter of the *Lotus Sūtra,* in which the Buddha says that although people believe that he had achieved buddhahood forty years earlier, he had in fact achieved buddhahood innumerable eons ago. Thus, the well-known biography of the Buddha in which Prince Siddhārtha takes the four chariot rides, leaves the palace under cover of darkness, practices asceticism for six years, and achieves enlightenment under the Bodhi Tree was just another case of his "skillful means," a display, an act, to inspire the world. We saw similar intimations of the Buddha's true identity in the *Play in Full.* The character who appeared in that drama would be called an "emanation body" by Mahāyāna exegetes.

It is this body that is adorned with the thirty-two marks and the eighty secondary marks of a superman (*mahāpuruṣa*), a strange grab bag of physical characteristics that do not paint a particularly pretty picture.[6] The alternative translation of *nirmāṇakāya* as "composite body" makes sense here. Many elements of the list are unremarkable: long fingers, smooth hands, glossy fingernails the color of bronze, long legs, round shoulders, a broad brow, blue eyes. There is particular interest in his teeth: even, evenly spaced, white, forty in number (eight more than usual), with canine teeth that are round, sharp, white, and even. He has no black moles on his body and his belly is round, clean, and flat, with a navel that turns to the right. The hair on his head is black, soft, thick, fragrant, and curls to the right. There are a number of animal similes: thighs like an antelope, upper body like a lion, jaws like a lion, eyelashes like a bull. He is said to have a stride like a lion, an elephant, a goose, and a bull, although each of those beasts walks rather differently from the others.

But then there are things that seem rather odd. Although no simian simile is evoked, the list of the thirty-two marks says that when he is standing upright his arms extend down to his knees. Although nowhere does it say that he is hung like a horse, he has a penis that retracts inside his body. He has a tuft of hair between his eyes from which he can emit beams of light that illuminate distant worlds. Although he never needs to swim, he has webbed fingers and toes; his tongue is so long that he can cover his face and lick behind his ears; and he has a protrusion on the top of his head whose circumference cannot be measured despite its perfect proportions.

And there are other physical characteristics of the Buddha that do not appear in the two lists of marks. Two famous scenes in the life of the Buddha describe his retrospection, his backward looks. As already discussed, after his departure from the palace astride his horse Kaṇṭhaka, the prince stopped, wishing to take one last look at his city where he had spent the first twenty-nine years of his life, where his wife and newborn son lay sleeping. Rather than turn around in the saddle, the gods pivoted the circle of earth where the horse stood so that the prince could see Kapilavastu without turning his head. Fifty years later, as his passage into nirvāṇa approached, the Buddha left the city of Vaiśālī. Wishing to see the site of so many of his teachings for the last time, he turned to look at the city with what the texts call the "elephant's gaze" (*nāgāvalokita* in Sanskrit, *nāgāpalokita* in Pāli), that is, rather than turning his head, he turned his body to face the city. This is because a buddha, like a *cakravartin,* does not have vertebrae in his neck but a single bone, which makes it impossible for him to turn his head. What could be the reason for this skeletal abnormality? Perhaps it is because it would be undignified for a buddha or a universal monarch to have to turn his head; whoever comes into his presence should stand before him. It may be that a Buddha never looks back, or, apart from these poignant moments, never has a reason to look back, at least with his body; he is constantly looking back with his mind, knowing all of the past deeds not only of his own lives, but of the lives of all of the beings in the universe.

One could write an entire book composed of descriptions of the lists of the qualities of the Buddha. In *The Temptation of Saint Anthony,* Flaubert mentions the "eighteen substances." He is likely referring to the eighteen "unshared qualities" (*āveṇikadharma*), qualities that are "unshared" in the sense that the rest of us do not possess them. Here we learn, for example, that the Buddha is never worried about things like tigers and thieves when he is traveling because he never takes the wrong road; he never shouts or bursts out laughing; he never forgets anything and is never late; his mind is always in direct realization of the nature of reality; he does not make an ultimate distinction between saṃsāra and nirvāṇa; he never neglects the welfare of sentient beings; his love and compassion are constant; he is willing to travel to buddha lands equal in number to the grains of sand on the banks of the Ganges to benefit a single sentient being; he is constantly aware of the various mental capacities of sentient beings and how best to teach them; he knows how to teach the eighty-four thousand collections of doctrine in ways that are appropriate to sentient beings; his state of having abandoned all obstructions never deteriorates; he moves in ways that are always appropriate; he has unimpeded knowledge of the past; he has unimpeded knowledge of the present; he has unimpeded knowledge of the future.[7]

Elsewhere, we learn that the Buddha's senses are cross-functional, that he can place an entire world into a hair pore without changing the size of either; that every hair on his body directly realizes all objects of knowledge; that when he speaks, he just says *a*, the first letter of the Sanskrit alphabet, and each member of his audience hears a different discourse, intended specifically for them, in their native tongue. We read in a text call the *Hundred Legends* (*Avadānaśataka*) that when the Buddha smiles, blue, yellow, red, and white rays of light emerge from his mouth, some going down, some going up. Those that go down descend into the eight hot hells and eight cold hells; the rays of light bringing coolness to the hot hells and warmth to the cold hells. The rays of light that emerge from the Buddha's mouth and rise upward ascend to the realms of the twenty-three Buddhist heavens, places whose gods become attached to their sublime pleasures. The rays of light turn into sounds that say: "This is impermanent; this is suffering; this is empty."[8]

So much for the Buddha's body. What of his mind? We should not be surprised that it also has its own special qualities, enumerated in yet more lists. One of the most famous, and among the shortest and least technical, are the five or six *abhijñā*, the superknowledges. They are: (1) the knowledge of thaumaturgy (*ṛddhividhijñāna*), which includes such things as the ability to produce manifold forms, to appear and disappear, to walk through walls and mountains, to walk on water, to fly in the cross-legged posture, to touch and stroke the sun and moon with one's hands, and to physically travel as far as the world of Brahmā, a heaven located in the Realm of Form; (2) the divine ear (*divyaśrotra*), or clairaudience; (3) the knowledge of others' minds (*parasya cetaḥparyāya jñāna*), or telepathy; (4) the knowledge of former abodes (*pūrvanivās ānusmṛti jñāna*), or the memory of one's own former lives; (5) the divine eye (*divyacakṣu*), which sees the present karmic fate of beings throughout the various universes and realms of rebirth; and (6) the knowledge of the destruction of the defilements (*āsravakṣaya jñāna*), that is, the knowledge that one has put an end to future rebirth.[9] The last three of these figure in the account of the Buddha's enlightenment.

So many of these strike us as qualities of a god, or even God, rather than qualities of a human. What prevents the Buddha from being God is that he does not create the world. And yet, he does create a world; it is said that when a buddha achieves enlightenment, he also creates the domain for his teaching, called a buddha field (*buddhakṣetra*). These worlds are mentioned often in the Mahāyāna sūtras, with the Land of Bliss (Sukhāvatī), the buddha field of Amitābha, being only the most famous. Our world is not like these buddha fields. Or perhaps it is. In a famous scene at the beginning of the *Vimalakīrti Sūtra*, Śāriputra asks the Buddha (or, more accurately, the Buddha causes Śāriputra to ask him) why our world is so impure, unlike the marvelous domains of other buddhas. The Buddha touches the ground with his toe, and it is suddenly transformed into a bejeweled paradise. The Buddha tells the astonished assembly, who find themselves each seated on a jeweled lotus, "My buddha-domain, Śāriputra, is always like this, but it is in order to mature inferior living beings that the Realized One makes it appear marred by so many defects."[10] He then touches the ground again and the world reverts to its familiar impure state. The theological implications of this scene are too profound to consider here, apart from the question: "In what way is the Buddha human?"

As discussed in Chapter 7, during the first watch of the night of his enlightenment, the Buddha remembered all of his past lives in specific detail. The clinical psychologist might compare the Buddha's recollection with documented cases of extraordinary reminiscence, such as incidents of incontinent nostalgia brought about by anamnestic seizure in the temporal lobe, in which scenes or sounds from the long-forgotten past are replayed in vivid hallucination, or the forced reminiscence induced by the drug L-dopa in which the most trivial details of the past are brought into present awareness.[11] These cases have suggested to some researchers that all humans constantly carry in the brain "fossilized memory sequences" of all past experiences which remain indefinitely, and that these dormant memories can be reactivated under special conditions, such as those brought about by brain injury, the electrical stimulation of epileptogenic points in the cerebral cortex, or states of extreme excitement.[12] There is also hyperthymesia, also known as HSAM (Highly Superior Autobiographical Memory), in which a person can recall an extraordinary number of events from their life in vivid detail. These memories are usually involuntary, triggered by something beyond the person's control, and the flood of memories is often unwelcome. MRI studies indicate that individuals with this extremely rare condition have an enlarged temporal lobe and caudate nucleus.

But the Buddha remembers the events not only of this life but of an infinite number of past lives. And his reminiscences differ significantly in tone from those just described. The memories experienced through the stimulation of the temporal lobe are described in the language of presence and possession, with events recounted as if they are being fully relived in the moment. And the memory of the famous Russian mnemonist known to science simply as S was of a synesthetic character in which all the senses were stimulated by a sound or visual object.[13]

The comparison of the Buddha to modern mnemonists can be taken to its parodic extreme with the case of the twins described in Oliver Sacks's *The Man Who Mistook His Wife for a Hat.* Variously diagnosed as severely retarded, psychotic, or autistic, each of the twins had an extraordinary memory, their ability to recall past events seemingly closest to that of the Buddha. The twins could instantly and correctly tell you the day of the week of any date over a period of 80,000 years. Yet their skill was not one of mere computation, for they could also recount the weather, the news, and their experiences of any day of their life when specified by date.[14] As we read in the *Visuddhimagga,* when buddhas recall a specific moment of the past, they "descend with the lion's descent wherever they want, even skipping over many millions of aeons as though there were an elision in the text."[15] The Buddha's recollection of his former lives is topographically flat, without affect, with none of the imagery of eidetic memory, with none of the wistfulness of reminiscence, with none of the spontaneity of *mémoire involontaire,* with none of the forgetfulness of selective memory whereby the past is woven each day and unraveled each night.[16] The memory of the Buddha is comprehensive, disinterested, continuous, closed, dissolving singular events into a formula.

Yet when we imagine what it would be like to actually have such a memory, we learn that those who experienced incontinent nostalgia or forced reminiscence suffered from neurological disorders that result from injury or disease. The Russian mnemonist's synesthetic memory of things barred him forever from the world of ideas, and the twins remained seated in the corner of a psychiatric ward communicating with each other in twenty-digit prime numbers. The great fictional mnemonist, Borges's "Funes the Memorious," suffered an equestrian accident that caused him to perceive everything in vivid detail and then to remember it all, rendering him incapable of abstraction: "It was not only difficult for him to understand that the generic term *dog* embraced so many unlike specimens of differing sizes and different forms; he was disturbed by the fact that a dog at three-fourteen (seen in profile) should have the same name as the dog at three-fifteen seen from the front."[17]

The rise and fall of religions is rarely the result of rhetoric. Scholars continue to debate why Buddhism had disappeared, at least as an institution, from India by the fourteenth century. The Muslim incursions that began in 1001 were certainly a factor, but Buddhism had been in decline for centuries before that. Whatever their specific effect might have been, it is clear that philosophical attacks by Hindu authors also played some role. The famed Vedānta master Śaṅkara was an ardent opponent of Buddhism. Buddhist sources, however, seem to have been more concerned with the proponents of the Mīmāṃsā school, the school of Vedic literalists. In the last great compendium of Indian philosophy by a Buddhist master, the *Compendium of Principles* (*Tattvasaṃgraha*), the eighth-century monk Śāntarakṣita devotes almost half of his massive text to Mīmāṃsā. Proponents of this school uphold the Vedas as the primordial source of truth, famously arguing that they have no human author, having existed for all time as sound, sound that was later heard by Vedic sages, who then proclaimed it to the world. The Vedas are thus literally non-human (*apauruṣeya*). As we have noted, the Mīmāṃsā authors argued that the fact that the Vedas were not composed by humans is one of the reasons for their infallibility; because there is no record of their authorship or their composition, the Vedas are eternal. For them, the Buddhist sūtras are fallible because they had a human author.

Buddhist attempts to counter these claims may be one explanation for what we might call the superhumanization or, perhaps, the dehumanization of the Buddha: he teaches the dharma without the slightest operation of thought, like a wheel set in motion;[18] he is not subject to the faults of mortal beings because he is beyond the cycle of rebirth and thus immortal;[19] the scriptures attributed to him need not be actually spoken by him, and sometimes even emanate from walls. He is not the author of the sūtras, only their supervisor.[20] Indeed, one of the early Indian Buddhist schools, the Vaibhāṣika, asserts that the words of the Buddha are *apauruṣeya,* "non-human."[21]

The schools of Indian philosophy had different views on the number of sources of valid knowledge. For example, Mīmāṃsā includes sound (*śabda*), referring to the Vedas. The Buddhists famously count only two, direct perception and inference, in some cases, again in keeping with their Vedic opponents, adding a third: scriptures (*āgama*), that is, the word of the Buddha. Still, the central focus of Buddhist philosophy is direct perception and inference, with the first valued over the second, especially as it pertains to the achievement of enlightenment. Inference is a form of *vikalpa,* often translated as "thought," but sometimes meaning "misconception" or even "doubt." It is devalued for its inability to perceive things directly in their vivid detail, forced instead to understand the world through generic images, lacking the immediacy of sense perception and especially of the yogic direct perception required to see the nature of reality and achieve enlightenment. From this perspective, it is not particularly surprising that the Buddha has no thoughts; the tradition used its imagination to imagine a founder without imagination.

Yet when we imagine what it would mean for someone to live only in direct perception, without abstraction and forgetfulness, we think of Funes, lying on his bed in the darkness so as to protect himself from the sensory onslaught. His affliction seems a morbid parody of yogic direct perception. Nietzsche argued that "there could be no happiness, no cheerfulness, no hope, no pride, no *present* without forgetfulness. The man in whom this apparatus of repression is damaged and ceases to function properly may be compared (and more than merely compared) with a dyspeptic—he cannot 'have done' with anything."[22] And as the poet reminds us, "If all time is eternally present / All time is unredeemable."[23] It is forgetting that makes narrative possible. Perhaps it is because the Buddha remembers everything that it is so difficult to create a narrative of his life.

The Argentine writer reminds us of how horrible it would be to remember everything. An Englishwoman using a male pseudonym reminds us of what it would be like to know the minds of others (another of the Buddha's powers). In George Eliot's novella *The Lifted Veil,* published in 1859, the narrator, named Latimer, suffers a childhood illness that grants him the ability to hear the thoughts of others. This is not a blessing but a curse. The thoughts of others "would force themselves on my consciousness like an importunate, ill-played musical instrument, or the loud activity of an imprisoned insect." He calls this ability a "superadded consciousness," an appropriate translation for the *abhijñā* described in Buddhist texts. But for Latimer it is an affliction, becoming a source of intense pain and grief when he hears the thoughts of friends and family, "when the rational talk, the graceful attentions, the wittily-turned phrases, and the kindly deeds, which used to make the web of their characters, were seen as if thrust asunder by a microscopic vision, that showed all the intermediate frivolities, all the suppressed egoism, all the struggling chaos of puerilities, meanness, vague capricious memories, and indolent make-shift thoughts, from which human words and deeds emerge like leaflets covering a fermenting heap."[24]

But what of the Buddha's compassion? Again, it is difficult to overstate the importance of the Vedas and the Hindu conviction that they are eternal and not of human origin as an influence, not just on the deification, but on the dehumanization of the Buddha. One of the Mīmaṃsā critiques of the Buddha as an infallible source of knowledge is that he is consistently described as compassionate. Their claim, in brief, is that any religion whose teacher is compassionate is false because their teacher is fallible. That teacher is fallible because it is impossible to have compassion without passion (*rāga*). Dharmakīrti, the greatest of the Buddhist logicians, responded that the Buddha was without passion and yet had compassion. The reason? Dharmakīrti was a proponent of the Yogācāra position that the external world does not exist, everything is "mind only." The subject-object dichotomy is an illusion created by ignorance. Because the Buddha has destroyed all ignorance, his compassion has no external object. Thus, the Buddha could have compassion without passion because ultimately there were no beings to feel compassion for. This kind of compassion is called "great compassion," a compassion that does not recognize the distinction between self and other.[25]

For the Buddha to be immune from critique, then, he must be stripped of his humanity, of his personhood. Indeed, it is explained that the Buddha is not a person, a *pudgala* in Sanskrit, because a person is "filled with contamination," a direct translation of *gang zag,* the Tibetan rendering of the term.[26] He is, therefore, in many ways *apauruṣeya,* not a person, the term used to describe the Vedas. He is, instead, an eternal principle of enlightenment, appearing from time to time in history to do the same things, to teach the same things.

The horror of enlightenment arises from this compulsive compounding of these qualities, these dharmas, sutured together to produce a body that is unimaginable, not because it is wondrous but because it is somehow monstrous. Perhaps this is why we feel the appeal of the "historical Buddha," the austere teacher invented by European scholars in the nineteenth century, who attempted the impossible: to visualize him without the bump on his head. Perhaps this is why we see the appeal of Zen masters like Dōgen, who said that to sit in the posture is to be the Buddha. Perhaps this is why we are inspired by the buddha nature sūtras, which tell us that there has always been a buddha inside us. We just don't know it. Perhaps this is why we remain transfixed by early Buddhist sculpture, where the Buddha is simply not there.

For like the empty seat under the Bodhi Tree depicted on the stone slabs decorating a stūpa, the Buddha becomes invisible again, his teachings emanating from walls, as if he was never there, granted not just the power to live for an eon or until the end of the eon but an immortality in the Mahāyāna sūtras that gave him the power to teach anything in any form to anyone forever. And yet there are those footprints, signs of his past presence, marks of his absence.

Since we began this chapter with a statue, let us end with a statue. Oscar Wilde knew the work of Flaubert well. Flaubert's short story "Hérodias," published three years after *The Temptation of Saint Anthony*, in 1877, was one of the inspirations for Wilde's play *Salomé* in 1893. But to bring us back to the Buddha, we must turn to another French work, Joris-Karl Huysmans's *À rebours* ("Against Nature"), published in 1884, a decade after Flaubert's *Saint Anthony.* It is the story of a young man named Jean des Esseintes. Like the Buddha, he is from an aristocratic family, and like the Buddha, he is repulsed by the world. Yet, unlike the Buddha, he devotes himself to aesthetic practice, retreating not into the forest but into his study where he lives in a realm of the senses of his own careful construction, immersing himself, in turn, into what he regards, after much study and meditation, as the most refined experiences of the rarest of wines, of cuisine, of perfumes, of flowers (both natural and artificial), and of painting, all described in meticulous detail. He is not simply a sensualist, however. He knows, and has strong opinions, about centuries of Latin theology and French literature. A series of illnesses bring him close to death. His doctor tells him that in order to survive he must return to the world "and live an ordinary mode of existence by amusing himself like others." That is, to avoid death he must not renounce the world but return to it, he must leave the sublime and embrace the ridiculous, he must abandon the pure and live among the polluted. The novel ends with his lament, "O Lord, pity the Christian who doubts, the sceptic who would believe, the convict of life embarking alone in the night, under a sky no longer illumined by the consoling beacons of ancient faith."[27]

The first full English translation of Huysmans's novel appeared in 1926 as *Against the Grain,* where we read on the title page, "The Book that Oscar Wilde Loved and that Inspired Dorian Gray," an advertisement that Wilde would have disputed. *À rebours* was a key piece of evidence in Wilde's trial in 1895 for sodomy, where lengthy passages were read aloud in court by Lord Edward Carson, asking Wilde whether the "yellow book" that inspires Dorian Gray to descend into aesthetic depravity is *À rebours.* Although Wilde equivocated on the stand, disputing Carson's description of the French novel as "a sodomitical book," *À rebours* is clearly the yellow book.

In the 1945 film of Wilde's novel, Dorian Gray is confronted by his young friend Basil Hallward, the painter of the eponymous portrait whom Dorian later stabbed before stabbing the painting and thus killing himself. Visiting Dorian after he has begun his descent into depravity, Basil sees the yellow book on the table, and says, "It's vile, evil, corrupt, decadent. I detest it."

Dorian: What would you like me to read, Basil?

Basil: Since you ask me. *(Removes a book from his pocket.)*

Dorian: *The Light of Asia.*

Basil: I'm never without it.

Dorian: It's the story of Buddha, isn't it?

Basil: Yes, the story of Buddha, a good man. Promise me you'll read it, Dorian.

Dorian: I promise.

But Dorian does not read it, and Basil and Dorian are soon dead. *The Light of Asia*, published in 1879, is Sir Edwin Arnold's Victorian bestselling life of the Buddha. Was it artistic license for the 1945 screenplay to insert the Buddha into a scene that does not appear in the novel? In 1888, two years before the publication of *The Picture of Dorian Gray*, Wilde published a book of children's stories called *The Happy Prince and Other Tales*. The tale of the title tells the story of a prince who never leaves his palace. He lives surrounded by beauty in the Palace of Sans-Souci, where he plays with his friends by day and dances in the Great Hall at night. So content is the carefree prince that he never asks what lies beyond his garden wall, living and dying in his palace. After his death, his people commission a gilded statue of the prince and mount it on a tall column. It is only then that the prince, now a statue, can see the miseries of the world. Although his heart is made of lead, he cannot help but weep.

To relieve the suffering that he saw, he asks a swallow to remove the ruby from the hilt of his sword and carry it to a poor woman nursing her sick son. He asks the swallow to pluck out one of his ruby eyes and carry it to a young writer, so hungry and cold that he cannot finish his play. The bird takes the other eye to a little girl who gives it to her father so that he will not beat her. The prince then asks the swallow to peck off the gold that covers his statue, leaf by leaf, and take it to the poor. One day the swallow dies of the cold and the beautiful statue of the prince, now bereft of its beauty, is removed from its lofty pedestal and thrown into a furnace to be melted down. When the fire goes out, all that remains is its broken heart of lead. Unlike us in our search for the historical Buddha, when all of the wondrous qualities are removed, Wilde finds a core. Perhaps our quest to remythologize the Buddha is more like the swallow's, who takes the precious stones and bits of gold that adorn the statue and uses them to enrich the world.

Whether the person whom we call the Buddha ever lived, his image, whenever it originated, has lived on, not as a single image but as countless images, images that, when properly consecrated, come alive, said to be able to dispel all manner of sorrow and bestow all manner of blessing to those who wander in this world of suffering. It is an image that has traveled around the world, imbued with stories and teachings and doctrines that have inspired millions for centuries, all sealed safe inside an icon.

Linguists have identified the properties that distinguish human language from the languages of other creatures. One of these is called "displacement," the capacity of human language to transport the referents of words outside the present. We note that the verb here is not "place" but "displace," suggesting an intentional transportation outside a natural setting. Displacement is the ability to place things elsewhere, to name things that do not exist in present time and present space, that is, the ability to articulate the presence of absence. And so, unlike other sentient beings, we can describe the past, we can describe the future, and we can describe things that don't exist at all.

Religions, and perhaps especially Buddhism, put these three skills to good use. We think immediately of the central importance of past lives and future lives, of buddhas of the past and buddhas of the future. We recall that Buddhism's signature philosophical claim, and from the Buddhist perspective, its liberating insight, is an articulation of absence, the declaration that the self does not exist. Thus, to speak about what does not exist need not entail falsehood. To say that the Buddha did not exist is not to say that he is false. We recall that the Buddha's most profound form is the *dharmakāya,* often translated as "truth body."

Notes

Introduction

1. Bhikkhu Ñāṇamoli, *The Life of the Buddha According to the Pāli Canon* (Seattle: BPS Pariyatti Editions, 2001), xiii.

2. *Introduction to the Domain of the Inconceivable Qualities and Wisdom of the Tathāgatas* (*Tathāgataguṇajñānācintyaviṣayāvatāranirdeśa*), 1.23–29, translated by Karen Liljenberg and Ulrich Pagel, in *84000: Translating the Words of the Buddha*, first published 2020, current version v 1.0.22 (2024), https://84000.co/translation/toh185#UT22084-061-005-translation.

3. *The Book of Ser Marco Polo the Venetian Concerning the Kingdoms and Marvels of the East*, 2 vols., trans. and ed. by Sir Henry Yule, 3rd ed., revised by Henri Cordier (New York: AMS, 1986), reprint of 1926 London edition, vol. 2, 316–319. See also the extensive notes of Yule and Cordier, 320–330.

4. For an anthology of European descriptions of the Buddha from Clement of Alexandria to Eugène Burnouf, see Donald S. Lopez Jr., *Strange Tales of an Oriental Idol: An Anthology of Early European Portrayals of the Buddha* (Chicago: University of Chicago Press, 2016).

5. See Donald S. Lopez Jr., *From Stone to Flesh: A Short History of the Buddha* (Chicago: University of Chicago Press, 2013).

6. David Friedrich Strauss, *The Life of Jesus, Critically Examined*, vol. 1, trans. by George Eliot (Cambridge: Cambridge University Press, 1846), 35.

7. Letter to Frédéric Baudry, June 24, 1871, in Yvan Leclerc and Danielle Girard, eds., "Correspondance: Édition électronique," *Correspondence de Flaubert* (Rouen: Centre Flaubert, Université de Rouen, 2017), https://flaubert.univ-rouen.fr/correspondance/correspondance/24-juin-1871-de-gustave-flaubert-à-frédéric-baudry/?year=1871&person_id=126&storage_place_id=6.

8. In her introduction, Mrosovsky writes that "the Buddha still has little chance of retaining his dignity while in the grip of Flaubert's mature undermining irony," creating "a thorough deflating portrait." See Gustave Flaubert, *The Temptation of Saint Antony,* trans. by Kitty Mrosovsky (Ithaca, N.Y.: Cornell University Press, 1981), 42. She seems to have derived this impression from reading some of the relevant passages of Burnouf and likely did not consult what is clearly Flaubert's main source, the *Lalitavistara,* which had been translated from the Tibetan by Burnouf's student Foucaux.

9. Flaubert, *The Temptation of Saint Antony,* 16.

10. *The Middle Length Discourses of the Buddha: A New Translation of the Majjhima Nikāya,* original translation by Bhikkhu Ñānamoli; translation edited and revised by Bhikkhu Bodhi (Boston: Wisdom, 1995), 167. For a recent attempt to prove the historical existence of the Buddha as rationalist philosopher, see Andrew Wynne, "Did the Buddha Exist?" *Journal of the Oxford Center for Buddhist Studies* 16 (2019): 98–148.

11. Frederic Prokosch, *The Seven Who Fled* (New York: Harper & Brothers, 1937), 329.

1
The Appearance of the Buddha

1. Gustave Flaubert, *The Temptation of St. Anthony,* trans. by Lafcadio Hearn (New York: Alice Harriman, 1911), 159–160.

2. See Maurice Walshe, *The Long Discourses of the Buddha* (Boston: Wisdom, 1995), 441–460.

3. On the Buddha's crown protrusion, see the chapter "Buddha" in Donald S. Lopez Jr., ed., *Critical Terms for the Study of Buddhism* (Chicago: University of Chicago Press, 2005), 13–36.

4. Flaubert, *The Temptation of St. Anthony,* 160.

5. Ibid., 153.

6. See Donald K. Swearer, *Becoming the Buddha: The Ritual of Image Consecration in Thailand* (Oxford: Oxford University Press, 2004).

2
A Child Is Born

1. Gustave Flaubert, *The Temptation of St. Anthony,* trans. by Lafcadio Hearn (New York: Alice Harriman, 1911), 160–161.

2. Henry Clarke Warren, *Buddhism in Translations* (Cambridge: Harvard University Press, 1956), 14, 15.

3. Ibid., 14–15, n. 2.

4. See Jan Nattier, *Once Upon a Future Time: Studies in a Buddhist Prophecy of Decline* (Berkeley: Asian Humanities, 1991), 7–26.

5. On the five considerations, see N. A. Jayawickrama, trans., *The Story of Gotama Buddha (Jātaka-nidāna)* (Oxford: Pali Text Society, 2002), 64–66.

6. On Queen Māyā's qualifications to be the bearer of the Buddha, see Reiko Ohnuma, *Ties that Bind: Maternal Imagery and Discourse in Indian Buddhism* (New York: Oxford University Press, 2012), 70–71.

7. For the description of Queen Māyā's womb in the *Gaṇḍavyūha Sūtra,* see Phyllis Granoff, trans., "Māyā, Mother of the Buddha," in Donald S. Lopez Jr., ed., *Buddhist Scriptures* (New York: Penguin, 2004), 129–135.

8. See Louis de la Vallée Poussin, trans., *Abhidharmakośabhāṣyam,* vol. 2, English trans. by Leo M. Pruden (Berkeley: Asian Humanities, 1988), 382.

9. Athanasius Kircher, *China Illustrata,* trans. by Charles D. Van Tuyl (Bloomington: Indiana University Research Institute, 1987), 141–142. Urs App has traced the story as far back as a Jesuit text written in Spanish in 1556, *Sumario de los errores.* See his *The Cult of Emptiness: The Western Discovery of Buddhist Thought and the Invention of Oriental Philosophy* (Rorschach: UniversityMedia, 2012), 38.

10. Eugène Burnouf, *Introduction to the History of Indian Buddhism,* translated by Katia Buffetrille and Donald S. Lopez Jr. (Chicago: University of Chicago Press, 2010), 366.

11. See André Bareau, "Lumbinī et la naissance du futur Buddha," *Bulletin de l'École française d'Extrême-Orient* 76 (1987): 69–81.

12. Flaubert, *The Temptation of St. Anthony,* 161.

13. See Michael J. Sweet, trans., *Mission to Tibet: The Extraordinary Eighteenth-Century Account of Ippolito Desideri, S. J.* (Boston: Wisdom, 2010), 395.

14. See Jayawickrama, *Story of Gotama Buddha,* 72. A lengthy account, in prose and verse, of Asita's meeting with the infant prince is found in the *Mahāvastu.* See J. J. Jones, trans., *The Mahāvastu,* vol. 2 (London: Luzac, 1952), 27–42.

15. See Louis de la Vallée Poussin, trans., *Abhidharmakośabhāṣyam,* vol. 2, English trans. by Leo M. Pruden (Berkeley: Asian Humanities, 1988), 484–487.

16. On the Buddha's sexuality, see José Ignacio Cabezón, *Sexuality in Classical South Asian Buddhism* (Somerville, Mass.: Wisdom, 2017), 326–333. See also John Powers, *A Bull of a Man: Images of Masculinity, Sex, and the Body in Indian Buddhism* (Cambridge: Harvard University Press, 2009).

17. See Jayawickrama, *Story of Gotama Buddha,* 76.

18. See Reiko Ohnuma, *Ties that Bind: Maternal Imagery and Discourse in Indian Buddhism* (New York: Oxford University Press, 2012), 79–82.

3
The Prince in the Palace

1. Gustave Flaubert, *The Temptation of St. Anthony,* trans. by Lafcadio Hearn (New York: Alice Harriman, 1911), 161.

2. Ibid., 161–162.

3. See Gregory Schopen, "Taking the Bodhisattva into Town: More Texts on the Image of 'the Bodhisattva' and Image Processions in the *Mūlasarvāstivāda-vinaya,*" in *Buddhist Nuns, Monks, and Other Worldly Matters: Recent Papers on Monastic Buddhism in India* (Honolulu: University of Hawai'i Press, 2014), 378–384.

4. See Bhikkhu Ñāṇamoli and Bhikkhu Bodhi, trans., "Greater Discourse to Saccaka (*Mahāsaccaka Sutta*)," in *The Middle Length Discourses of the Buddha: A New Translation of the Majjhima Nikāya* (Boston: Wisdom, 1995), 340.

5. See Samuel Beal, *The Romantic Legend of Sâkya Buddha* (London: Trübner, 1875), 74. In the *Buddhacarita,* the somewhat older Prince Siddhārtha has a similar reflection when riding his horse outside the palace, which leads him to meditate under a rose apple tree. See Patrick Olivelle, trans., *The Life of the Buddha by Ashva-ghosha* (New York: New York University Press, 2008), 125–129.

6. Flaubert, *The Temptation of St. Anthony,* 162.

7. *The Play in Full (Lalitavistara),* 12.65, translated by the Dharmachakra Translation Committee, in *84000: Translating the Words of the Buddha,* first published 2013, current version v 4.48.25 (2024), https://read.84000.co/translation/toh95.html.

8. See N. J. Krom, *Barabuḍur: Archaeological Description,* vol. 1 (The Hague: Martinus Nijhoff, 1927), 151–152. For other versions of the story, see J. J. Jones, trans., *The Mahāvastu,* vol. 2 (London: Luzac, 1952), 72–73, and *The Play in Full* (*Lalitavistara*), chap. 12.

9. Jones, *Mahāvastu,* vol. 2, 71–72.

10. Flaubert, *The Temptation of St. Anthony,* 162.

11. *The Play in Full,* 12.10 and 12.15.

4
The Great Departure

1. Gustave Flaubert, *The Temptation of St. Anthony,* trans. by Lafcadio Hearn (New York: Alice Harriman, 1911), 162.

2. *Buddhacarita,* 3.30, in Patrick Olivelle, trans., *The Life of the Buddha by Ashva-ghosha* (New York: New York University Press, 2008), 71.

3. *Buddhacarita,* 3.58, in Olivelle, *Life of the Buddha,* 79.

4. *Buddhacarita,* 3.61–62, in Olivelle, *Life of the Buddha,* 81.

5. N. A. Jayawickrama, trans., *The Story of Gotama Buddha (Jātaka-nidāna)* (Oxford: Pali Text Society, 2002), 79.

6. *Buddhacarita,* 4.88, in Olivelle, *Life of the Buddha,* 115.

7. J. J. Jones, trans., *The Mahāvastu,* vol. 2 (London: Luzac, 1952), 141.

8. *Buddhacarita,* 5.38, in Olivelle, *Life of the Buddha,* 139.

9. Jones, *Mahāvastu,* vol. 2, 154. The language of the original translation has been modernized.

10. See Ṭhānissaro Bhikkhu, trans., *The Buddhist Monastic Code I,* 2nd rev. ed. (Valley Center, Calif.: Metta Forest Monastery), 13.

11. Jones, *Mahāvastu,* vol. 2, 113.

12. *Buddhacarita,* 2.29–32, in Olivelle, *Life of the Buddha,* 45.

13. On the penis of the Buddha, see Nobuyoshi Yamabe, "The *Ocean Sūtra* as a Cross-Cultural Product: An Analysis of Some Stories on the Buddha's 'Hidden Organ,'" in Irisawa Takashi, ed., *The 100th Anniversary of the Otani Mission and the 50th of the Research Society for Central Asian Cultures* (Osaka: Toho Shuppan, 2010), 257–268.

14. See John S. Strong, "A Family Quest: The Buddha, Yaśodharā, and Rāhula in the *Mūlasarvāstivāda Vinaya,*" in Juliane Schrober, ed., *Sacred Biography in the Buddhist Traditions of South and Southeast Asia* (Honolulu: University of Hawai'i Press, 1997), 114.

15. Samuel Beal, *The Romantic Legend of Sâkya Buddha* (London: Trübner, 1875), 128.

16. *The Play in Full (Lalitavistara),* 14.44, translated by the Dharmachakra Translation Committee, in *84000: Translating the Words of the Buddha,* first published 2013, current version v 4.48.25 (2024), https://read.84000.co/translation/toh95.html.

17. *The Play in Full,* 14.43.

18. See John Strong, *The Experience of Buddhism: Sources and Interpretations* (Belmont, Calif.: Wadsworth, 1995), 11.

19. Tsugunari Kubo and Akira Yuyama, trans., *The Lotus Sutra* (Berkeley: Numata Center for Buddhist Translation and Research, 2007), 231.

20. *The Play in Full,* 13.26.

21. Jorge Luis Borges, *Collected Non-Fictions,* trans. by Eliot Weinberger (New York: Viking, 1999), 375.

5
Six Years of Austerities

1. Gustave Flaubert, *The Temptation of St. Anthony,* trans. by Lafcadio Hearn (New York: Alice Harriman, 1911), 162.

2. Ibid., 163.

3. See Bhikkhu Ñāṇamoli and Bhikkhu Bodhi, trans., "*Mahāsīhanāda Sutta:* The Greater Discourse on the Lion's Roar," in *The Middle Length Discourses of the Buddha: A New Translation of the Majjhima Nikāya* (Boston: Wisdom, 1995), 173–176.

6
The Attack of Māra

1. Gustave Flaubert, *The Temptation of St. Anthony,* trans. by Lafcadio Hearn (New York: Alice Harriman, 1911), 163–164.

2. See Toni Huber, *The Guide to India: A Tibetan Account by Amdo Gendun Chöphel* (Dharamsala, India: Library of Tibetan Works and Archives, 2000), 47.

3. N. A. Jayawickrama, trans., *The Story of Gotama Buddha (Jātaka-nidāna)* (Oxford: Pali Text Society, 2002), 94.

4. *The Play in Full (Lalitavistara),* 21.1, translated by the Dharmachakra Translation Committee, in *84000: Translating the Words of the Buddha,* first published 2013, current version v 4.48.25 (2024), https://read.84000.co/translation/toh95.html.

5. *The Play in Full,* 21.20–21.

6. J. J. Jones, trans., *The Mahāvastu,* vol. 2 (London: Luzac, 1952), 364.

7. David Friedrich Strauss, *The Life of Jesus, Critically Examined,* vol. 1, trans. by George Eliot (Cambridge: Cambridge University Press, 1846), 26.

8. *Encyclopedia Britannica,* 9th ed., vol. 4 (Cambridge: Cambridge University Press, 1910), 427, s.v. "Buddhism."

9. Flaubert, *The Temptation of St. Anthony,* 164.

10. *The Play in Full,* 21.139.

11. E. B. Cowell, trans., *Buddhist Mahāyāna Texts, Part 1: The Buddhakarita of Asvaghosha* (London: Clarendon, 1894), 162.

12. For a discussion of this scene and its connection to the Buddha's founding of the order of nuns, see Liz Wilson, *Charming Cadavers: Horrific Figurations of the Feminine in Indian Buddhist Hagiographic Literature* (Chicago: University of Chicago Press, 1996), 36–37.

7
The Night of Enlightenment

1. Gustave Flaubert, *The Temptation of St. Anthony,* trans. by Lafcadio Hearn (New York: Alice Harriman, 1911), 165.

2. Bhikkhu Ñāṇamoli and Bhikkhu Bodhi, trans., "*Ariyapariyesanā Sutta:* The Noble Search," in *The Middle Length Discourses of the Buddha: A New Translation of the Majjhima Nikāya* (Boston: Wisdom, 1995), 256.

3. The names of the Buddha's meditation teachers, Ārāḍa Kālāma and Udraka Rāmaputra in Sanskrit, are accordingly rendered in Pāli here.

4. Ñāṇamoli and Bodhi, "*Ariyapariyesanā Sutta:* The Noble Search," 259–260.

5. Bhikkhu Ñāṇamoli and Bhikkhu Bodhi, trans., "*Bhayabherava Sutta:* Fear and Dread," in *The Middle Length Discourses of the Buddha,* 102–107. In addition to these two versions of the enlightenment in the Nikāyas, there are, of course, many others in Sanskrit literature. For an exegesis of the extant accounts from the mainstream schools and a discussion of their relative chronology, see André Bareau, *Recherches sur la biographie du Buddha dan les Sūtrapiṭaka et les Vinayapiṭaka anciens: de la quête de l'éveil à la conversion de Śāriputra et de Maudgalyāyana,* Publications de L'École Française d'Extrême-Orient 51 (Paris: École Française d'Extrême-Orient, 1963), 75–91.

6. Ñāṇamoli and Bodhi, "*Bhayabherava Sutta:* Fear and Dread," 105.

7. *Buddhacarita,* 14.3, in Patrick Olivelle, trans., *The Life of the Buddha by Ashva-ghosha* (New York: New York University Press, 2008), 403.

8. Ñāṇamoli and Bodhi, "*Bhayabherava Sutta:* Fear and Dread," 105.

9. "*Aggivacchagotta Sutta,* To Vacchagotta on Fire," in *The Middle Length Discourses of the Buddha,* 591. For a discussion of these questions, see Steven Collins, *Selfless Persons: Imagery and Thought in Theravāda Buddhism* (Cambridge: Cambridge University Press, 1982), 131–137.

10. The preceding discussion is adapted from Donald S. Lopez Jr., "Memories of the Buddha," in Janet Gyatso, ed., *In the Mirror of Memory: Reflections on Mindfulness and Remembrance in Indian and Tibetan Buddhism* (Albany: State University of New York Press, 1992), 21–46.

11. Ñāṇamoli and Bodhi, "*Bhayabherava Sutta:* Fear and Dread," 106.

12. Ibid.

13. *Dhammapada* 11, 153–154, in Acharya Buddharakkhita, trans., *The Dhammapada: The Buddha's Path to Freedom* (Kandy, Sri Lanka: Buddhism Publication Society, 1985), 58.

14. On Yaśodharā's extended pregnancy, see Max Deeg, "Chips from the Biographical Workshop—Early Chinese Biographies of the Buddha: The Late Birth of Rāhula and Yaśodharā's Extended Pregnancy," in Linda Covill, Ulrike Roesler, and Sarah Shaw, eds., *Lives Lived, Lives Imagined: Biographies of Awakening* (Somerville, Mass.: Wisdom, 2010), 49–87.

15. See Donald K. Swearer, *Bimbā's Lament,* in Donald S. Lopez Jr., ed., *Buddhism in Practice* (Princeton: Princeton University Press, 1995), 550–551.

8
Seven Weeks in the Forest

1. J. J. Jones, trans., *The Mahāvastu,* vol. 3 (London: Luzac, 1956), 269.

2. On the story of Trapuṣa and Bhallika and the various significances of the hairs of the Buddha, see John S. Strong, *Relics of the Buddha* (Princeton: Princeton University Press, 2004), 72–82.

3. Bhikkhu Ñāṇamoli and Bhikkhu Bodhi, trans., "*Ariyapariyesanā Sutta:* The Noble Search," in *The Middle Length Discourses of the Buddha: A New Translation of the Majjhima Nikāya* (Boston: Wisdom, 1995), 260.

4. See R. A. E. Coningham et al., "The Earliest Buddhist Shrine: Excavating the Birthplace of the Buddha, Lumbini (Nepal)," *Antiquity* 87 (2013): 1104–1123.

9
To the Deer Park

1. *The Middle Length Discourses of the Buddha: A New Translation of the Majjhima Nikāya,* original translation by Bhikkhu Ñānamoli; translation edited and revised by Bhikkhu Bodhi (Boston: Wisdom, 1995), 263.

2. G. P. Malalasekara, *Dictionary of Pāli Proper Names* (London: John Murray, 1937), s.v. "Upaka."

3. Gustave Flaubert, *The Temptation of St. Anthony,* trans. by Lafcadio Hearn (New York: Alice Harriman, 1911), 165.

4. *The Play in Full (Lalitavistara),* 13.33–34, translated by the Dharmachakra Translation Committee, in *84000: Translating the Words of the Buddha,* first published 2013, current version v 4.48.25 (2024), https://read.84000.co/translation/toh95.html.

5. Walter Benjamin, *Illuminations* (New York: Schocken, 1968), 108–109.

6. Flaubert, *The Temptation of St. Anthony,* 165–166.

7. See Maurice Walshe, *The Long Discourses of the Buddha* (Boston: Wisdom, 1995), 246–247.

10
Passage to Nirvāṇa

1. Gustave Flaubert, *The Temptation of St. Anthony,* trans. by Lafcadio Hearn (New York: Alice Harriman, 1911), 166.

2. *The Play in Full (Lalitavistara),* 8.9, translated by the Dharmachakra Translation Committee, in *84000: Translating the Words of the Buddha,* first published 2013, current version v 4.48.25 (2024), https://read.84000.co/translation/toh95.html.

3. Flaubert, *The Temptation of St. Anthony,* 166.

4. See Michael Radich, *The Mahāparinirvāṇa-mahāsūtra and the Emergence of the Tathāgatagarbha Doctrine* (Hamburg: Hamburg University Press, 2015), 112.

5. Kosho Yamamoto, trans., *The Mahayana Mahaparinirvana Sutra,* 580; http://www.nirvanasutra.org.uk.

6. See Maurice Walshe, *The Long Discourses of the Buddha* (Boston: Wisdom, 1995), 246. Walshe's rendering of the Pāli *kappa* as "century" has been changed to "eon." The Pāli commentary says that *kappa* means *ayukappa,* or "lifespan." According to that reading, the Buddha is saying here that a buddha has the power to live to the end of the human lifespan, which, at that point in Buddhist cosmology, was said to be one hundred years. According to this reading, if Ānanda had asked the Buddha to do so, he could have lived an additional twenty years, from age eighty to age one hundred. This seems a rather paltry power of the Buddha and little reason for an earthquake.

7. Walshe, *The Long Discourses of the Buddha,* 251–252.

8. On the doctrinal controversies regarding the Buddha's ability to live for an eon, see Padmanabh S. Jaini, "Buddha's Prolongation of Life," *Bulletin of the School of Oriental and African Studies, University of London,* 21.1/3 (1958): 546–552.

11

Times and Teachings

1. Gustave Flaubert, *The Temptation of St. Anthony,* trans. by Lafcadio Hearn (New York: Alice Harriman, 1911), 159.

2. Ibid.

3. Ibid., 166.

4. Eugène Burnouf, *Introduction to the History of Indian Buddhism,* translated by Katia Buffetrille and Donald S. Lopez Jr. (Chicago: University of Chicago Press, 2010), 533.

5. See Heinz Bechert, ed., *When Did the Buddha Live?: The Controversy on the Dating of the Historical Buddha* (Delhi: Sri Satguru, 1995). For a useful review, see L. S. Cousins, "The Dating of the Historical Buddha: A Review Article," *Journal of the Royal Asiatic Society* 3.6.1 (1996): 57–63. On Tibetan calculations, see also David Seyfort Ruegg, "Notes on some Indian and Tibetan Reckonings of the Buddha's Nirvāṇa and the Duration of his Teaching," in *The Dating of the Historical Buddha,* part 2, ed. Heinz Bechert (Göttingen: Vandenhoeck and Ruprecht, 1992), 263–290.

6. Among the large body of scholarship on Aśoka, see John S. Strong, *The Legend of King Aśoka: A Study and Translation of the Aśokāvadāna*

(Princeton: Princeton University Press, 1983); Patrick Olivelle, Janice Leoshko, and Himanshu Prabha Ray, eds., *Reimagining Aśoka: Memory and History* (New Delhi: Oxford University Press, 2012); Nayanjot Lahiri, *Ashoka in Ancient India* (Cambridge: Harvard University Press, 2015); and Patrick Olivelle, *Ashoka: Portrait of a Philosopher King* (New Haven: Yale University Press, 2024).

7. *Introduction to the Domain of the Inconceivable Qualities and Wisdom of the Tathāgatas* (*Tathāgataguṇajñānācintyaviṣayāvatāranirdeśa*), 1.66, 1.100, translated by Karen Liljenberg and Ulrich Pagel, in *84000: Translating the Words of the Buddha,* first published 2020; current version v 1.0.23 (2024), https://read.84000.co/translation/toh185.html.

8. Étienne Lamotte, "The Assessment of Textual Authenticity in Buddhism," *Buddhist Studies Review* 1.1 (1983–1984): 6.

9. See Oskar von Hinüber, "The Foundation of the Bhikkhunīsamgha: A Contribution to the Earliest History of Buddhism," *Annual Report of the International Research Institute for Advanced Buddhology at Soka University for the Academic Year 2007* 11 (March 2008): 3–29.

10. Caroline Rhys Davids published a biography of the Buddha (presented as his autobiography) in *Gotama the Man,* published in 1928. Here, and in *Sakya or Buddhist Origins,* published in 1931, she sought to portray the original teachings of the Buddha before they were distorted by generations of monks. For her discussion of the relationship between supernormal powers achieved through meditation and the ability to converse with divine powers, see *Sakya or Buddhist Origins* (London: Kegan Paul, Trench, Trubner, 1931), 180 ff. On Caroline Rhys Davids, see Dawn Neal, "The Life and Contributions of CAF Rhys Davids," *The Sati Journal* 2 (2014): 15–31.

11. For a detailed discussion of the "Schism Edict" and its possible meanings, see Herman Tieken, "Aśoka and the Buddhist *Saṃgha:* A Study of Aśoka's Schism Edict and Minor Rock Edict I," *Bulletin of the School of Oriental and African Studies* 63, no. 1 (2000): 1–30.

12. For a discussion of possible correlates to all seven texts, see Patrick Olivelle, *Ashoka: Portrait of a Philosopher King* (New Haven: Yale University Press, 2024), 117–122.

12
Stūpas and Sūtras

1. See Gregory Schopen, "Immigrant Monks and the Protohistoric Dead," in *Buddhist Monks and Business Matters: Still More Papers on Monastic Buddhism in India* (Honolulu: University of Hawai'i Press, 2004), 373.

2. See G. P. Malalasekhara, *Dictionary of Pāli Proper Names,* vol. 2 (Delhi: Munshiram Manoharlal, 1998), 294–305.

3. See R. A. E. Coningham et al., "The Earliest Buddhist Shrine: Excavating the Birthplace of the Buddha, Lumbini (Nepal)," *Antiquity* 87 (2013): 1104–1123.

4. See Li Rongxi, trans., *The Great Tang Dynasty Record of the Western Regions,* BDK English Tripiṭaka 79 (Berkeley: Numata Center for Buddhist Translation and Research, 1996), 118. On the various versions of what the Buddha taught during his heavenly sojourn, see Peter Skilling, "*Dharma, Dhāraṇī, Abhidharma, Avadāna:* What Was Taught in Trayastriṃśa?" *Annual Report of the International Research Institute for Advanced Buddhology at Soka University for the Academic Year 2007* 11 (March 2008): 37–60. On the staircase itself, see John S. Strong, "The Triple Ladder at Saṃkāśya: Traditions about the Buddha's Descent from Trayastriṃśa Heaven," in *From Turfan to Ajanta: Festschrift for Dieter Schlingloff on the Occasion of his Eightieth Birthday,* Eli Franco and Monika Zin, eds. (Lumbini: LIRI, 2010), 967–978.

5. Hermann Oldenberg, *The Gṛihya-Sūtras: Rules of Vedic Domestic Ceremonies, Part 1,* Sacred Books of the East, vol. 29 (Oxford: Oxford University Press, 1886), 246.

6. For a useful study of ancient Indian funerary practices as evidenced in iconography, see Giuseppe De Marco, "The Stūpa as a Funerary Monument: New Iconographical Evidence," *East and West* 37, no. 1/4 (December 1987): 191–246.

7. Schopen, "Immigrant Monks and the Protohistoric Dead," 372.

8. Maurice Walshe, trans., *The Long Discourses of the Buddha: A Translation of the Dīgha Nikāya* (Boston: Wisdom, 1995), 264–265.

9. For a detailed study and analysis of this story and its several versions, see John S. Strong, *Relics of the Buddha* (Princeton: Princeton University Press, 2004).

10. For a beautifully illustrated study of the works that adorned Buddhist stūpas in India, see John Guy, *Tree and Serpent: Early Buddhist Art in India* (New York: Metropolitan Museum of Art, 2023).

11. Étienne Lamotte, *History of Indian Buddhism from the Origins to the Śaka Era,* trans. by Sara Webb-Boin (Louvain: Peters Press, 1988), 15.

12. Jonathan Duncan, "An Account of the Discovery of Two Urns in the Vicinity of Benares," in *Asiatic Researches,* vol. 5 (London, 1799), 132. I am grateful to John Strong for this reference.

13. See Himanshu Prabha Ray, *The Return of the Buddha: Ancient Symbols for a New Nation* (New Delhi: Routledge, 2014), 57–58.

14. James Prinsep, "Discovery of the Name of Antiochus the Great, in Two of the Edicts of Asoka, King of India," *Journal of the Asiatic Society of Bengal* 7 (1838): 156.

15. For a study of this transformation, see Donald S. Lopez Jr., *From Stone to Flesh: A Short History of the Buddha* (Chicago: University of Chicago Press, 2013).

16. See Tsong-kha-pa, *The Great Treatise on the Stages of the Path to Enlightenment,* vol. 1 (Ithaca, N.Y.: Snow Lion, 2000), 273.

17. *The Play in Full (Lalitavistara),* 6.40, translated by the Dharmachakra Translation Committee, in *84000: Translating the Words of the Buddha,* first published 2013, current version v 4.48.25 (2024), https://read.84000.co/translation/toh95.html.

18. As has been noted, there is no single full biographical account of the Buddha, from his exit from Tuṣita to his entrance into nirvāṇa, in the Pāli canon, but episodes of the Buddha's (or a buddha's) life are set forth in such works as the *Mahāpadāna Sutta* (DN 14), which recounts the life of the previous buddha Vipassī; the *Mahāparinibbāna Sutta* (DN 16), which recounts the Buddha's final days; the *Ariyapariyesanā Sutta* (MN 26), the most detailed of the canonical accounts, where he describes his practice of asceticism, his enlightenment, and his first teaching to the group of five; the *Mahāsaccaka Sutta* (MN 36), where he also describes his practice of asceticism and enlightenment; and the *Acchariya-abbhūta Sutta* (MN 123); a short text that describes the future Buddha's descent from the Tuṣita heaven, the time in his mother's womb, and his birth.

19. See Bhikkhu Ñāṇamoli and Bhikkhu Bodhi, trans., *The Middle Length Discourses of the Buddha: A New Translation of the Majjhima Nikāya* (Boston: Wisdom, 1995), 256.

20. On Bareau's Buddha, see Bernard Faure, *The Thousand and One Lives of the Buddha* (Honolulu: University of Hawai'i Press, 2022), 37–39. Bareau's numerous essays on the life of the Buddha, drawing on a wide range of previously neglected sources, remain an invaluable resource. Many of those essays are collected in André Bareau, *Recherches sur la biographie du Buddha dans les Sūtrapiṭaka et les Vinayapiṭaka anciens* (Paris: Presses de L'École Française d'Extrême-Orient, 1995). His own biography of the Buddha is *En Suivant Bouddha* (Paris: Philippe Lebaud, 1985).

21. David Friedrich Strauss, *The Life of Jesus, Critically Examined,* vol. 1, trans. by George Eliot (Cambridge: Cambridge University Press, 1846), 1.

22. Ibid., 26.

23. On the Pāli commentaries, see John S. Walters, "The Buddha's Bad Karma: A Problem in the History of Theravāda Buddhism," *Numen* 37.1 (June 1990): 70–95. For this example from a Mahāyāna sūtra, see Mark Tatz, trans., *The Skill in Means (Upāyakauśalya) Sūtra* (Delhi: Motilal Banarsidass, 1994), 81–83.

24. Ñāṇamoli and Bodhi, *The Middle Length Discourses of the Buddha,* 263.

25. In his response to David Drewes's argument that the Buddha was not a historical figure—David Drewes, "The Idea of the Historical Buddha," *Journal*

of the International Association of Buddhist Studies 40 (2017): 1–25—the distinguished Pāli scholar Oskar von Hinüber presents the account of the encounter with Upaka as evidence for the Buddha's historicity. At the end of his essay, von Hinüber quotes approvingly the statement by Erich Frauwallner that "Those who refuse to give credence to the tradition until a diary kept by Ānanda has been found . . . will have long to wait. They may pride themselves on the strictness of their method, but they will be forced to admit that such systems would paralyze all scientific inquiry." The advances made in Buddhist Studies since Frauwallner wrote those words in 1957 would suggest that this is not the case. For von Hinüber's full argument in favor of the Buddha's historicity, see Oskar von Hinüber, "The Buddha as a Historical Person," *Journal of the International Association of Buddhist Studies* 42 (2019): 231–264.

26. R. Gordon Wasson and Wendy Doniger O'Flaherty, "The Last Meal of the Buddha," *Journal of the American Oriental Society,* 102.4 (Oct.–Dec. 1982): 591–603.

27. Mettanando Bhikkhu and Oskar Von Hinüber, "The Cause of the Buddha's Death," *Journal of the Pali Text Society,* 26 (2000): 105–117.

28. See John S. Strong, "Explicating the Buddha's Final Illness in the Context of His Other Ailments: The Making and Unmaking of Some Jātaka Tales," *Buddhist Studies Review* 29.1 (2012): 17–33.

29. For a discussion of this story, with references to its several versions, see John S. Strong, "Overstory: First There Is a Buddha, Then There Is No Buddha, Then There Is," in Vanessa R. Sasson and Kristin Scheible, eds., *The Buddha: A Storied Life* (New York: Oxford University Press, 2024), 215–229.

30. See Yang-Gyu An, *The Buddha's Last Days: Buddhaghosa's Commentary on the Mahāparinibbāna Sutta* (Bristol: Pali Text Society, 2021), 122. For a study of this famous meal, see Strong, "Explicating the Buddha's Final Illness."

31. Maurice Walshe, trans., *The Long Discourses of the Buddha: A Translation of the Dīgha Nikāya* (Somerville, Mass.: Wisdom, 1995), 256–257.

32. N. A. Jayawickrama, trans., *The Story of Gotama Buddha (Jātakanidāna)* (Oxford: The Pali Text Society, 2002), 91.

33. See Gregory Schopen, *Buddhist Monks and Business Matters: Still More Papers on Monastic Buddhism in India* (Honolulu: University of Hawai'i Press, 2004), 398.

34. Schopen, *Buddhist Monks and Business Matters,* 400.

13
The Forest of Theories

1. See Donald S. Lopez Jr., *Buddhism: A Journey Through History* (New Haven: Yale University Press, 2024), 112–123.

2. Robert Spence Hardy, prefatory remarks in Wong Puh and S. Beal, "Text and Commentary of the Memorial of Sakya Buddha Tathagata," *Journal of the Royal Asiatic Society of Great Britain and Ireland* 20 (1863): 135.

3. Rupert Gethin, *The Foundations of Buddhism* (Oxford: Oxford University Press, 1998), 16.

4. Francis Xavier, *The Letters and Instructions of Francis Xavier*, translated and introduced by M. Joseph Costelloe, S.J. (St. Louis: Institute of Jesuit Sources, 1992), 337.

5. Simon de la Loubère, *A New Historical Relation of the Kingdom of Siam* (Oxford: Oxford University Press, 1986), 138.

6. Paulinus Bartholomaeo, *Viaggio alle Indie orientali*, published in English in 1800 as *A Voyage to the East Indies, containing an account of the manners, customs, &c. of the natives, with a geographical description of the country. Collected from observations made during a residence of thirteen years, between 1776 and 1789, in districts little frequented by the Europeans* (London: J. Davis, 1800), 332. Elsewhere, he writes, "However, that first and original Budha is nothing other than a spirit and the planet Mercurius, apparently the residue of a cult of the ancient celestial army, viz. the sun, moon, and planets, which once existed among all peoples. In fact, it is not possible that one and the same Budha alone taught so many great peoples and refined the Chinese, Indians, the kingdom of Pegu, Tibet, Egypt and finally the entire North in cult, religion, sciences, and law. Thus, he can only be an allegorical and astronomical numen, somehow the fictitious and common tree of basic human institutions." See Bartholomaeo, *Systema Brahmanicum liturgicum mythologicum civile: Ex Monumentis Indicis Musei Borgiani Velitris Dissertationibus Historico-Criticis* (Rome: Fulgoni, 1791), 161. I am grateful to Isrun Engelhardt for locating this passage and translating it from the Latin.

7. Professor [H. H.] Wilson, "On Buddha and Buddhism," *Journal of the Royal Asiatic Society* 16 (1856): 229.

8. Ibid., 247.

9. Ibid., 248. We should note that Wilson seems not to have admired Buddhism. To conclude his lengthy essay, he writes, referring to Christian missionaries, "Various agencies are at work, both in the north and the south, before whose salutary influence civilisation is extending; and the ignorance and superstition which are the main props of Buddhism, must be overturned by its advance" (265).

10. See Hajime Nakamura, *Gotama Buddha: A Biography Based on the Most Reliable Texts*, vol. 1 (Tokyo: Kosei, 2000), 215.

11. For a survey of European debates about whether or not the Buddha was a historical figure (with the author concluding that he was not), see David Drewes, "The Idea of the Historical Buddha," *Journal of the International Association of Buddhist Studies* 40 (2017): 1–25.

12. Cited in Siglinde Dietz, "The Dating of the Historical Buddha in the History of Western Scholarship up to 1980," in Heinz Bechert, ed., *When Did the Buddha Live? The Controversy on the Dating of the Historical Buddha* (Delhi: Sri Satguru, 1995), 63–64.

13. Nakamura, *Gotama Buddha,* vol. 1, 20.

14. Nakamura, *Gotama Buddha,* vol. 2 (Tokyo: Kosei, 2005), 200.

15. Stephen Batchelor, *After Buddhism: Rethinking the Dharma for the Secular Age* (New Haven: Yale University Press, 2017), 91.

16. Hans Penner, *Rediscovering the Buddha: Legends of the Buddha and Their Interpretation* (New York: Oxford University Press, 2009).

17. Bernard Faure, *The Thousand and One Lives of the Buddha* (Honolulu: University of Hawai'i Press, 2022), 60.

18. Ibid., 62.

19. See K. R. Norman, "Theravāda Buddhism and Brahmanical Hinduism: Brahmanical Terms in Buddhist Guise," in Tadeusz Skorupski, ed., *The Buddhist Forum: Volume II, Seminar Papers 1988–90* (Tring, U.K.: Institute of Buddhist Studies, 2012), 194.

20. See Gregory Schopen, "Doing Business for the Lord," in *Buddhist Monks and Business Matters: Still More Papers on Monastic Buddhism in India* (Honolulu: University of Hawai'i Press, 2004), 73–77.

21. These points have been made by Oskar von Hinüber in his essay "The Foundation of the Bhikkhunīsamgha: A Contribution to the Earliest History of Buddhism," *Annual Report of the International Research Institute for Advanced Buddhology at Soka University for the Year 2007* 11 (March 2008): 3–29.

22. On the evolution of Hindu views toward images of deities, see Phyllis Granoff, "The Absent Artist as an Apology for Image Worship: An Investigation of Some Medieval Indian Accounts of the Origins of Sacred Images," in Olle Qvarnström, ed., *Jainism and Early Buddhism: Essays in Honor of Padmanabh S. Jaini, Part I* (Fremont, Calif.: Asian Humanities, 2003), 441–459.

23. See Robert DeCaroli, *Image Problems, The Origin and Development of the Buddha's Image in Early South Asia* (Seattle: University of Washington Press, 2015), 30–43. Gregory Schopen has found passages in the monastic code in which the Buddha permits images depicting him when he was a bodhisattva—that is, during the years preceding his enlightenment—to be carried in procession. See Gregory Schopen, "Taking the Bodhisattva into Town: More Texts on the Image of 'the Bodhisattva' and Image Processions in the *Mūlasarvāstivāda-vinaya,*" in *Buddhist Nuns, Monks, and Other Worldly Matters* (Honolulu: University of Hawai'i Press, 2014), 390–403.

24. See DeCaroli, *Image Problems,* 12–16.

25. The argument that the Piprahwa relics are the actual relics of Śākyamuni Buddha is made by Harry Falk in "The Ashes of the Buddha," *Bulletin of the Asia Institute,* New Series, vol. 27 (2013): 43–76.

14
The Horror of Enlightenment

1. On the Jowo statue, see Cameron David Warner, "Re/Crowning the Jowo Śākyamuni Statue: Texts, Photographs, and Memories," *History of Religions* 51.1 (August 2011): 1–30.

2. See G. P. Malalasekhara, *Dictionary of Pāli Proper Names,* vol. 2 (Delhi: Munshiram Manoharlal, 1998), 294–305.

3. Tsugunari Kubo and Akira Yuyama, trans., *The Lotus Sutra* (Berkeley: Numata Center for Buddhist Translation and Research, 2007), 177.

4. For a useful study of the three (and four) bodies of a Buddha, and Indian and Tibetan debates about them, see John J. Makransky, *Buddhahood Embodied: Sources of Controversy in India and Tibet* (Albany: State University of New York Press, 1997).

5. Bhikkhu Bodhi, trans., *The Connected Discourses of the Buddha: A New Translation of the Saṃyutta Nikāya,* vol. 1 (Boston: Wisdom, 2000), 939.

6. The thirty-two marks and eighty secondary marks were discussed at length by Eugène Burnouf in Appendix 8 of his translation of the *Lotus Sūtra.* See Eugène Burnouf, *Le Lotus de la bonne loi* (Paris: L'Imprimerie Nationale, 1852), 553–647. For a study of the possible origins of the list, see Nathan McGovern, "On the Origin of the 32 Marks of a Great Man," *Journal of the International Association of Buddhist Studies* 39 (2016): 207–247.

7. This version of the list is provided by the Dalai Lama in *Opening the Eye of New Awareness,* trans. by Donald S. Lopez Jr. (Boston: Wisdom, 1985), 106–107. For a study and analysis of the various qualities of the Buddha, see Paul J. Griffiths, *On Being Buddha: The Classical Doctrine of Buddhahood* (Albany: State University of New York Press, 1994).

8. Adapted from Burnouf, *Introduction to the History of Indian Buddhism,* translated by Katia Buffetrille and Donald S. Lopez Jr. (Chicago: University of Chicago Press, 2010), 219–221.

9. This standard list occurs in full at Maurice Walshe, *The Long Discourses of the Buddha* (Boston: Wisdom, 1995), 105. For a discussion of various enumerations of the powers, see Har Dayal, *The Bodhisattva Doctrine in Buddhist Sanskrit Literature* (Delhi: Motilal Banarsidass, 1975), 112–116.

10. Luis Gómez and Paul Harrison, trans., *Vimalakīrtinirdeśa: The Teaching of Vimalakīrti* (Berkeley: Mangalam, 2022), 16.

11. Such cases are discussed by Oliver Sacks in *The Man Who Mistook His Wife for a Hat* (New York: Harper and Row, 1987), 132–152.

12. See Sacks, *The Man Who Mistook His Wife for a Hat,* 152.

13. See A. R. Luria, *The Mind of a Mnemonist,* trans. by Lynn Solotaroff (Cambridge: Harvard University Press, 1968), 81.

14. See Sacks, *The Man Who Mistook His Wife for a Hat,* 198.

15. Bhadantācariya Buddhaghosa, *The Path of Purification (Vissuddhimagga)*, 4th ed., trans. by Bhikkhu Ñāṇamoli (Seattle: BPS Pariyatti Editions, 2010), 405.

16. The image of Penelope is drawn by Walter Benjamin in his essay on Proust in *Illuminations* (New York: Schocken, 1968), 202.

17. Jorge Luis Borges, *A Personal Anthology* (New York: Grove, 1967), 42. The four preceding paragraphs are adapted from Donald S. Lopez Jr., "Memories of the Buddha," in Janet Gyatso, ed., *In the Mirror of Memory: Reflections on Mindfulness and Remembrance in Indian and Tibetan Buddhism* (Albany: State University of New York Press, 1992), 21–46.

18. *Tattvasaṃgraha*, ślokas 3368–3369. For the Sanskrit, see Dvārikādāsa Śāstri, ed., *Tattvasaṃgraha*, 2 vols. (Varanasi: Bauddha Bharati, 1968). This edition also contains Kamalaśīla's *Tattvasaṃgrahapañjikā*. For an English translation of both works, see Ganganatha Jha, trans., *The Tattvasaṅgraha of Shāntarakṣita with the Commentary of Kamalashīla*, 2 vols., repr. ed. (Delhi: Motilal Banarsidass, 1986).

19. *Tattvasaṃgraha*, 3550–3551.

20. *Tattvasaṃgraha*, 3606–3611.

21. See Padmanabh S. Jaini, "The Vaibhāṣika Theory of Words and Meanings," *Bulletin of the School of Oriental and African Studies* 22 (1959): 107.

22. Friedrich Nietzsche, *On the Genealogy of Morals*, trans. by Walter Kaufmann and R. J. Hollingdale (New York: Random House, 1969), 58.

23. T. S. Eliot, "Burnt Norton," in *Four Quartets* (New York: Harcourt, 1943), 13.

24. George Eliot, *The Lifted Veil* (1859; New York: Penguin, 1985), 20.

25. See Cristina Pecchia, "Is the Buddha Like 'a Man in the Street'? Dharmakīrti's Answer," *Wiener Zeitschrift für die Kunde Südasiens* 51 (2007–2008): 163–192.

26. For the Sanskrit etymology, see Louis de la Vallée Poussin, *Abhidharmakośabhāśyam*, vol. 4, trans. by Leo Pruden (Berkeley: Asian Humanities, 1988), 1357, n. 3.

27. Joris-Karl Huysmans, *Against Nature (À rebours)*, trans. by John Howard (New York: Simon and Brown, 2013), 202.

Index

Abhidharmakośa (*Treasury of Knowledge*), 196
Abhiniṣkramaṇa (*Great Renunciation*), 9, 54, 62, 87
Acchariya-abbhūta Sutta, 232n18
Account of Origins (Buddhaghosa), 86, 87, 96, 172
Account of Origins (*Nidānakathā*), 4
Afghanistan, 158, 190
After Buddhism (Batchelor), 182
Against the Grain (Huysmans), 217
Agañña Sutta, 93
Ājīvika sect, 114–115, 146, 160, 167–168, 192
Alexander the Great, 158, 190
Amitābha (Ameda), 177, 209
Ānanda, 23, 122, 126–128, 154, 168, 170–171, 173, 174, 184, 197, 229n6, 232–233n25
Anāthapiṇḍada, 175
Anattalakkhana, 118
Anglo-Afghan War, 158
Antiochus II, 158
Antiquities of the Jews (Josephus), 135
Ārāḍa Kālāma, 72–73, 77, 78, 89, 110, 227n3
Aratī/Arati, 86
À rebours ("Against Nature," Huysmans), 216–217
Ariyapariyesanā Sutta (*The Noble Search*), 99, 159–160, 168, 232n18
Arnold, Edwin, 11, 135, 218
Asiatic Researches (Duncan), 157
Asiatic Society of Bengal, 158
Asita, 36–39, 41
Aśoka, Emperor, 35, 138, 144, 146–149, 152–158, 186–187, 196, 199
Aśokāvadāna, 196
Aśvaghoṣa, 11, 53–54, 60, 90, 188. See also *Buddhacarita* (Aśvaghoṣa)
Aśvajit, 114, 198
Aṭṭhakavagga, 191, 193, 199
Avīci hell, 166
Axial Age, 156

Babylonian captivity, 167
Bareau, André, 35, 161
Batchelor, Stephen, 182
Baudry, Frédéric, 7
Beal, Samuel, 9, 11

Being and Time (Heidegger), 197
Benares, King of, 157
Benjamin, Walter, 122
Bhallika, 87, 107, 110, 112
Bharhut stūpa, 186
Bhayabherava Sutta, 90
Bimbā, 50. *See also* Yaśodharā
Bimbisāra, 69–70
Bimbā's Lament, 102
Bodh Gayā, 109, 122, 147, 151–152
Bodhi Tree, x, 104, 105, 110, 112, 114, 115, 166, 181, 194, 205, 216
Book of Songs (*Shijing*), 137
Borges, Jorge Luis, 68, 212, 214
Bosch, Hieronymus, 6
Boudhanath Stūpa, 149
Brahmā, 34, 65, 82, 109, 132, 160, 167, 171, 184, 209
Brahmajāla Sutta, 192
British East India Company, 23, 157, 158
Bruegel, Pieter (the Elder), 6
Bucephalus (horse), 158
Buddha, The: His Life, His Doctrine, His Order (Oldenberg), 12
Buddhacarita (Aśvaghoṣa), 46, 66, 87, 90, 126, 188
Buddhaghosa, 86, 115, 172, 194; *Account of Origins,* 86, 87, 96, 172
Buddhavaṃsa (*Chronicle of the Buddhas*), 4, 162
Buddhist Publication Society, 1
Burma, 142
Burnouf, Eugène, 2, 4, 6, 7, 11, 20, 34–35, 136, 157, 178, 222n8

Campin, Robert, 32
Caravaggio, 200
Carson, Edward, 217
Cathedral of Lhasa, 201
Ceylon, 142, 158, 177
Chandaka, 52, 53, 54, 63, 65, 66, 187
China, 3, 137, 169
Chronicle of the Buddhas (*Buddhavaṃsa*), 4, 162
Ciñcamānavikā, 165, 166
Clement of Alexandria, 2
Compendium of Principles (*Tattvasaṃgraha*), 212
Conan Doyle, Arthur, 143
Confucius, 156
Coomaraswamy, Ananda Kentish, 190
Cowell, E. B., 11
Cunda, 169, 171

Dalai Lama, 14
Dalí, Salvador, 6
Deeds of the Buddha (*Buddhacarita*) (Aśvaghoṣa), 11, 53–54, 60–61
Deer Park, 8, 110, 115, 126, 167–168
Desideri, Ippolito, 36, 93
Devadatta, 48, 119, 161, 165–166
Dharmakīrti, 215
Dharmaśāstras, 92
Diamond Sūtra, 140
Dīgha Nikāya, 115, 192
Dīpaṅkara (buddha), 27, 109
Discourse on Fear and Dread (*Bhayabherava Sutta*), 90
Dōgen, 216
Dostoevsky, Fyodor, 143
Droṇa, 154
Duncan, Jonathan, 157
Durkheim, Emile, 183

East India Company, 23, 157, 158
Elijah (biblical), 156

Eliot, George, 214
Epic of Gilgamesh, 137

Fall of the Idols and the Triumph of Christianity, The (Laureti), 125
Faure, Bernard, 183
Faxian, 20
First Council, 173–174
Foley, Alethea, 8
Formless Realm, 37, 70–74, 110
Foucaux, Philippe Édouard, 7, 11
Foucher, Alfred, 190
Francis Xavier (saint), 177
Frauwallner, Erich, 232–233n25
Freud, Sigmund, 59, 62
From Stone to Flesh (Lopez), 2, 11

Gandhāra, 111
Ganeśa, 17
Gethin, Rupert, 177
Gopā, 50, 62. *See also* Yaśodharā
Gopikā, 61
Gospel of Luke, 38, 43
Gospel of Mark, 135
Gospel of Matthew, 35, 58
Gospel of Pseudo-Matthew, 125
Gotama Buddha (Nakamura), 182
Grand Inquisitor (Dostoevsky), 143
Great Chronicle (*Mahāvaṃsa*), 138, 158
Great Discourse on the Final Nirvāṇa (*Mahāparinibbāna Sutta*), 11, 126, 136, 153–154, 171, 186, 232n18
Great Discourse on the Lion's Roar (*Mahāsīhanāda Sutta*), 13
Great Discourse to Saccaka (*Mahāsaccaka Sutta*), 45, 76–77, 159, 232n18
Great Renunciation (*Abhiniṣkramaṇa*), 9, 54, 62, 87
Gṛhyasūtras, 152–153
Guhyasamāja Tantra, 60
Guy, John, ix

Happy Prince and Other Tales, The (Wilde), 218–219
Hardy, Robert Spence, 177
Hearn, Patrick Lafcadio, 7–8, 11, 21–22, 23, 35
Heart Sūtra, 140
Heaven of the Thirty-three, 20, 36, 65, 150, 152, 176
Heidegger, Martin, 197
Herod, 135
Hesiod, 137
Highly Superior Autobiographical Memory (HSAM), 210
Hilarion (saint), 17, 18, 25, 38, 43, 58, 125, 131, 132
Hinüber, Oskar von, 232–233n25
Hirakawa, Akira, 137
History of Indian Buddhism, A: From Śākyamuni to Early Mahāyāna (Hirakawa), 137
History of Indian Buddhism from the Origins to the Śaka Era (Lamotte), 156
Homer, 156
Hundred Legends (*Avadānaœataka*), 208
Huysmans, Joris-Karl, 11, 216–217

Indra (Śakra), 34, 65, 82, 184
Infinite Consciousness, 71, 72
Infinite Space, 71, 72
Introduction to the Domain of the Inconceivable Qualities and Wisdom of the Tathāgatas (*Tathâ gataguṇajñânâcintyaviṣayâvatâra nirdeúa*), 2, 139
Introduction to the History of Indian Buddhism (Burnouf), 34–35
Islam, 197, 212

Jainism, 18, 30, 78, 134, 141, 146, 149–150, 159, 179, 188, 192, 199
Jambudvīpa, 31, 126, 150
Jaspers, Karl, 156
Jātaka tales, 10, 91, 93, 121, 188
Jeremiah (biblical), 156
Jerusalem, 167
Jetavana monastery, 125, 150, 161
John the Baptist, 135, 164
Jokhang, 201–202
Jones, J. J., 11
Joseph (biblical), 125
Josephus, 135
Judaism, 197
Julien, Stanislas, 120

Kālacakra Tantra, 137
Kāḷadevala, 36
Kanakamuni (Konāgamana), 148, 149, 150
Kaṇṭhaka, x, 54, 63–64, 65, 103, 206
Kāśyapa, 148, 149, 150
Kauṇḍinya (Koṇḍañña), 39, 41, 117
Khantivāda, 121
Kierkegaard, Søren, 96
Kipling, Rudyard, 48
Kircher, Athanasius, 34
Koizumi, Setsuko, 8
Koizumi, Yakumo, 8
Kṛṣṇa, 132, 188
kṣatriya caste, 151, 203
Kuśinagara, 151–152, 153, 154, 170–171

Lalitavistara. See *Play in Full* (*Lalitavistara*)
Lamotte, Étienne, 140, 156
Land of Bliss (Sukhāvatī), 209
Laos, 84
Laozi, 156
L'Art Gréco-Bouddhique du Gandhâra (Foucher), 190
Laureti, Tommaso, 125
Laws of Manu, 23
Legend of Aśoka (*Aśokāvadāna*), 138
Lévi-Strauss, Claude, 183
Life of the Buddha According to the Pāli Canon (Ñāṇamoli), 1
Life of Jesus, Critically Examined, The (Strauss), 5, 12, 163
Lifted Veil, The (Eliot), 214
Light of Asia, The (Arnold), 11, 135, 218
Light of the World, The (Arnold), 135
Lokāyata school, 192
Lokottaravāda, 9
Lotus Sūtra, 7, 20, 67, 140, 188, 203, 205
Loubère, Simon de la, 178
Lumbinī Garden, 34, 35, 111, 147, 148, 151–152, 195, 196

Macquarrie, John, 197
Madhyadeśa, 31
Mahāsaṅghika, 9
Mahābhārata, 153
Mahādeva, Prince, 121
Mahākāśyapa, 173
Mahāmāyā. *See* Māyā, Queen
Mahāpadāna Sutta, 232n18
Mahāparinibbāna Sutta, 11, 126, 136, 153–154, 171, 186, 232n18
Mahāparinirvāṇa Sūtra, 11, 126
Mahāprajāpatī, 42
Mahāsaccaka Sutta, 45, 76–77, 159, 232n18
Mahāsattva, Prince, 158
Mahāsīhanāda Sutta (*Great Discourse on the Lion's Roar*), 13

Mahāvaṃsa (*Great Chronicle*), 138, 158
Mahāvastu (*Great Matter*), 4, 8–9, 60, 83, 106
Mahāvīra, 18, 30, 134, 149–150, 179, 188
Mahāyāna sūtras, 14, 126, 140–141, 142, 165, 177, 209, 216
Maitreya, 30, 123, 148
Majjhima Nikāya, 88
Manikyala, 158
Man Who Mistook His Wife for a Hat, The (Sacks), 211
Māra, 13, 58, 80–87, 105, 106, 122, 127, 151, 159, 166, 168–169, 181
Mary (mother of Jesus), 36, 42, 125, 200
Mauss, Marcel, 183
Māyā, Queen, x, 32–35, 42, 77, 111, 152, 159–161, 173, 176, 179, 184, 185, 187
Merode Altarpiece (Campin), 32
Mīmāṃsā school, 193, 212, 213, 215
Minor Rock Edict I, 138, 146, 186
Minor Rock Edict III, "Schism Edict," 186
Mohenjo-daro, 137
Moses, 101
Mount Meru, 20, 30, 36, 65, 71, 107, 122, 124, 150, 161, 176, 184, 185
Mṛgajā, 61
Mṛgāramātā, 175
Mrosovsky, Kitty, 7
Mucilinda/Mucalinda, x, 106, 112, 166
Mūgapakkha, Prince, 188
Muhammad, 101, 167, 197
Mūlasarvāstivāda school, 61, 62, 174

Nāgāsena, 165, 170
Nakamura, Hajime, 137, 182
Ñāṇamoli (Osbert Moore), 1
Nanda (half-brother of Siddhārtha), 189
Neither Perception nor Non-Perception, state of, 71, 73
Nepal, 148
New Testament Studies, 5
Nietzsche, Friedrich, 214
Nigali Sagar, 148, 149
Noble Search, The (*Ariyapariyesanā Sutta*), 88, 159–160, 168, 232n18
Northern Black Pottery (NBP), 195
Nothingness, 71, 72, 73

Oldenberg, Hermann, 4, 12

Pakistan, 140, 190
Palazzo Doria Pamphilj (Rome), 200
Pali Text Society, 143
Pārāyanavagga, 191
Path of Purification (*Visuddhimagga*), 92, 211
Paul (apostle and saint), 135
Paulinus of St. Bartholomew, 178
Peak of Existence, 71, 73
Penner, Hans, 182–183
Picture of Dorian Gray, The (Wilde), 217–218
Piprahwa relics, 195, 235n25
Play in Full (*Lalitavistara*), 7, 9–10, 37, 47–50, 62, 67–68, 72, 76, 77, 78, 80, 81–82, 86, 87, 90, 99, 101, 102, 107, 108, 120, 122, 124–126, 205
Polo, Marco, 3–4
Pontius Pilate, 135, 167
Prasenajit, 175

Prinsep, James, 158
Prokosch, Frederic, 14

Questions of Milinda, 92, 165

Rāga, 86
Rāhula, 55–59, 61, 63, 96, 102, 103, 119, 144, 206
Rāhulamātā, 50
Rati, 86
Realm of Desire, 70–72, 74, 81, 117
Realm of Form, 70–74, 209
Rediscovering the Buddha (Penner), 182–183
Rest on the Flight into Egypt (Caravaggio), 200
Ṛg Veda, 92, 180, 193
Rhys Davids, Caroline, 143
Rhys Davids, Thomas W., 85, 143
River of the Arrow, 48
Romantic Legend of Sākya Buddha, The (Beal), 9, 11
Royal Asiatic Society, 179
Rudrayāna, King, 176

Saccaka, 159
Sacks, Oliver, 211
Śākya clan, 195, 196
Salomé (Wilde), 216
Sāma Veda, 180
Sāṃkāśya, 152, 176
Saṅgītisutta, 141
Śaṅkara, 212
Sāṅkhya, 192
Śāntarakṣita, 212
Śāriputra, 97, 114, 141, 176, 198, 209
Sarnath, 151–152, 157, 160
Schism Edict, 144, 186
Second Pillar Edict, 145
Section on the Schism in the Saṅgha (*Saṅghabhedavastu*), 62–63
Senart, Émile, 180–181
Seven Who Fled, The (Prokosch), 14
Shijing (*Book of Songs*), 137
Shrine of the Steadfast Gaze, 110
Shwedagon Pagoda, 108
Siam (Thailand), 25, 84, 178
Śibi, King, 120
Simeon (biblical), 38, 43
Śiva, 132
Spiritualism, 143
Śrāvastī, 13, 161, 175, 183–184
Sthāvarā (earth goddess), 83–84
Strange Tales of an Oriental Idol (Lopez), 2
Strauss, David, 5, 11, 12, 84, 163
Subhadra, 173, 174
Śuddhodana, King, 32, 34, 36, 38–39, 41, 124–125, 179
Sudinna, 59
Sujātā, 77, 111, 166, 167
Sukhāvatī, 209
Sumedha, 27, 28–29, 31, 55, 109
Sūtra on the Fourfold Assembly (*Catuṣpariṣat*), 105
Sūtra on the Great Renunciation (*Abhiniṣkramaṇa Sūtra*), 46
Sūtra on the Marks (*Lakkhaṇa Sutta*), 19
Suttanipāta, 191
Synoptic Gospels, 125, 135

Tanhā, 86
Tathāgata, 116, 127, 139, 175, 198
Tathâgataguṇajñânâcintyaviṣayâvatâranirdeúa (*Introduction to the Domain of the Inconceivable Qualities and Wisdom of the Tathāgatas*), 2, 139
Tattvasaṃgraha (*Compendium of Principles*), 212

Temptation of Saint Anthony, The (*La Tentation de Saint Antoine*) (Flaubert), 6–8, 12, 17, 131, 134, 216
Tevijja Sutta, 90, 180
Tezuka, Osamu, 3
Thailand (Siam), 25, 84, 178
Theogony (Hesiod), 137
Therīgāthā (*Songs of the Sisters*), 81
Thomas Aquinas (saint), 196
Thorani, 84
Trapuṣa, 87, 107, 110, 112
Treasury of Abhidharma (Vasubandhu), 196
Tṛṣṇā, 86
Turnour, James, 158
Tuṣita heaven, 30, 42, 152, 159, 160, 165, 183, 191
Twilight Zone, 46, 48–49

Udāyin, 54
Udraka Rāmaputra (Uddaka Rāmaputta), 73, 75, 77, 78, 89, 110, 227n3
Upaka, 114, 115, 160, 167–168
Upāli, 174–175
Upaniṣads, 96, 134, 192
Uṣṇīṣavijayā, 20

Vasubandhu, 196
Vedas, 29, 132, 148, 179, 193, 212, 213,
Vimalakīrti Sūtra, 209
Visuddhimagga, 92, 211
Voltaire, 198
Vulture Peak, 69

Warren, Henry Clarke, 11, 27
Wencheng (Chinese princess), 201
Wilde, Oscar, 11, 216, 217–219
Wilson, Horace Hayman, 178–179, 234n9

Xaca (Śākya), 177–178
Xuanzang, 48, 108, 120, 152

Yajur Veda, 180
Yama, 81
Yangon, 108
Yaśas, 118
Yaśodharā, 49–50, 55–59, 61, 62, 96, 102–103, 119, 160, 184, 206; dreams of, 62–63
Yogācāra, 215

Zen masters, 216
Zoroaster, 156